Paying for Welfare

Paying for Welfare
Towards 2000

Third Edition

Howard Glennerster

 PRENTICE HALL

HARVESTER WHEATSHEAF

London   New York   Toronto   Sydney   Tokyo   Singapore
Madrid   Mexico City   Munich   Paris

First published 1985
Second edition published 1992

This third edition, first published 1997 by
Prentice Hall Europe
Campus 400, Maylands Avenue
Hemel Hempstead
Hertfordshire, HP2 7EZ
A division of
Simon & Schuster International Group

Typeset in 10/12pt Times
by Dorwyn Ltd, Rowlands Castle, Hants

Printed and bound in Great Britain by
T. J. Press (Padstow) Ltd, Padstow, Cornwall

Library of Congress Cataloging-in-Publication Data

Glennerster, Howard.
    Paying for welfare : towards 2000 / Howard
    Glennerster.
        p.   cm.
    Includes bibliographical references and index.
    ISBN 0-13-442013-6
    1. Public welfare—Great Britain—Finance.
    2. Public welfare—Economic aspects—Great
    Britain.   I. Title
    HV245.G523   1996
    338.4'336194—dc20   96–20582
                                               CIP

British Library Cataloguing in Publication Data

A catalogue record for this book is available from the
British Library

ISBN 0–13–442013–6

  2 3 4 5   01 00 99 98

CONTENTS

List of tables   vii
List of figures   ix
List of abbreviations   xi
Preface   xiii

Part I   Welfare and the state: theories and concepts   1

1   Mixed modes of finance   3
2   The theoretical basis for the state funding of services   15
3   Quasi-markets for welfare?   30

Part II   The controlling institutions   47

4   Setting the limits at the centre   49
5   Containing the locals   77
6   Setting the limits locally   100

Part III   The sources of funds   111

7   Taxes   113
8   Fees and charges   135
9   Charity and giving   148

Part IV   Financing the services   165

10   Paying for health services   167
11   Paying for personal social services   191

12 Paying for education   208
13 Paying for housing   236
14 Paying for social security   258

Part V   The future: towards 2000   283

15 Can we afford the welfare state?   285

Bibliography   299
Index   331

TABLES

1.1	Sources of funds for welfare	13
4.1	General government expenditure: budget plans	68
7.1	Sources of tax revenue in the United Kingdom, 1948–1994/5	119
7.2	Taxes as a percentage of gross income, by income group in the United Kingdom, 1994/5	129
7.3	Total taxes and social security contributions as a percentage of GDP, 1993	132
10.1	Health-care spending: international variations, 1992	173
12.1	Public expenditure on education as a percentage of GDP (at factor cost) in the United Kingdom, 1950–94	212
12.2	Public expenditure on education by level, 1993/4	213
14.1	Relative levels of social protection benefits in Europe, 1992	267
14.2	Average income of pensioners by source, 1979 and 1992	268
14.3	National Insurance Fund, 1993/4	270
15.1	Attitudes to the state in different countries, 1988	295
15.2	Those wanting more state spending on various services in different countries, 1988	296
15.3	Attitudes in Britain to raising taxes, 1983–94	297

FIGURES

1.1   The finance–provision distinction   6
1.2   Welfare finance in a simple economy   9
1.3   Welfare finance by cash redistribution   9
1.4   Welfare finance: mixed methods   11
2.1   A political economy view   25
4.1   NHS spending in real and volume terms, 1982/3 to 1992/3   61
4.2   UK government welfare spending, 1973/4 to 1994/5   63
5.1   Central resource levers   83
7.1   Gains or losses as a percentage of post-tax income: the consequences of tax changes, 1978/9 to 1994/5   130
10.1   Hospital and community health services gross current expenditure per head by age, 1992/3   174
10.2   Allocating the Health Service budget in England, 1994/5   178
11.1   Personal social services spending by client group in England, 1992/3   197
11.2   Real and volume terms spending on local authority social services, 1982/3 to 1994/5   198
12.1   Public expenditure on education as a percentage of GDP: international comparisons, 1991   213
12.2   Sources of funds for education in the United Kingdom, 1993/4   214
12.3   The operation of the local management of schools (LMS)   217

12.4 The sources of funds for higher education in the   224
      United Kingdom
13.1 Public expenditure on housing, 1973/4 to 1995/6   243
13.2 Sources of funds for housing, 1993/4   245
14.1 Benefit expenditure by group   266
14.2 Sources of funds for social security, 1993/4   268
15.1 The political market for social services   287
15.2 The dependent age population of the United   289
      Kingdom, 1941–2001
15.3 Ratio of people of working age to retired people in   291
      different countries, 1990–2030

ABBREVIATIONS

ACG   Annual capital guideline
AEF   Aggregate external finance
AIDS   Acquired Immune Deficiency Syndrome
BCA   Basic credit approval
BMA   British Medical Association
BUPA   British United Provident Association
CIPFA Chartered Institute of Public Finance and Accountancy
CPRS   Central Policy Review Staff
CTC   City technology college
DES   Department of Education and Science
DHSS   Department of Health and Social Security (replaced by DoH and DSS)
DoE   Department of the Environment
DoH   Department of Health
DSS   Department of Social Security
EEC   European Economic Community
EU   European Union
FIS   *Either* the financial information system operated by the Treasury *or* family income supplement
GDP   Gross domestic product (the value of goods and services produced in the economy)
GGE   General government expenditure
GLC   Greater London Council
GNI   General Needs Index (for housing purposes)
GNP   Gross national product (as gross domestic product but with the addition of net property income from abroad)

GRE	Grant-related expenditure figures which helped determine local authorities' entitlement to rate support grant
HAG	Housing association grant
HEFC	Higher Education Funding Council
HMI	Her Majesty's Inspectors of Schools
HMO	Health maintenance organisation
HRA	Housing revenue account
IAF	Industry Act forecasts
ILEA	Inner London Education Authority
LEA	Local education authority
LMS	Local management of schools
MSC	Manpower Services Commission
NHS	National Health Service
NNDR	National non-domestic rate
OECD	Organisation for Economic Co-operation and Development
PAR	Programme analysis and review
PARR	Health service formula for allocations in N. Ireland
PAYE	Pay As You Earn (tax collection)
PES	Public expenditure survey: the annual round of negotiations between the Treasury and spending departments
PESC	Public Expenditure Survey Committee
PPA	Private patients' association
PSB	Potential schools budget
PSBR	Public sector borrowing requirement
RAWP	Resource Allocation Working Party (on NHS funding in England)
RSG	Rate support grant (later revenue support grant)
RTIA	Receipts taken into account
SCA	Supplementary credit approval
SCRAW	Scottish resource allocation formula for health services
SERPS	State earnings-related pension scheme
SMR	Standardised mortality ratio or death rate
TEC	Training and Enterprise Council
UFC	Universities Funding Council
UGC	University Grants Committee
VAT	Value added tax
WPA	Western Provident Association
WRVS	Women's Royal Voluntary Service (previously WVS)

PREFACE

In 1984, having lectured for many years to undergraduates at the London School of Economics on the finance of the social services, I became increasingly frustrated by the fact that there was no single directly relevant textbook. The only answer seemed to be to write one. There are, of course, very useful traditional texts on public finance for economics students, but they are very thin on the institutional background – how money actually reaches schools and hospitals and housing associations. This is not an economics textbook but it is designed to be complementary to basic public finance texts.

At the same time as I was writing the first edition my colleague, Dr Barr in the economics department at the LSE, also decided to write up his more theoretical lectures on *The Economics of the Welfare State*. We conceived these as complementary texts for our students and hoped they might be for others too!

Now this text has reached its third edition and I have received many helpful suggestions on changing it from users – students and teachers alike. In the second edition I introduced an extended discussion of the economic theories underlying market failures on the one hand and 'government failures' on the other. The latter led to the introduction of quasi-markets across the social services in the 1990s and the concept is treated more fully in this edition. The future funding of the welfare state has moved to the centre of politics and the literature has grown enormously. I have tried to use and reference what I thought to be the most useful additions.

The book is aimed at undergraduates in political science, social policy and economics, and at those on professional training courses who will need to know how the services in which they work are financed – how their salaries at the end of the month get paid, to put it crudely. This should apply to teachers, social workers, housing managers, doctors and nurses. But it is also aimed at the more general public who have become more interested and concerned with the quality of their services as a result of the changes since Mrs Thatcher took office. There was a time when the finance of local services was a bore. Not any more. Between the first and the second edition of this book an ancient tax – the poll tax – was reintroduced and withdrawn after much protest. As I write there is much discussion of ministers getting off 'Scott free'. A scot was a local medieval tax. Hence scot-free meant tax free. The history of taxation, it seems, never loses its interest.

Acknowledgements

I am grateful to John Hills and all the members of the Welfare State Programme and the Department of Social Policy at the LSE with whom I have worked and who are a continual source of expertise and inspiration. Each year the students give my lectures and book a thorough going over and not much escapes them. Above all, there is all I owe to Ann who suffers my addiction to writing with such affection.

London School of Economics, 1996

PART I

Welfare and the state:
theories and concepts

CHAPTER 1

MIXED MODES OF FINANCE

This book is deliberately entitled *Paying for Welfare* and not *Paying for the Welfare State*. That title would have begged the fundamental questions: Need welfare be provided by the state? Does something that is *financed* by the state have to be *provided* by the state? Does the state necessarily imply a central governmental agency? The answer to each of these questions is 'no', not only in theory, but also increasingly in practice. These questions are now at the centre of debate about the future of welfare states in most parts of the world. This first chapter describes the wide variety of ways in which human services can be financed. We begin with some definitions and concepts that will be used throughout the book.

Definitions

What do we mean by welfare? To the American on the sidewalk it means cash handouts to hoodlums. To the professional economist it is a collective term for happiness, utility, or that which individuals desire. The word itself dates from the seventeenth century at least, and means the same as 'fare well' – to remain in good health and sufficiency (*Shorter Oxford English Dictionary*). That does point us to the essence of its modern meaning. The proclaimed objective of welfare provision in most societies is to ensure a basic standard of living for their citizens. This will usually entail a

3

minimum income and access to food, shelter, education, health care and support if they are sick or disabled. It leaves open how that objective is to be achieved and what the motives are – humane or sinister.

Probably the most important achievement in the thirty years after the Second World War was that of near full employment. The labour market ensured the welfare of most of the population for most of their working lives. Thus work is part of welfare, not its antithesis (Sinfield, 1983). The firm can ensure that its employees fare well when they are temporarily sick, or compensate them when they have an accident at work and ensure that they continue to fare well in their retirement. Many firms in this country have done so for part of their workforce for many years and are now obliged to make pension provision and to pay sickness and maternity benefits for a minimum period. In Japan, occupational welfare of this kind in the largest firms is more extensive. In Europe, industrywide pension schemes are more common. Then, of course, individuals can buy their own insurance against calamity – to try to secure their own family's wellbeing. Charitable organizations, friends, family and neighbours can all help in adversity, but the state in most countries steps in to secure a minimum income and access to basic services. In short, the maintenance of people's welfare lies in the power of many agencies and individuals, *including* local, regional and national organs of government.

Cash or kind?

Ensuring a minimum standard of living can also be achieved in a variety of ways. A firm, charity or government can give a dependent person or poor family cash, and leave them to buy what they need, or it can give the family goods or service free. We can give disabled people a cash allowance to pay for their transport or a small car to get about in. We can give the family or elderly person next door a donation of cash or go in and do the shopping. We can look after our own children all day or buy a place in a nursery. Provision for people's welfare can be in cash or in kind or in service done or in time that could be spent doing other things – opportunity time costs, economists call it.

Regulation or provision?

Government can pass laws which require firms or individuals to do things, like provide sick pay or ramps for disabled people, without spending any money itself. This does not of course mean that no one pays. The activity is financed privately but is forced on individuals or firms by government. It is in all respects like a tax, a compulsory levy, but it does not count as such in the national accounts.

Finance or provision?

Another crucial distinction runs throughout all discussions on the finance of the social services – the distinction between *finance* and *provision*. A typical layman's error is to assume that if a service like education or residential care is provided by a public agency it must also be financed out of public funds, by taxation, or conversely that if a service is provided by a private agency it must be financed privately, by fees. These are in fact only two of a wide range of possible alternatives. For example, a local authority old people's home charges fees. Some of these fees are paid by individuals themselves, some are paid out of pensions the old people receive from central government. The sources of funds are mixed – public and private. Government or firms can issue quasi-cash – say, luncheon vouchers or school vouchers – which enable one to buy a particular service in a particular market. The service is thus financed by one agency but provided by another.

Since this important distinction will reappear throughout the succeeding chapters, it is worth spending time now being clear about it. Much public discussion of the 'privatization' issue is hopelessly confused on this matter. Figure 1.1 sets out the logical possibilities in their simplest form. First, there is the question: What kind of agency provides the service? The column headings in the figure indicate this. A service can be provided by public sector bodies. These may be central government or a local agent of central government, like a district health authority, or services may be run by a locally elected council. In the 1980s, legislation passed by Mrs Thatcher's Government hived off institutions like hospitals

Provision

		Public sector bodies			Private organizations		Private – informal
		Central government	Public trusts	Local government	Profit	Non-profit	
Types of institution		e.g. NHS hospitals	e.g. NHS hospital trusts, grant-maintained schools, colleges	e.g. LEA schools, old people's homes, council houses	e.g. language schools, clinics, nursing homes	e.g. church schools, universities, housing associations, Barnardo homes	Families, neighbours, households, self-help groups
Finance	Public	Grants to health authorities from the Exchequer	Grants from central government, purchases by local government	Grants from central government, council tax	Social security payments to meet nursing home fees, LEA purchase of boarding-school places	Government grants to housing associations, universities, church schools, and places bought for children by LEAs	Social security payments to carers of disabled people, payment by local authorities to foster parents
	Private	Income from private pay beds, prescription charges	Fees paid by private users, households or companies	Charges by old people's homes	Fees paid by households	Rents to housing associations	Income lost in giving up work to care for a family member

Figure 1.1 The finance–provision distinction

and some schools from direct central or local government management control and created hybrid agencies like the Benefits Agency.

Then again, a service can be *privately provided* by a non-statutory agency. This may be a private profit-making company, a non-profit agency, or a self-help group, or by one individual for another. Various profit-making hospitals, language schools and nursing homes for old people come in the first group. Dr Barnardo's homes, the Family Service Units and church schools count as non-profit agencies, playgroups or informal groups of AIDS sufferers as self-help groups. Help for relatives or spouses or neighbours counts as informal care – provision by private households.

Second, we must turn to the question: Who finances the service? The rows in Figure 1.1 distinguish this. Welfare agencies can be financed out of public funds, or privately or a mixture of the two. National Health Service hospitals used to fall into the top left-hand category. Now Trusts are financed by central government money given to district health authorities or health commissions. However, some money comes from private individuals who pay for private care in private pay beds in these hospitals. Some hospitals have small private funds and most receive voluntary help from people in the local community. Local schools are paid for out of a mixture of local revenue – the council tax *and* by central government grants – but they are forbidden by law from charging fees. Local further education colleges, however, provide training courses and charge for the courses. The fees may be paid by the individual or the firm, perhaps. Both count as private sources of income.

The pure case of private welfare provision entirely financed privately is less easy to find than one might imagine. Language schools are an example. Private schools have pupils paid for out of public funds and receive indirect state aid in the form of tax relief. Private nursing homes have patients financed out of social security benefit. Universities are private bodies largely funded from central government but with elements of private fee paying and private research funding. We find a whole range of 'voluntary' or non-government agencies providing social care services – case work, counselling, care of the elderly and handicapped – that are heavily dependent on public funds. Individuals who perform caring duties may receive help from social security benefits if the person being cared for is disabled. Foster parents are paid by the local social services department.

Thus in practice, most provision of health and education is in the hands of a public authority with mixed sources of funding. Large parts of the social caring services are privately provided and publicly funded. Moreover, the largest part of social spending takes the form of cash given to individuals in social security benefits that they spend on privately produced goods and services. We already have a mixed economy of welfare. In later chapters of the book we shall unravel this complex situation of finance. It is enough to note that there is no one dominant mode of financing welfare in the United Kingdom or indeed anywhere in the world.

'To privatize', it may be noted, ugly as the phrase is, must logically mean to move any service from a box in the top left-hand corner of Figure 1.1 either downwards, introducing an element of private funding, or to the right to introduce an element of private provision within a publicly financed service like the NHS, to hive off services to a private body. Or the move may be diagonally down to the right – to do a little of both. These distinctions are too frequently confused. The case for and against each, as we shall see, is rather different. (For a discussion on these lines, see Klein, 1984.)

The flow of funds

We now present a formal model that is capable of describing the finance of any system of welfare in any economy. In the very simplest economy of all, a pure market economy, incomes are generated by households or workers, and enterprises or capital. The first kind of income we call wages, the second, profit. Incomes are spent on the outputs of other enterprises or on services provided by individuals. Welfare providers are either private profit-making firms, charitable non-profit-making bodies, or households. They are paid by other households purchasing services for a fee, by firms doing so for their employees and by charitable gifts. No government transfers take place. This simple economy can be illustrated in a flow of funds diagram (see Figure 1.2).

Government may decide that it cannot leave all society's casualties to the mercy of private charity, employers and family, for

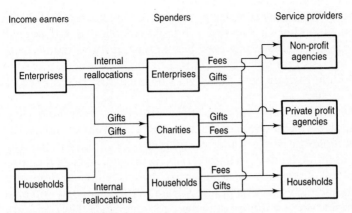

Figure 1.2 Welfare finance in a simple economy

reasons we shall discuss in Chapter 2. It can take the minimum step of intervention, impose taxes and give the proceeds away in cash or even quasi-cash such as vouchers, which tie the money to a particular kind of purchase. In this case the flow of funds model can be elaborated (see Figure 1.3). Taxes flow to the Treasury to be allocated back to needy households in either cash or quasi-cash. Households then spend their enhanced income on housing, schooling or food, provided by private institutions. Households are the sole or main final spenders.

Many would like to see the world in terms as simple as this. It is not. What has grown up in all industrial and post-industrial

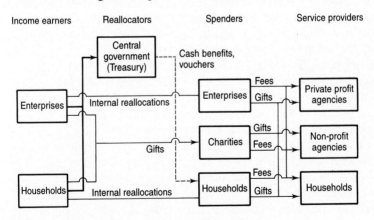

Figure 1.3 Welfare finance by cash redistribution

societies is a highly complex pattern of welfare finance. We sketch the main outlines in Figure 1.4. It looks complicated, but we shall take it slowly, describing each part in turn. It forms the basis for the analysis that follows in the rest of the book and is therefore important to grasp here. It derives from an earlier study (Peacock *et al.*, 1968).

As in the simpler versions of the world, we begin on the left-hand side with the incomes that are generated in any economy – by households or workers and by enterprises or firms. We end with the users of funds – welfare service providers, including central and local government institutions like schools or homes. Remnants of the simple world of a purely private welfare economy still exist alongside these statutory providers. In some fields they dominate. What government in its various forms does is to introduce an intermediary – a reallocative system of finance, beyond the household. Central or local government raises revenue from households and firms through taxation. It may decide not to tax some individuals or households as heavily as others because they are doing things the government approves of and wants to encourage, like owning their own house or having a private pension scheme. This is essentially a cash subsidy to that individual. Economists call this a 'tax expenditure' and we discuss it later in the book.

Central and local governments are not the only agents of the state who have power to take money and redistribute it. The courts do the same. They may be redressing a private wrong that one person or employer has done another through compensation. More central to our concerns here, the courts have the power to require one partner of a broken marriage to support the other and the children of the marriage. The court-based system of income support for many years ran alongside the social security system with little relationship between the two. This was authoritatively discussed by the Finer Committee (1974). However, if individuals knew that the social security system would meet their ex-partner's needs, settlements could be arranged which assumed this, minimized the ex-husband's costs and let the taxpayer pay. Many wives were unable to recover the money that was owed to them. It was this situation that led to the creation of the Child Support Agency, which was to recover payments from partners who had a responsibility to maintain children of a previous relationship. For a fuller discussion of the tax-like powers of the Agency see Garnham and Knights (1994) and Lewis

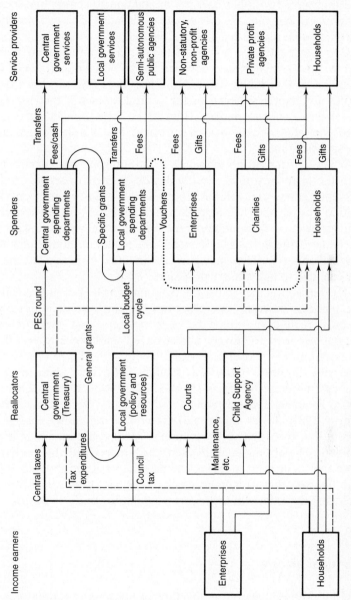

Figure 1.4 Welfare finance: mixed methods

(1995) for the changing social policy in this field during this century. We thus have two other agencies in addition to central and local government that can take money and reallocate it. This explains the set of flows on the left-hand side of Figure 1.4.

Once having decided how much to raise in taxes the government has to allocate that money between the spending departments. It does this in the Public Expenditure Survey (PES) which we describe in Chapter 4. Some of the central taxes will then be redirected to local government. This may be done through a general subsidy to all their activities – a general grant – or a special activity – a specific grant.

When it receives the money, a local authority may decide to transfer the money to its own housing department or schools, or it may give grants to a voluntary organization – a non-profit organization – or pay fees to a private organization to provide a service. The government may require them to do this. They may, however, do none of these, but may instead give money to households to spend themselves. They may give cash in a tied form as a voucher, for example to buy nursery provision.

The horizontal line across the diagram, which ends in fees paid for services, describes the processes by which households earn income, reallocate income between partners, and spend it on various services. Relatively unrecognized until recently was the reallocation that takes place within family units. There is now an emerging literature on the way families redistribute their money amongst different members (Becker, 1976; Pahl, 1980; Piachaud, 1982; Rimmer, 1982; Brannan and Wilson, 1987; Pahl, 1989; Morris, 1989; Davies and Joshi, 1994). As yet we know very little, except that the original distribution of income between men and women is highly unequal, to men's advantage, and that women nevertheless do most spending on items like food and clothing. It is also the case that women do much of the *caring* for dependants, including the elderly in the family – a point to which we return.

The total picture

The purpose of elaborating this flow of funds approach has been partly to provide a framework for succeeding chapters, but it also

Table 1.1 Sources of funds for welfare

Sources of funds	1978/9 (%)	1993/4 (%)
Earmarked taxes: National Insurance	20	18
General taxes	31	35
Local authority taxes	10	8
Total taxes	**61**	**61**
Tax reliefs	5	6
Fees and charges for public services	5	3
Enterprise welfare	12	8
Other private spending	17	22
Total	100	100
£ billions[1]	(167)	(262)

Note: [1] At 1993/4 prices.
Source: Hills (1995b).

emphasizes the wide range of options open to us in paying for welfare. Provision by state-run institutions financed out of taxation is only one of a very large range of alternatives. In the following chapters we shall describe what happens in Britain today and how the system has evolved. However, we end this chapter by using the framework we have just outlined to analyze the total flow of funds in the UK case, private and public, and to show the changes that have taken place recently. I am indebted to John Hills for all the work needed to produce these figures.

Table 1.1 shows the total expenditure in the United Kingdom devoted to financing pensions, health care, education and housing, whether provided in the public or the private sector. If we define the total welfare budget in these terms, it amounted to £262 billion or about 48 per cent of the gross domestic product in 1993/4. Only 61 per cent was financed from taxation. No less than a fifth was financed directly from individuals' own pockets, and much of the rest by employers' 'enterprise welfare', or 'occupational welfare' as Titmuss (1958, 1976) called it.

What is perhaps surprising is that the tax share has not changed since 1978/9. There has been a significant rise in private household payments for pensions and housing and medical care, but there has been a corresponding fall in employer-funded welfare.

Having looked at the many various ways in which welfare can be financed, we now examine the theories that have tried to explain why it is financed in the way it is.

Further reading

The following publications are recommended for further reading: J. Hills (1995), 'Funding the welfare state', *Oxford Review of Economic Policy*, **11**, no. 3, pp. 27–43; J. Falkingham and J. Hills (eds) (1995), *The Dynamics of Welfare: The welfare state and the life cycle*, Hemel Hempstead: Harvester; E. Papadakis and P. Taylor-Gooby (1987), *The Private Provision of Public Welfare: State, market and community*, Hemel Hempstead: Harvester; and G. Parker (1990), *With Due Care and Attention: A review of research on informal care*, 2nd edn, London: Family Policy Studies Centre.

CHAPTER 2

THE THEORETICAL BASIS FOR THE STATE FUNDING OF SERVICES

Despite the fact that the market allocates most goods, services and incomes in modern societies, governments have continued to raise large sums in taxes to sustain social welfare spending. Most countries spend between a fifth and a third of their national income on tax or contribution-based social welfare and some spend rather more. (See Chapter 7 for the comparative figures.) How are we to explain this persistent scale of state spending on welfare?

Different schools of economic thought have different answers to that question. They can be broadly grouped under four headings: traditional economic theories about *market* failure; a more recent emphasis on *information* failures in some kinds of market; Marxist economists' concern with the larger role of welfare spending in sustaining capitalist economies; and economists on the radical right who emphasize the self-interest of government employees and the nature of *political* markets.

Market failure

Philosophers may justify public finance of basic human services for reasons of social justice or equity. Economists have a more hard-nosed approach. Whatever the equity of the case, they say, are there any economic efficiency grounds for the state intervening? Is the market not the best allocator or are there efficiency limits to the market's role?

Traditional economic thought has always accepted that markets do not work perfectly in all circumstances. Adam Smith, writing in 1776 (see 1974 Penguin edition), clearly recognized this, and modern economists have a standard set of circumstances in which they agree that market exchange fails to produce the most efficient outcome. A famous American economist Kenneth Arrow (1963: 947) summed up his explanation for non-market social institutions thus: 'I propose here the view that, when the market fails to achieve an optimal state, society will, to some extent at least, recognise the gap, and non market social institutions will arise in attempting to bridge it.'

Some of the most common types of market failure are discussed below. Economics students will want to consult the further reading at the end of the chapter if they do not already know it.

Social or public goods

The most widely accepted limitation of market exchange derives from the inherent nature of some services or activities. For a market to exist, a particular object which is bought by me has to be, thereby, unavailable to someone else who wants to buy it. If my neighbour will benefit equally from my having a hose-pipe in the garden he is likely to leave the buying to me. I may make the same calculation and no one buys. The logical thing to do is to club together and buy it between us – a mini social good.

Social goods have particular properties. One is that of non-excludability. A product will not be produced in quantities that maximize the efficient gain to society if people can benefit whether they pay or not. Clean air is the standard example, so is general policing of an area. Each family would leave it to others in the street to pay the local bobby to walk down the street, yet every one gains if the whole area is secure. You could ask for a voluntary charge for the service but few would pay and the level of service would be suboptimal. Another characteristic of a social good is non-rivalry. If I drive along an uncrowded road it is not costing others any extra for me to do so. I am not using resources at the expense of others. There should be no charge on that road. When the road becomes crowded, however, the conclusion would be different. Non-excludability from benefit is one reason for defining a social good, non-rivalry another.

Economists often limit their examples of such cases to defence or police or environmental issues. Measures of public health, sanitation and the control of infectious disease were recognized by the Victorians as vital social goods. The common education of all children in a nation to achieve 'nation building' or social cohesion, would be another example.

The existence of a social good suggests some kind of public action may be necessary. It does not tell us exactly what. Laws to require sanitation in your house may be enough. In other cases a state service, for example police, may be needed. Unfortunately, knowing that a service can only be provided collectively does not tell us how much to spend on it. Because no market bargains can be struck or exchange take place, there is no unambiguously right level of spending, at least in terms of traditional economic theory. All we can hope for is an open and informed electoral process.

Externalities

The number of pure public or social goods is small; see Foster *et al.* (1980) for a discussion of this in relation to local government services. There is another set of situations in which economists recognize market failure. Activities may be undertaken or products bought in the market but their price may not reflect the whole benefit or costs to the society. If the benefits are private to the purchaser a price paid in a free market will lead to an efficient allocation of resources on grounds that any first-year economics text will explain. However, my car may affect your and the wider public's welfare in a number of ways: the lead in the exhaust fumes may harm your health, the gases may affect the ozone layer and the good of future generations; driving a car down a crowded street may cause delays to others driving the same way. These are all negative externalities or social costs. Only if they are reflected in the price or in some charge upon me will my actions in the marketplace represent a truly efficient allocation of resources – efficient, that is, for the whole community. If a congestion tax is levied on me as a car driver in a city centre, I shall only drive in if the gain to me in convenience is greater than the cost of the congestion I have caused. In the same way I will not take into account the benefits to the wider society of my child being able to communicate with others. I may not invest enough in her education from society's point of view. So some market decisions may produce too much activity (car fumes) and others too little (education). Insanitary housing may be all a poor person can buy from a landlord but the public health hazard is a cost to neighbours. As a parent who sees his daughter's future confined to motherhood, I may see no point in educating her to be other than a mother. Society as a whole, as well as the child, would be the loser. Secondary education is a necessary requirement for a democratic society and for individual self-fulfilment, but there is no reason why parents should wish to buy that amount of education or be able to. Once more, collective action of some kind is called for. It may be regulation, it may be taxation, it may be state provision.

Monopoly and imperfect competition

Completely efficient allocations of resources only occur where there is perfect competition. These conditions rarely, if ever, exist and much public policy is concerned to limit monopoly power and introduce as much competition as is politically feasible. In many areas a local secondary school or a district general hospital will enjoy a *geographical monopoly*. This is not just because the state has made it so, but because economies of scale require a big institution. A smaller one would not be able to enter the market and compete the larger out of existence. The travel costs and difficulty of going to the next school or hospital are such as to give the institution the same kind of power as a commercial monopoly. This may argue for close state regulation of standards in such schools, or a case may be made for local political control. Economic theory cannot help us here. It does suggest an unregulated market will not produce the most efficient outcome.

Charity or income externalities

We have seen that my activity, driving with lead in my petrol, may affect you directly. My low income or starving family may also affect your happiness. You may be greatly disturbed by the fact that the market has not resulted in my family having enough to live on. Your utility, or happiness, may be a function not just of your income but of mine too. The classic statement of this theorem was set out by Hochman and Rodgers (1969). In a two-person world you can solve this by giving me part of your income. There are problems, however. I may feel resentful of such personal charity. My utility is not enhanced, it may even be worsened by the shame. If your real concern is with my utility you will not have benefited either. One way round this may be for individuals to use the agency of the state to impersonalize the giving and seek to remove the stigma by creating a set of rights to benefit.

More fundamentally, in a non-two-person world, where poverty is generally disliked, others will benefit from your generosity and may be tempted to leave it all to you. They will free-ride on your charity. Alternatively, they might all agree to contribute, sharing the burden. It can be argued that what concerns people is the overall pattern of income distribution and that the state is the only agency capable of taking action to achieve this.

There is a converse problem. It much concerned the Victorians and has its modern counterpart. By your charity you may make a beggar of me. I shall never work again and my family's morals may be corrupted. I will trade on your susceptibilities. The Victorians concluded that some collective regulation of charitable giving was called for; if not, society would descend into beggary.

The difficulties of charitable giving are not at an end. You may want to see me and my family with enough to eat but would be upset if I spent the cash you gave me on beer or drugs. You may want to tie the support you give to particular purposes. Private charities can do this by giving clothes or food, but the indignity may rise in line with the specificity of the gift. The state may be able to give tied benefits, like food stamps, but people will probably find ways to trade them for money.

These kinds of justification for state activity on grounds of market failure have been recognized by economists for many years. They do not, however, add up to an overwhelming case for widespread social service provisions of the kind that exist in most countries today. Services like schools, hospitals and pension provision are clearly not public or social goods in the narrow economic sense. Large private markets exist for all these activities, even more so in the case of housing. There are public good *elements* in many services like education, however, and certainly externalities.

More recent advances in economic theory have elaborated further deficiencies in markets that arise from information failures. This literature has been summarized and developed by Barr (1992, 1993) and the following section draws heavily on his work.

Information failure

Markets require perfect information to work perfectly. The less perfect the knowledge, the less well the market works. This is true generally and may be countered by attempts to improve consumer knowledge, for example. There are, however, a class of problems that are more deep seated and difficult to remedy by simple consumer protection measures.

Consumer knowledge limits

Consumers of health care, to take one example, lack information that would enable them to make rational choices for themselves in several ways:

1. It is unclear to the immediate consumer what service he requires, if any. Are you really ill or imagining it? If there is something wrong, what is it? What treatment is called for? The patient's capacity to judge the doctor's advice on this is limited in the extreme. You may take your car to several other garages to get second and third opinions. To some extent this happens in health care, especially in more consumer-conscious systems like the United States. In practice, the importance of trust between doctor and patient and a sense of continuity, the anxiety that surrounds illness, mean that consumer loyalty is high and important. In urgent cases such shopping around is in any case impossible. Similar problems arise with the choice of school. The need for continuity in a child's education precludes continual changes of school to ensure the best buy. The problems posed by the mentally infirm or disabled are greater still.

2. Even when it has been decided what service is needed, the consumer may face great difficulty measuring the quality and comparing it with what might have been received elsewhere. So many of the circumstances are personal. How well my child does depends on individual capacities and family situation. How well the school is doing, taking these factors into account, is a highly complex exercise to determine, as we shall see in the next chapter. Where a producer is making a standard product that can be tested, comparisons are possible. What characterizes most social services is their highly personal nature, and this makes simple, widely available measures of quality difficult to produce.

3. Quality is not the only thing consumers need to know about in the marketplace; they will need accurate pricing information too. They will need to know whether paying a little more for such an operation is going to increase their chances of survival, and by how much. It is not just that such information is difficult to give because of the high degree of uncertainty attaching to the individual case, it is also costly to acquire. A full medical examination and cost information and prediction undertaken more than once by different hospitals will be necessary. The transaction costs, as economists call this, of getting the information necessary to act as a rational consumer, are high.

4. Consumers may need to know about the probability of events occurring far into the future and of a kind they would rather not think about, such as becoming infirm in advanced old age. Few people insure for the very high costs of long-term care in old age even in the United States (Rivlin and Wiener, 1988).

Individual consumers thus face a more difficult prospect operating in these kinds of market than in the everyday high-street shop. These reasons all have to do with limited and uncertain information available to the user.

Provider information

Service providers in a market also face difficulties. They may know less than their customer about their customer's characteristics, yet need perfect or good information about their potential patient or client to be able to quote a competitive price.

Adverse selection

An individual with a poor health record has every incentive to hide the fact from a private health insurer. The insurer needs to know what the probabilities are of that individual being a costly patient. If he is costly the insurer will ask a higher premium or price for the health insurance cover. A health maintenance organization that promises to provide care for a flat-rate payment per year will want the same information in order to adjust its annual charge. The patient will have every incentive to lie or modify the truth. In response, insurance companies try to find out as much as they can about applicants in order to isolate high-risk individuals and either charge them a higher premium or exclude them altogether. If that company does not, its competitor will. A company that fails to exclude high-cost patients will have to charge higher premiums to everyone and that will put it at a disadvantage in competing for the custom of the most sought after, the low-risk client. If the company is more attractive to the high-risk patient a downward spiral will set in, whereby it loses healthy patients and acquires less healthy ones, becoming less and less competitive (Rothschild and Stiglitz, 1976; Atkinson, 1989; Laffont, 1989).

As one head of marketing for an American health insurer put it to me a few years ago: 'Let's face it, competition in health care is all about making sure you don't have ill people on your books.' These problems of 'cream skimming' have forced non-profit health insurers in the United States, like Blue Cross and Blue Shield, to adapt their policies. They have forced many HMOs out of business as private profit-making concerns, competing with them, not on the basis of providing more efficient services (E-competition), but by selecting out or creaming off the low-risk individuals (S-competition). If the gain to a firm from S-competition is greater than that from competing on efficiency, it will of course choose the former. This does not, in theory, destroy the case for competition in health care, for it may be possible to identify risk factors and government may compensate firms, HMOs or general practitioners who take on high-risk groups (van de Ven and van de Vliet, 1990; Matsaganis and Glennerster, 1994). Such formulas are very difficult to produce, however, especially if the whole range of health cover is involved. GPs, for example, may try to avoid taking on patients who are costly in time, even in a non-cash-market situation, but it is more serious where the patient carries a price tag too.

The formal economic literature on adverse selection is largely confined to health services and insurance, but precisely the same problem arises in other welfare services. Indeed, it may be the one common factor that runs through all forms of social provision. Old people's homes and residential care for children from broken homes exhibit exactly the same response to similar incentives. More dependent people will not be taken on unless a higher price can be paid. Those not yet dependent but with a higher risk of becoming so will be excluded.

Schools face similar incentives. Given a flat fee for educating a child a rational school will take the most educable child if it wishes to maximize its exam ratings or competitive edge in the market-place (Glennerster, 1991). It will cream off those from homes or with previous school performance scores that suggest it can get good results with minimum input. For more discussion of this point see Chapter 3.

Moral hazard

Drawing again on examples from insurance, economists point to the poor information insurance firms have about the insured's behaviour and the impact that being insured will have on that behaviour (Pauly, 1974). If I am insured against theft I may be less careful about locking up my house; in extremis, if hard up, as a house owner I may indulge in deliberate arson. This does not make market insurance impossible but it makes it more expensive. This is not a problem that is confined to private insurance. If I know that either the state or my family will look after me if I do become elderly and infirm, I may be less willing to pay for insurance to support myself. If I have sickness insurance, state or private, I may be prepared to take more time off work or ignore the need to keep healthy. If there were insurance against marriage breakdown, would there be more breakdowns? Some would argue that social security has encouraged the breakdown of marriage. It was exactly that kind of logic that lay behind the creation of the Child Support Agency. Men should not be able to walk out on a wife and expect the state to pay. If young men had financially to support the children produced by thoughtless sex they might be more likely to wear a condom.

The effects are largest in what economists call third-party insurance systems. My car is insured against accident. So when I have an accident and my car is damaged I am happy to go along with whatever the garage charges, so long as the insurance company will pay. This drives up costs. Precisely this situation obtains in health-care insurance in many countries, thus driving up health-care prices. The response has been for insurance companies to insist on patients paying part of the price of their treatment, a co-payment, and to insist on very close regulation of treatment given.

Attempts have also been made to increase the competition between health providers. Private markets in health care tend to
generate very high prices, which competition has been unable to
check at all effectively.

Certainty and uncertainty

A chronically sick person, for example, will find it difficult to obtain insurance because of the certainty of very high-cost care. At
the other extreme, when there is no basis for predicting outcomes,
insurance markets will not work either. As Barr (1993) points out,
the impossibility of predicting future levels of inflation over a retired person's life makes it almost impossible for private insurance
companies to offer fully inflation-proofed pension schemes without some kind of government support.

Taken together, these information failures go a long way towards explaining why social institutions have evolved that try to
mitigate their consequences. Their salience clearly varies from one
service to another. What they do is to provide a framework to
which we shall return in discussing each service later in the book.
Before that we review some less conventional economic theories
that give different reasons for the existence and growth of social
welfare.

A political economy view

Traditional economic analysis concentrates on particular failures
in what is otherwise seen as a natural and efficient system of exchange – the market. For Marxist writers, and others besides, the
whole system of market exchange is flawed. The role the welfare
state plays is to rescue, albeit temporarily, capitalist market systems from collapse. This may not be a fashionable view in the
1990s, especially in the light of the failure of non-market command
economy systems in eastern Europe. But it is equally impossible to
point to pure capitalist modes of exchange coexisting with democratic governments that possess no form of state income support or
other welfare provision. In the 1980s the government forced
through a major economic restructuring designed to make the UK
more competitive. Whatever the judgements about its success, it

would not have been possible if the three million people whom it made unemployed had had no form of income support. Much the same lesson is being learnt in the eastern European nations. If they want to move to a free labour market system they must have some way of giving income to those thrown out of work in the period of adjustment. This was the message brought by none other than the World Bank (Barr, 1994).

Many Marxists, prior to the 1960s, had ignored the welfare system. Some did see it as a partial victory for the working class but others saw it as a sop that bought off the labour movement from seeking real change. For a self-critical review of Marxists' work on welfare see Lee and Raban (1988). It was not until the 1970s that a coherent political economy view emerged, stimulated especially by the work of O'Connor (1973) in the United States and Gough (1979) in the United Kingdom. These authors maintained that welfare spending by the state was both essential for the functioning of a capitalist economy *and* bound to grow inexorably to the point that a capitalist economy would be unable to finance the scale of spending required. There was, in short, a basic contradiction built into the western economic system and welfare spending was at its heart.

The essence of the first leg of the argument is set out in Figure 2.1. There are two broad categories of public expenditure: *social capital* and *social expenses*. The first category has a direct economic payoff. It helps to sustain the economic infrastructure and thus sustains private capital. It has an *accumulation function*. This kind of activity can be further subdivided. There is the creation of

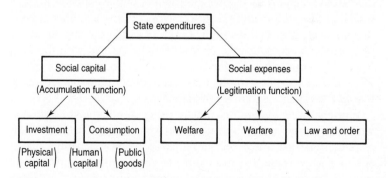

Figure 2.1 A political economy view (Source: Judge, 1982b)

new capital or investment by the state which can be of two kinds again. There is physical capital – roads, railways, airports, power generation. Then there is human capital – investment in education, in training, in health to produce a healthy labour force, support for families to enable them to reproduce a new labour force. O'Connor (1973) distinguished that kind of state spending from expenditure on the urban structure. Money for recreation, parks, concerts and services that the suburban middle class enjoy is largely denied to the inner-city classes. Then there are what he called social expenses, which are a drag on productive output but are necessary to keep the whole capitalist edifice in place. These mitigate the grossest inequalities. They take starving children from the streets, and old people from desperate penury. Without that, the political legitimacy of the state would be undermined. The defence forces, the police and the secret service are the hard hand of legitimation.

There was nothing new about this analysis except its emphasis on the cost of such activities. The actual categories and their boundaries were disputed, for example by Gough (1979). What was new was the dynamic element in O'Connor's theoretical analysis. It suggested that the levels of spending needed to sustain the capitalist system would grow steadily. The rate of profit was declining and would need more and more injections of state support, he argued. Unemployment would grow and cost steadily more, and the costs of services would be pushed up by workers in the state sector following the wage increases won by trade union activity in the private sector. Drawing on the analogy of a then nearly bankrupt New York City, he forecast that the whole state apparatus would not be able to raise the taxes to support this growing burden of public expenditure. The working class were being asked to pay increasing amounts in taxation and were able to resist both politically and by passing on the tax increases in wage demands. Here O'Connor agreed with the New Right. He, unlike them, believed that any attempt to rein back the level of state spending would, in the end, undermine the accumulation of capital and legitimacy of the state.

Written during a period of rapidly rising spending and taxation as well as economic crisis, this analysis had wide appeal. The middle-way response was that the growth in public spending was neither inevitable nor irreversible. It was possible to sustain a necessary level of welfare spending within a mixed economy and to control that spending effectively. The means for doing so are outlined in Chapter 4.

They have proven very effective in the United Kingdom in the 1980s and 1990s. Marxists would ask whether this can continue.

In the 1970s and 1980s a very different set of ideas evolved on the radical right (see Glennerster and Midgley, 1991). These ideas have many strands, but part of them derives from a new kind of economics – *public choice theory*.

A public choice view

Mueller (1989) defines public choice as 'the economic study of non market decision making'. That is a very large and all-encompassing category. Here we concentrate on that part of the work which is concerned to explain public expenditure growth and begins with a seminal work by Niskanen (1971), who was building on previous work by Downs (1957, 1967) and Tullock (1965). This approach places the responsibility for the growth of welfare spending on imperfections in the democratic process and on the nature of the incentives that exist within government bureaucracies.

Pressure groups seeking to force government to create a new service will have something to gain of a significant kind. Their members may be prepared to spend many hours and much money lobbying for a new service or programme. The general taxpayer will only see a small marginal loss resulting from the higher taxes and will not spend the time organizing to oppose more spending. New programmes therefore are approved, even though the 'silent majority' do not really want them. Once in place, public programmes are very difficult to kill off because they have a constituency prepared to fight for them. Public budgets therefore have great inertia. Some go as far as to suggest that political choice is all but ruled out (Rose and Davies, 1994).

A public agency may begin with a legitimate purpose and then continue with no very obvious function: planting trees to provide pit props for the mines in the First World War, for example, which then developed as the Forestry Commission, creating nuisances, not least to fell walkers! The same may be true of welfare agencies. Once a social programme is in place those who run it have a direct interest not merely in keeping it going, but also in expanding the size of the activity. Public bureaucrats have the following possible gains from their jobs: 'salary, perquisites of the office, public reputation, power, patronage, output of the bureau, ease of making changes and ease of running the bureau' (Niskanen, 1971). With the exception of the last two, Niskanen claims that all these possible personal gains are directly and positively linked to the size of the agency budget. Hence it is not surprising to find heads of services, like directors of social service departments, always arguing for more money. What is more, they are likely to have the best, or only, information about the social problem they are responsible for meeting, and therefore can exaggerate its size and their impact. They are in a powerful position to persuade legislators or councillors to spend more. What is worse, they have no pecuniary advantage in the efficient running of the organization. Thus public organizations tend to be both large and inefficient.

This kind of reasoning underpinned much Conservative opinion in the 1980s. More recently, the assumptions and reasoning have come under powerful counterattack (Dunleavy, 1991; Self, 1993). The interests and motivations of those who work in public services are not reduced that simply to a pecuniary base. Nor is it clear that senior bureaucrats are necessarily closely tied to spending more money. Their careers may be advanced by gaining a reputation for tough management. Mrs Thatcher created a new set of incentives in the civil service and amongst her ministers by making it clear that preferment lay in cutting, not increasing, the size of your budget. The political climate will be critical, and so, too, will the institutional context.

Above all, the explanation, good as it may be for helping to understand one kind of demand for more spending, ignores the institutional and political constraints on spending that exist. It is important to realize that the authors draw largely on American experience, where the spending lobbies are more powerful and where Congress has a freedom to spend that the House of Commons does not (see Glennerster, 1975). We describe the considerable powers of the Treasury in the United Kingdom in Chapter 4.

The lack of incentives for efficiency, which exist in welfare services especially, are not so easily dismissed. There are four main difficulties:

1. There is no easy way to measure the output of social service agencies. It is therefore difficult to know whether the public is receiving good value for money. The price may be too high.

2. There is rarely a competitor with whom users or legislators can compare the quality of the service they are receiving.
3. Because there is no ready alternative provider of the service, the user or client cannot 'exit' easily. He or she cannot transfer their custom and therefore their cash. This puts the provider in a comfortable position, knowing that whatever happens the user will have to put up with their services, and this is unhealthy.
4. Because the service is free, consumers are less demanding than if they are paying. This puts them in a dependent position, tending to be grateful for the service received.

Taken together, it is possible to see these problems in parallel with the failings of the market and to classify them as 'government failures' (Wolf, 1979; Le Grand, 1991).

It is these kinds of consideration that lead some to advocate the extension of competition to social services and the creation of 'quasi-markets' that would combine the need for publicly funded services with the efficiency incentives provided by markets.

Further reading

The following publications are recommended for further reading: N. A. Barr (1992), 'Economic theory and the welfare state', *Journal of Economic Literature*, **30**, June, pp. 741–803; N. A. Barr (1993), *The Economics of the Welfare State*, 2nd edn (3rd edn expected), London: Weidenfeld; J. Le Grand (1991), 'The theory of government failure', *British Journal of Political Science*, **22**, pp. 423–42; and, for those with an economics background, D. C. Mueller (1989), *Public Choice II*, Cambridge: Cambridge University Press.

For a critique of the public choice view, see P. Dunleavy (1991), *Democracy, Bureaucracy and Public Choice*, Hemel Hempstead: Harvester Wheatsheaf; and P. Self (1993), *Government by the Market: The politics of public choice*, London: Macmillan. For an American Marxist political economy view, see J. O'Connor (1973), *The Fiscal Crisis of the State*, New York: St Martins Press. For a UK view, see I. Gough (1979), *The Political Economy of the Welfare State*, London: Macmillan.

A critical evaluation of the economic case for government intervention is provided by S. J. Bailey (1995), *Public Sector Economics*, London: Macmillan.

CHAPTER 3

QUASI-MARKETS FOR WELFARE?

We have seen in the previous chapter that though there are funda-mental difficulties with markets as a way of allocating health care, education and other human services, there are also problems with monopolistic state provision. This has led to an increasing number of experiments to introduce elements of competition into the de-livery of such services, not only in the United Kingdom, but also in other similar welfare states like those in Scandinavia and Canada (Saltman and von Otter, 1992, 1995; Jerome-Forget *et al.*, 1995).

Old assumptions

The accepted way of thinking about the delivery of welfare ser-vices in the United Kingdom, from the 1940s through to the 1970s, was to assume that state intervention implied that services should be both financed *and* provided by some agency of the state. That might be central or local government, or some body directly responsible to the central state like a new town development corporation.

It had not always been so. The state's involvement in education had begun, in the nineteenth century, with grants to private church schools. This aid was extended to private secondary grammar schools in the twentieth century. There was a widely held view in the nineteenth century that the state should not be in the business of providing schooling. If involved at all, it should confine its role to aiding the private voluntary sector. The development of state schools was a slow one (see Chapter 12).

Housing associations, not local councils, had been the first to respond to housing for the poor. Even when it came, state support for housing had begun with subsidies made available to both private builders and local authorities (see Chapter 13). Much of the care and support of elderly and disabled people had begun as a form of charity that gained public support and then became a statutory service – family case work is a good example. Yet increasingly, as the state began to finance services, so it began eventually to take over their administration too.

Reasons for the fusion of finance and provision

There were a number of technical reasons for the decline in state support for private agencies. Some of these are very similar to the kinds of reasons that led large corporations to absorb their suppliers – it was easier and cheaper to exercise direct control over these other companies than to make contracts with them. These factors are explored in the economic literature (Williamson, 1975). However, other reasons derived from the nature of public services and the need to ensure equity and accountability. We summarize both sets of factors as follows:

1. *Weak financial accountability* An early illustration can be drawn from housing finance. In the early years after the First World War subsidies were given to public and private builders alike to build houses for the poor. It proved very difficult to stop private builders making excessive profits out of state subsidies. Tough Treasury and audit controls were easier to apply if the agent, the body doing the work, was a statutory authority.
2. *Difficulties in quality control* Schools were an example of this different problem. To receive a grant, private schools had to come up to minimum standards set by school inspectors (see Chapter 12). Simply to rely on personal judgements by individual inspectors was not deemed sufficient. Schools had to put their children through a set of fairly crude tests, and each child had to pass them before the school could be paid a grant for that child. Teachers and the inspectorate itself objected that this

was a constraining and stultifying process, which led to too much time being spent on exam practice. Achieving the close quality control needed to dispense cash to independent agencies was difficult to do effectively without perverting what these agencies wished to do. Many voluntary organizations feel this today when faced with detailed contractual requirements from local authorities.

3. *Universality* Pressure grew for services to be equally and universally available, pressure that reached its peak during and after the Second World War. It seemed that the easiest way to achieve this was to do it through the agency of a single provider charged with the responsibility of providing a universal service with equal access nationwide. This motivation lay behind the National Health Service and the nationwide social security system introduced in 1948.

4. *Equity* Public organizations must be seen to be dealing fairly with all those who use the service. Like cases must be treated alike. The tight rules that result may be difficult to administer at one remove in a private or independent organization. Social security benefits are a good example.

5. *Unitary government* All social services were in the end the responsibility of the appropriate minister or secretary of state in Westminster because, unlike many other countries, the United Kingdom is a unitary state. That politician was held responsible for the service, and as such, he or she wanted mistakes minimized and political credit maximized. That was most readily achieved, especially in a period of expansion, by concentrating control and delivery in the hands of a statutory body over which the minister had ultimate charge. In a period of cuts, distance from the consequences may seem more attractive.

6. *Political climate* These partly technical, partly political factors were reinforced by a general climate of ideas which held public provision *per se* to be a good thing, an end in itself. This was not a view universally held, of course, but amongst those who favoured greater social equity, social provision as well as funding was the almost instinctive solution.

The 1940s saw the end to social insurance provided by voluntary societies and trade unions. It saw the rapid growth of housing provided by local authorities because there were no other agencies

large enough to undertake the rapid and massive housing programme needed after the war. Voluntary hospitals disappeared,
seen as a root cause of unequal provision of health care and facing
severe financial difficulties.

Organizational consequences

Bureaucracy and hierarchical control

Once a structure had emerged in which central government had
ultimate responsibility and in which equity and universality were
political goals, bureaucracy and hierarchical control were likely
outcomes. Neither term should be considered in a pejorative way,
for the following reasons:

1. Consistency requires rules commonly observed. That is what
   bureaucracy, in its strict sense, provides.
2. Accountability upwards to a political master means a chain of
   command downwards.
3. The dangers of non-compliance by local agencies to political
   goals and standards require tight supervision and inspection.

In an account of the US system of public schooling, Chubb and
Moe (1990) describe the impact of such factors in a very different
decentralized system.

Parallels in the private sector

In many ways these kinds of factors parallel, but are distinct from,
the kinds of factors that lead to the growing centralization or hierarchical structure of private firms (Williamson, 1975). Firms may
resort to manufacturing components or owning a subsidiary rather
than buying from another producer for a number of reasons:

1. *Complex contracts* It may be difficult to draw up a contract
   that covers all the possible contingencies and to enforce the

contract. The transaction costs, or the costs of negotiation, legal and administrative, may be high. The firm may wish to have the kind of flexible control that can be achieved within an organization as distinct from putting everything on paper in advance in a contract with another organization.

2. *Limited knowledge*   One organization may find it difficult to make a contract with another very different one just because it lacks the expertise. To think up a contract to cover all possible eventualities may be too difficult for any expert.

3. *Uncertainty*   It may be a service or product where future demands are highly uncertain. The contractor may want a very high price for giving the company an assured supply in those circumstances.

The costs of bureaucracy

There were efficiency costs associated with hierarchical organization in both the public and the private sectors:

1. In the private sector, large enterprises found it difficult to adapt to the economic uncertainties of the 1970s and 1980s. Restructuring large corporations with established ways proved difficult. Contracts with small but dispensable suppliers might be more flexible. Corporate decentralization came to be fashionable (Kanter, 1984).

2. Information technology could enable senior management to monitor local branches and independent suppliers more effectively without powerful intervening hierarchies.

3. The ambition to control organizations from the centre outran the centre's capacity to generate sensible information to plan and monitor institutions. How many university students did the country need? What was the output of different universities? Government made itself look very foolish in trying to answer these kinds of question and consistently getting them wrong (Barnes and Barr, 1988).

4. As the steady expansion of funds available to the welfare services ceased, efficiency in the use of those funds became more important.

5. Consumers became increasingly accustomed to wide choice in private markets. Their expectations of public services grew, even if the resources devoted to them by the political process did not.
6. The political climate changed with the economic crisis of the mid-1970s. Equity and universality came lower down the political list of priorities. Private sector models came to be taken as the norm.

In this situation, stress came to be laid on the weaknesses of the traditional model of delivering social and other public services, not only in the United Kingdom but also in the United States (Osborne and Gaebler, 1992; Glennerster and Le Grand, 1995).

Limitations to the traditional model

No incentives for efficiency

Economists distinguish two kinds of efficiency. *Allocative* efficiency exists in a situation where resources are distributed throughout the economy in ways that reflect the best possible fit between what consumers want and what can be produced. This concept is to be distinguished from *productive* efficiency. Are the firms producing the goods or services doing so in the most efficient way? Critics argued that public and social services fell down in both respects. We begin with allocative efficiency.

Allocative efficiency and choice

Because parents or patients or clients mostly had no choice of school or hospital, they had no way of expressing their preferences for one kind of service or another. In the marketplace it was in the interests of shops and firms to experiment in offering diverse products. The one that achieved the right mix received the most custom. This could not happen in a monopolist public service. Social service providers had no way of knowing what it was that consumers really wanted. Traditional supporters of the public service model responded by pointing out that the users of services had the vote and that political parties had an interest in finding out what users wanted. Economists claimed that representative power over the day-to-day running of services was minimal. The case was powerfully put in an influential book by an American economist, A. O. Hirschman (1970), called *Exit, Voice and Loyalty*.

Exit, Voice and Loyalty

Hirschman's book is often cited by those who seem to have read no more than the title, but the book merits more attention. He begins by asking why it is that inefficient organizations exist at all if the market really works as it is meant to? He claims that there are two kinds of sanction or power that consumers have over organizations to make them respond to what they want.

One is by taking their custom elsewhere, to a firm that is providing what they want or doing it more efficiently. That is what traditional economic theory suggests will happen. In fact, there are considerable limits to people's capacity to exit. It may be costly to change provider, to build up links and personal networks. He cites schooling as a case where the child may suffer from a move and certainly from frequent moves. Consumers of personal services, like patients of a family doctor, may have loyalty and trust in him or her that are important elements in the professional relationship. Thus 'exit' is limited by the nature of the service, not just by whether it is publicly or privately provided. There are inherent limits to competition. Nevertheless, exit is the most powerful sanction.

The alternative that users of public services have is 'voice'. This also has severe limitations. Voice is costly. It means attending parent–teacher meetings, standing for election, campaigning. It is conditional on influence and bargaining power. That may be poorly distributed amongst the users. Those with high status or power in the outside social structure will be able to exert more leverage through voice.

He ends by advocating a mixture of exit and voice in public services. Voice, through democratic institutions, has to be made more effective, and one way to do that is to introduce an element of exit. Consumers have to be able to change doctors, schools, landlords, and so on, to bring their dissatisfaction to bear.

Productive efficiency and markets

Another American economist, H. Leibenstein (1966) distinguished allocative efficiency from what he called X-inefficiency. By this he meant the tendency of firms to produce the kind of products people wanted, but in a more costly, less efficient way than they would in a really competitive climate. Working practices might be slack or management poor. Instead of monopolies working efficiently and their owners drawing supernormal profit, the surplus was, as it were, being consumed by those working in the organization. They were not forced to be as sharp, innovative and hard working as they would have to be in a competitive environment.

It was possible to apply that analysis to the public sector. Public services are virtual monopolies. As public sector bodies they could not earn supernormal profits but the employees could make life easy for themselves, as follows:

1. Staff could adopt procedures that were comfortable for them but inconvenient for the public. Schools are only open part of the day at times inconvenient to young mothers. There is little reason for them to change. Caretakers and staff on public housing estates may have little incentive to produce a good environment. Their jobs were secure, however bad a job they did.
2. The rules which governed procedures were designed to prevent abuse of funds or political embarrassment. That often meant, 'do not do anything new, take the safe way out'.
3. Those in positions of authority could abuse that power. The hospital consultant might spend his time at a private clinic or on the golf course and leave his junior colleagues to do the job.
4. Social services, in particular, made the assumption that the professionals who worked in them regulated their own standards and were motivated by altruism or notions of professional duty to their clients or patients. This had the convenient side effect of expecting them to work for low pay. Economists and social policy analysts argued that this view was unrealistic (Downs, 1967; Lees, 1966; Wilding, 1982). While some bureaucrats and professionals were altruistic, self-interest, individual gain and the quiet life were equally important motives. Public servants are not all 'knights or angels', as Julian Le Grand (1995) has put it, and some may be knaves.

Organizations that ignore this are likely to be inefficient and unresponsive to clients.

Markets as the answer

In a competitive private market, the argument ran, these dangers were minimized because, if they became too great, customers would go elsewhere and the firm would lose money. This tended to ignore the limits to competition in the private sector and compare the perfect model of a private market with the real and imperfect world of the public sector, but the essential case was a powerful one. The solution was to introduce into the public sector the same competitive rigour that, in theory, applied in the private sector. That meant putting out to competitive tender the functions that were traditionally undertaken by public services (Savas, 1977, 1982).

The equity case

Although the case for markets put by the right in politics had concentrated on choice and productive efficiency arguments, there was a line of reasoning developed by what might be called the new market left, which concentrated on equity or distributional issues.

The foundation for this view began with the observation that the welfare state had in many ways benefited the middle class more than it had the working class (Abel-Smith, 1958; Townsend and Bosanquet, 1972; Le Grand, 1982; Goodin and Le Grand, 1987). While cash benefits were highly redistributive, going largely to the poor, services in kind were different, Le Grand (1982) argued. The points he made were as follows:

1. Gaining access to services in kind could be costly, both in time and in earnings forgone. It could involve waiting for doctors, seeking a second opinion, persuading your GP to arrange for a bed in a London teaching hospital instead of your local hospital, seeing head teachers or local authority education department officials to persuade them to take your child at the best school. The poor could afford the time less than the rich and were less equipped to follow such strategies.

2. Such activities required confidence and high status. These at-
   tributes also tended to make such groups relatively more successful in bringing pressure to bear on governments to expand
   or defend those services that served the middle class most. The
   successful defence of free university education from the proposal to charge fees on a means-tested basis in the mid-1980s
   was an example that fitted the theory.

The same kinds of inequality of influence worked in favour of
those services where the middle class were the main service providers – health care, for example. The collective protests by the
Royal Colleges against cuts in the NHS in 1988 were taken a good
deal more seriously than complaints by local authority manual
workers or council house managers. The public expenditure cuts of
the 1980s might therefore be expected to affect least those services
that were supplied to the middle class by the middle class (Le
Grand and Winter, 1987).

One policy conclusion from this analysis was to shift more state
activity to cash benefits which could be targeted on the poor.
Where services in kind were necessary they could be financed by
tied cash payments – vouchers. These could be set at higher levels
for the poor: children from low-income families, for example. This
would mean that schools would take more notice of poor parents.
They would attract more resources to their school if they attracted
more poor children. To do that they would have to do a good job
with deprived children. This was the kind of distinctive case the
new market left made out for a market in welfare over and above
the efficiency case the New Right were making.

Different kinds of market

Cash in a private market

The most extreme variant of bringing the market to welfare was to
say that all state services should be abolished and their cash
equivalent given to individuals. Simply to give cash, however,
might lead to parents spending the money themselves and not
educating the child.

Vouchers

One way to minimize these difficulties, advocated by Milton Friedman (1962), was to add to individuals' purchasing power in ways that tied state assistance to the purchase of a particular service in the marketplace. This could be done, as described in Chapter 1, by issuing a voucher to an individual or family for them to spend on a defined service, rather like a luncheon voucher. Several examples of this kind of arrangement exist in the United Kingdom or have been proposed.

1. Parents can be given a voucher to help them buy pre-schooling in a public or private nursery, as the Conservative government announced it would do from 1996 on an experimental basis and generally from 1997.
2. A young person can be given a training voucher, take it to an employer and require some form of training on the job. Experiments of this kind have been taking place in the 1990s.
3. The family of a mentally disabled child could be given a voucher to pay for care or training and they would be free to spend it with any agency or mix of agencies they chose (Bosanquet, 1984) (see Chapter 11).
4. Parents of children under 5 could be given a voucher to spend on whatever form of child care seemed most appropriate (Hewitt, 1989; Glennerster, 1995).

Quasi-vouchers

Many of the reforms introduced by the Conservative government in the 1990s have resulted in administrative arrangements that produce results which are essentially the same as vouchers.

If consumers of a service have free choice of which school or GP to go to and the school or GP with whom they sign on automatically gets a given sum of money from the government or local authority, this *is* effectively a school or health voucher system in operation. The 1988 Education Act introduced this arrangement for state schools in England (see Chapter 12). The assisted places scheme had introduced what was essentially a means-tested voucher for children attending some private schools in 1981 (see Chapter 12). The 1990 National Health Service and Community Care Act did the same for GPs by increasing patients' capacity to change GP. GPs have always been paid a given sum for each patient on their list since the health service began, and indeed before that under the old panel system. The 1990 Act also extended a voucher-like system to hospital services through the introduction of GP fundholding (see Chapter 10). Formula funding plus choice equals an effective voucher.

Tax or other refunds for specified expenditure

Another way of achieving the same effect is for government to promise to give a tax refund to individuals who spend money on an approved social purpose. Housing, and pension contributions are well-established examples. Tax benefits were extended to encourage personal private pensions in the 1980s (see Chapter 14). Other examples are as follows:

1. Those who take out private health insurance were given tax relief if they were over 60 in the 1990 Finance Act (see Chapter 10).
2. Those who paid fees at a private nursing home could recover the cost from the social security system. This type of arrangement spread rapidly after 1983 but was ended for new residents after April 1993 (see Chapter 11).
3. Housing benefit is another variant. Cash is given to individuals to pay their housing costs (see Chapter 13).

Quasi- or internal markets

Where the inequality of market knowledge between purchaser and provider was not too great, market reformers were prepared to advocate these kinds of change. Where that inequality was great, as in the case of health care, different solutions were advanced. The basis of the 'reforms' to the National Health Service embodied in the National Health Service and Community Care Act 1990 was to pull apart the purchaser and provider role in the NHS. It was accepted that the central Exchequer should continue to finance health care for anyone who wanted to use the NHS. District health authorities were charged with the responsibility of ensuring that the populations in their areas had available a high standard of care free at the point of use. However, instead of seeking to provide all the services themselves, the districts were free to buy services from hospitals in other districts, from the newly independent hospital trusts, or from the private sector. The influential American advocate of this reform, Alan Enthoven (1985), argued that districts could 'use the possibility of buying outside as bargaining leverage to get better performance from their own providers'.

Some general practitioners were also given certain limited powers to purchase services from whichever hospital they chose. For details of these changes see Chapter 10. Districts and fund-holding general practitioners were to act as informed purchasers of health services on the patients' behalf. The same principle was applied to social services departments in the same Act. They were to become purchasing agencies for community care services in their areas. District health authorities and social services departments would make contracts with their own or other units to provide a specific service at a given price. All of these moves to introduce elements of consumer exit power have been given the generic title of '*quasi-market* reforms' (Le Grand and Bartlett, 1993).

A fundamental change

The social policy legislation introduced by the Conservative government between 1988 and 1990 thus embodied a fundamental change in the social administration paradigm that had dominated thinking for a generation. It marked a complete break with the social administration principles of the 1940s to 1980s. The fusion of finance and control was to be replaced by competition and a contract culture. The role of local authorities was substantially downgraded. They were to become contractors not providers. Other powers and budgets were delegated down to schools or housing estates. This left central government and its civil servants relatively more powerful (Glennerster *et al.*, 1991; Glennerster and Le Grand, 1995).

The market had come to welfare and its origins were not entirely those of the right in politics. The changes looked as if they could be long-lasting.

Limits to quasi-markets

Just as there are limits to markets and market failures of the kind
we discussed in the last chapter, so there are limits to quasi-
markets. The importance of these limits varies in the case of each
service and they are discussed in more detail in the service chapters later in the book. Here some general issues are highlighted.
For any market to perform, certain conditions have to be satisfied.
That is as true of quasi-markets as real ones.

Multiple providers and free entry?

If providers are to feel that if they do not do a good job they will
lose the contract next year, there have to be other providers able
to step in. There has to be genuine competition between, ideally,
numerous organizations, for example all seeking to provide health
care to a district. In many instances – some would say most – this is
not a realistic picture outside the largest population centres and
often not even there. Because of what were seen to be the economies of scale associated with grouping functions in a large district
general hospital, distinct health authorities concentrated services
in units that serve large catchment areas. That process has continued after the reforms too. There may be, at the moment, no
effective competitors for many procedures or for emergency care
in many areas. However, for most non-emergency procedures, for
laboratory testing, and for outpatient and community health care
there certainly is a potentially contestable market. Similar problems arise in the case of secondary schools or voluntary care agencies, especially in rural areas.

Free entry?

If there are few existing competitors, markets need new entrants
who are able to enter the market readily, set up business, provide
something new and more efficient, and attract custom. Yet the
Treasury has kept tight control on new capital expenditure for
hospitals, schools and caring services. Even hospital trusts will find
it difficult to gain Treasury approval for speculative ventures

designed to put other public providers out of business. Private investors are likely to be wary of putting up money to compete where existing public agencies have a head start, unless there is clear evidence of additional demand which the state wants to meet. A tight budgetary climate is not conducive to speculative ventures. Conditions for free entry may not apply.

An even playing field?

For competition to be fair, district health authorities or local education or social service authorities would have to be indifferent to the fate of schools or facilities that they run in competition with a private unit in another area. This seems unlikely to happen, because the local authority would bear the brunt of criticism if a local facility is closed. The Conservative government's response may be to turn all schools and hospitals over to independent trusts, but as it stands, locally elected purchasing bodies are in an ambiguous position. Nor is it easy to see that even central government can readily walk away from the political fallout from a hospital closing, for example. Yet without the sanction of closure or bankruptcy, market discipline will not work.

A well-informed purchaser

Consumers, purchasers, need good information on service outcomes and quality, which does not exist in most areas of social policy. Though the need for it by purchasers may generate more and better information, this will be costly. The same applies to price information. In the NHS this was almost totally absent. Similar issues arise in education. One of the important outcomes of the market reforms has been to increase the demand for and supply of good information about costs and outcomes. There is still a very long way to go (Maynard, 1991).

A free market for labour

One of the characteristics of health, education and social work is that they are provided by professional groups which restrict entry to their professions. They also negotiate salaries as a group. This tends to mean that they have monopoly power in negotiating rewards for their services. We can see the most costly results in the United States where doctors' incomes are high relative to those in this country.

In the United Kingdom one outcome of the centralized system of service provision has been that the government has the ability to take a tough line, facing the professions with a single buyer of their services – a monopsonist position. Where multiple sellers of services have to make their own bargains with a monopoly professional body, the result could be an escalation in pay and costs in those services concerned (Barr *et al.*, 1988; Mayston, 1990). In fact, local bargaining and pay setting has been very slow to come. The government has been reluctant to let go and central unions are fearful of losing their power.

Making contracts stick

In the private world of contracting, simple contracts can be repeated with little cost, for example buying a house, though it may not seem that way! We saw in the first part of the chapter that one of the original reasons why firms came to integrate their activities was the cost, complexity and risks of contracting. These factors have not gone away. Many health and social care contracts have been very simple broad-brush, block, contracts which have done no more than regularize in contractual language what used to happen. This is changing as authorities gain more experience. Increasingly, a health authority will take a small group of services and review them in detail, and then make a longer-term contract and build a relationship with that provider. This reduces the costs of contracting, but it makes the relationship less like that of a crude market.

Cream skimming

Competition between public and private providers of services will create the same kinds of problems as in traditional markets. Cream skimming is the most obvious. If a general practitioner is paid a flat sum of money in a competitive situation to take a patient, there will be an incentive to refuse to take potentially less healthy patients. Competition to exclude the unhealthy could be as potent as it is in a private insurance market (Matsaganis and Glennerster, 1994). It may be possible to create counterincentives by paying GPs, for example, more to take potentially more expensive patients, and this is already happening to some extent. Very similar arguments apply in the case of schools (Glennerster, 1991; Vandenburghe, 1995).

The general advantages quasi-markets may bring and the limits and costs they can entail vary from one type of service to another. Later chapters explore how far markets have been introduced into each type of service and what they may mean in the long term.

Further reading

A good summary of the relative pros and cons of contracting versus hierarchical structures to deliver social services is provided in W. Bartlett (1991), 'Quasi-markets and contracts: a markets and hierarchies perspective on NHS reform', *Public Money*, **11**, no. 3, pp. 53–61. An early account of the quasi-market reforms of the 1990s is given in J. Le Grand and W. Bartlett (eds) (1993), *Quasi Markets and Social Policy*, London: Macmillan, which reviews American experience and gives a good theoretical framework; the same theme is covered, but more briefly, in J. Le Grand, H. Glennerster and A. Maynard (1991), 'Quasi-markets and social policy', *Economic Journal*, **101**, no. 408, pp. 1256–67.

An American hard sell of the case for improving the efficiency of the public sector through competition and decentralization is contained in D. Osborne and T. Gaebler (1992), *Reinventing Government: How the entrepreneurial spirit is transforming the public sector from schoolhouse to statehouse, city hall to Pentagon*, Reading, Mass.: Addison-Wesley.

The original and very influential book that makes the case for privatizing services like refuse disposal, and is most important conceptually, is E. S. Savas (1982), *Privatising the Public Sector: How to shrink government*, Chatham, NJ: Chatham House.

Finally, an account of why Scandinavian and British health services came to adopt the purchaser–provider split is given in R. Saltman and C. von Otter (1992), *Planned Markets and Public Competition*, Milton Keynes: The Open University. More importantly, this book makes a theoretical case for empowering consumers of social services through markets *within* the public sector.

PART II

The controlling institutions

CHAPTER 4

SETTING THE LIMITS AT THE CENTRE

There are three separate but interacting processes which determine how much we pay for welfare from the public purse. First, discussed in this chapter, is the procedure by which central government decides upon the total level of public expenditure it believes should be financed out of taxation. This not only determines what central government will spend itself, but also influences what other public agencies, including local authorities, will spend. Second, there is allocation of central funds to local authorities and the interaction between central government and local councils who provide services. Third, there is the budget process within those local authorities.

Before tracing the developments of public spending control at the centre, it is worth setting out briefly the contrasting ways in which other academics have sought to analyze it in order to make my own theoretical framework explicit.

Alternative views of spending control

The *pluralist* tradition is probably dominant in political science writing on budgeting. It is best exemplified in Wildavsky's work (Wildavsky, 1975, 1979; Heclo and Wildavsky, 1981). It sees public expenditure and taxing decisions as the outcome of competition between interest groups. Some represent users and others providers of services. They exert leverage where their pressures can be most effective. In America, Congressional Committees are important. In the United Kingdom, users and providers focus their attention on the spending departments in Whitehall. Parliament itself is relatively passive. Other economic interests wish to restrain public spending. These are articulated, in particular, through finance and economic affairs departments – the Treasury in the United Kingdom. In Whitehall the contest between the spenders and the controllers is largely played out behind closed doors (Heclo and Wildavsky, 1981). These writers scorn attempts to make budgeting a 'rational strategic' process. Budgets shift forwards or backwards by small 'increments', reflecting the balance of interests. More recently, writers in the pluralist tradition have come to emphasize the importance of 'inheritance' in budgeting (Rose and Davies, 1994). Past legislation forms the basis for the next budget round and is relatively infrequently repealed, especially in the social policy field. Mrs Thatcher inherited over 3,000 pieces of law, over half of which dated from before the Second World War. Only 11 per cent of her government's total expenditure was spent on legislation it initiated. Even at the end of the Attlee government's period of welfare state building in 1951, over 80 per cent of its social policy budget dated from before the war. This is not, in fact, an irrational consequence of lazy politicians. Especially in the case of social policy, individuals' and families' lifetime choices are made on the basis of expectations about what the state will provide. Family budgets would be devastated if parents suddenly found that they were expected to pay for their children's school fees, for example. Electorates are uncomfortable with rapid change or reversals of policy.

The *managerialist tradition* has produced numerous attempts at budgetary reform designed to encourage a more technical appraisal of spending choices, to produce longer-term spending plans and management systems that link the goals of departments to measurable outcomes, or to delegate budgetary control to cost centres or external agencies and hold them accountable using new methods of computerized financial information (Novick, 1965; Schick, 1966; Goldman, 1973; Cmnd 9058, 1983; Likierman, 1988; OECD, 1987; Thain and Wright 1995). It sees government faced with the same task of managing and controlling spending as any large business. The techniques used by business can therefore be adapted to government. In 1988 the UK Efficiency Unit, reporting to the Prime Minister, took the argument to its logical conclusion. Those parts of the civil service that provided services to the public, like the social security department, should be 'hived off' into separate agencies to get on with the job free of day-to-day political interference. The title of the Unit's report was *Improving Management in Government: The next steps*. The new agencies – like the Social Security Benefits Agency – came to be called 'Next Steps Agencies'. They should be run much as private companies, with chief executives and management boards. Work should be organized in a way that focused on the job to be done and there must be 'real and sustained pressure on and within each department for continuous improvement in the value for money obtained in the delivery of policies and services' (UK Efficiency Unit, 1988: 7).

The *Marxist tradition* emphasizes the dominance of capital in the economy of western nations. Government spending and taxing strategies are therefore subservient to economic interests, but the state is also trying to contain pressures from the working class for more services and benefits. It is this conflict that is reflected in the Whitehall spending battle. Parts of the economy need more spending in order to sustain profits, but all need to be taxed less. These contradictions explain the recurrent expenditure crises. The control of public spending therefore becomes central to the sustenance of the capitalist system (Gough, 1979). Faced with unpopular cuts, the government increased central control while leaving much of the responsibility for making the cuts to local government, thus fragmenting opposition (Flynn, 1988).

In what follows, we adopt what might be called a neo-pluralist approach (Hall *et al.*, 1975; Dunleavy and O'Leary, 1987). The process of expenditure control can be seen as a competitive game between spending departments and the Treasury, but the rules of the game reflect the economic context. As the economic crisis has deepened the rules have shifted increasingly in the Treasury's favour and the centre's power to contain local spending has grown. The nature of the economic system and the conflicts within it influence the changing rules of the game.

The institutions of control

In the seventeenth and eighteenth centuries, it was the Crown's desire to spend and Parliament's desire to limit the tax burden which led to regular conflicts between the king and Parliament. The House of Lords lost its powers of financial scrutiny in the 1911 Parliament Act but the House of Commons continued to be jealous of its power to scrutinize ministers' proposals for expenditure. In theory that role persists. A government department can only spend money specifically approved by the House of Commons. The government's taxing agents, the Inland Revenue, or Customs and Excise officials, levy taxes only with the House of Commons' approval. Local authorities may levy taxes only under Parliament's approval. The House of Commons Public Accounts Committee and its 'spies' (officials of the National Audit Office) make sure that money is not spent on purposes and in amounts that Parliament has not authorized. They also seek to ensure that it is spent with due 'economy, efficiency and effectiveness'. The Audit Commission performs the same functions as far as local authorities and the National Health Service are concerned. It has a Scottish equivalent, the Commission for Local Authority Accounts.

In practice, however, as party discipline grew, the institutional battle over the level of spending and taxing took place more and more *within* the government machine. In the end, the choices rest with the Cabinet and lie at the heart of modern politics. The Cabinet has as members ministers who are running major departments, want to see the service for which they are responsible improved, but are aware that collectively their joint demands could ruin their party's chances in the next election. Too large an increase in personal taxation could lose them votes and deny them further ministerial office. The Chancellor, the Chief Secretary to the Treasury, and the Prime Minister, have the task of pointing out the financial realities of life to their colleagues. The detailed battles go on between Her Majesty's Treasury, whose constitutional role is to contain spending, and the spending departments who are responsible for the individual services, and who are aware of demands they are under and the nature of the rising costs to which they are subject.

To a large extent the spending authorizations that emerge are the result of the interplay between the Treasury and the 'spending' ministries. The complex rules of this game that have grown, been discarded and then developed in another form, are all part of a continuous struggle between the spenders and the controllers. The Treasury will develop a system of control that temporarily contains the pressures; the spending departments will adapt, and may actually turn the new rules to their advantage. The Treasury responds with another, more effective weapon. The present system of bargaining and control is therefore best understood by tracing its origins and developments. From Gladstone's period as Chancellor in the middle of the last century onwards, a set of rules or constitutional conventions evolved that gave the Treasury its central position as guardian of the public purse, as follows:

1. No individual MP can make a proposal to spend public money or raise taxes. Under Standing Orders of the House of Commons no proposal to spend money can be tabled for discussion unless it is countersigned by a Treasury minister. This is in contrast to the United States, for example, where individual Congressmen can initiate spending proposals.
2. No proposal involving additional spending can be discussed by Ministers in Cabinet or Cabinet subcommittee unless it is accompanied by a Treasury paper on the cost consequences.
3. No spending proposals may be developed by a department from the earliest stages without consultation with the Treasury.
4. No department can spend money without Treasury approval.

The Treasury has staff to keep a continual watch over each department's spending. It is their business to know the strengths and weaknesses of each department's case. They are the individuals who must be given early warning if a new spending proposal is in the pipeline. Their opposite numbers in the spending departments are the principal finance officers. They act as go-betweens, representing their department's best case but also educating their own administrators and professional staff in the realities of a confined budget. As Heclo and Wildavsky (1981) emphasized in their classic account of the 'Whitehall village', there must be a strong element of trust. Each set of actors must respect the other's role and be as open as possible – not with the public, but with each other.

Even given good behaviour between gentlemen, spending departments have evolved some relatively effective tactics and strategies in pressing their cause with the Treasury or Cabinet (Glennerster, 1975):

1. Use the 'thin edge of the wedge' – press a proposal that has small short-term financial consequences but bigger long-term ones.

2. Appoint a committee of specialists to report on an aspect of a service. Its members, all interested in improving the service, are likely to produce an impressive case for expansion. The Ministry of Education and its successor, the Department of Education and Science, did this with great effect in the 1950s and 1960s.
3. Use a crisis or scandal constructively. Damaging revelations about conditions in mental subnormality hospitals were used by the Minister, Richard Crossman, to gain funds to improve conditions in mental hospitals in the late 1960s.
4. Work with pressure groups in your field. The poverty lobby may be critical, but they may also be helpful in creating a constituency for your department's proposals. In the Thatcher period this lobby lost its influence and private corporate interests replaced it, especially those with an interest in privatization.

If the climate of opinion is sympathetic and the Cabinet favourable, these tactics and strategies may be successful. At the end of the 1950s, the Treasury and its ministers came to believe that they were losing too many of the battles. Lowe's (1989) account of the spending departments' rout of various Treasury attempts to curb social spending in the mid-1950s illustrates this well. The Chancellor and his team resigned. The House of Commons Select Committee on the Estimates (1958) argued that the whole system of Treasury control was breaking down and advocated a committee of inquiry. The result was an internal committee with an external chairman – Lord Plowden. His report (Cmnd 1432, 1961) resulted in major reforms in the system of Treasury control, many of which remain in place today, though substantially modified in the intervening years. The report's diagnosis, as well as its proposals, are important for understanding the procedures that followed.

Plowden's diagnosis

The system of setting limits to public spending had broken down because:

1. The old climate of political opinion that was broadly hostile to the public sector had changed. The Treasury was swimming against the tide.

2. Proposals for new projects tended to 'bubble up' to Cabinet one at a time. Each on its own seemed admirable and only a small addition to the government's total expenditure. No total view of the consequences of all the commitments emerged until it was too late.
3. Policies were embarked upon with little notion of the long-term consequences on spending.
4. The overall effect was that total spending and hence taxation tended to rise faster than the Cabinet really wanted in the long term. This led to sudden and wasteful cuts in spending and cancellation of capital programmes.

Plowden's remedy

To put this right, Plowden proposed a new system of control that would force the Cabinet collectively to set limits to its ambitions, as follows:

1. There should be regular surveys of the long-term expenditure implications of current and proposed policies. The aim would be 'to ensure that the long-term rate of expansion in public expenditure was properly aligned with prospective resources'. Cabinet was to be asked to look at the probable growth in the economy, and the amount of tax revenue it wished to generate and *then* decide what in total it could afford to spend. Within that total, ministers would bid for funds, but that total, to which they had collectively agreed, should not be breached. We can call this the *control function* of the new system. It was to extend beyond controlling central government's direct spending and was to embrace the capital spending of nationalized industries and local authority spending too.
2. The second goal was 'to achieve greater stability in public spending decisions'. The limits to spending would be set out with a long-term perspective. Spending departments would be told how much they could spend in real terms in the next four years. This was a kind of *quid pro quo* for the spending departments. They could expect to receive a given level of real resources and plan accordingly for the medium term. We can call this the *planning function* of the new system.

3. The third objective was for the Treasury 'to improve the tools for making choices'. At the time this was barely spelt out, but as the 1960s progressed, the Treasury began to introduce from America a range of new budgeting and cost benefit techniques that can be seen as the means of implementing this objective. It could be called the *efficiency function* of the new system.

The Plowden reforms remain the basis of public spending control to this day. It has become fashionable to argue that the post-Plowden, long-term planning of public spending proved a disaster and actually helped to increase the growth of public spending, though in the early 1970s an American observer thought the system one of the most sophisticated and successful in the world (Wildavsky, 1975).

It was, in fact, the rapid inflation of the early 1970s that gave the system its bad reputation. It had been designed in a period of relative economic stability and was not fitted for such tumultuous times. The economic crisis of 1976 and the advent of Mrs Thatcher's Conservative government in 1979 was to change all that. The assumption from which the Treasury began, that the world was against them, changed. The key other actor, the Prime Minister, was with them all the way – on containing public expenditure, at least. In the mid-1970s individuals' real take-home pay fell for several years running, and the climate of public opinion, too, moved towards reducing taxes, showing less enthusiasm for spending though support for the NHS remained high (Whiteley, 1981). The political climate in which the Treasury was working in the 1980s and 1990s was different from the 1950s and 1960s and proved of crucial importance.

The changing rules of the game – Plowden's legacy

During the early 1960s government departments were asked to produce fairly crude estimates of their spending four years ahead in constant prices. A new expenditure division in the Treasury was created to co-ordinate and develop these forecasts. Total claims from spending departments were set against expected growth targets in the economy to check their feasibility. A new minister, the Chief Secretary to the Treasury, was appointed to oversee the whole exercise. Called the public expenditure survey, it gave its name to the whole process – PES.

By the economic crisis of 1967 it was clear the system had failed to prevent an even more rapid rise in public spending than before 1961. The plans had been based on overoptimistic assumptions of the potential growth of the economy and hence of revenue. From 1968 onwards, the economic growth targets became somewhat lower but continued to be too optimistic. The estimates from each department became more detailed and were spelt out for each of the future years. The results of the whole exercise were published in an annual White Paper and it or its successors have been published every year since. In 1970 the Heath government sought to fit in the third piece of the Plowden jigsaw – the efficiency function.

In a White Paper issued shortly after they came to office the new Conservative administration reviewed the development of the PES system to date and argued that there should be regular in-depth reviews of spending programmes, on both a departmental and interdepartmental basis. What emerged was a system that also became known by its initials, 'PAR' – programme analysis and review. To help administer it was a body called the Central Policy Review Staff (CPRS) which reviewed policies interdepartmentally. It was a small group attached to the Cabinet Office, comprising mainly younger civil servants, academics, and other outsiders seconded for brief periods. Some important issues were explored, from race relations and pre-school policy to issues of population change and the family, and the CPRS sought to establish a formal regular examination by Cabinet of social policy issues. It was called the Joint Framework for Social Policy (CPRS, 1975; Klein, 1988). It was not to last for long. Mrs Thatcher's administration eventually wound up both the PAR system and CPRS. (For an account and evaluation of the work of the CPRS by two people involved, see Blackstone and Plowden, 1988.)

Individual departments also developed a series of service planning systems. The aim was to ensure that local authorities developed plans that were consistent with the government's spending target (Glennerster, 1981b).

By the mid-1970s, therefore, the main elements of Plowden reforms were in place and had developed in sophistication, yet they failed, at that point, to prevent the fastest-ever growth in public spending outside wartime. The reason lay in the large economic changes that were affecting the world economy, the government's own responses, and the particular nature of the new machinery of control. In a turbulent economy, the planning and control functions turned out to be mutually incompatible. Departments' spending plans that were bargained over and eventually published in the annual public expenditure White Papers were expressed in constant prices or 'volume terms'. They excluded the effect of any general rise in prices or any rises specific to that service. Thus, if education were promised a rise in its allocation at 2 per cent a year, this would mean a real increase – in its capacity to employ teachers or build schools – of 2 per cent a year. Having fixed these 'volume' targets at the beginning of its period of office, a government would seek to hold to them even if the economy expanded faster or slower than expected, or if prices or wages rose. In these circumstances it was necessary for central government to pass supplementary estimates asking Parliament to vote more money to the Health Service or to local authorities. Public spending came to take a larger share of the nation's resources even though each service was keeping to its real volume target. It gave a degree of certainty to public sector managers in the short run, but when the tax costs began to mount, governments resumed their sudden cuts – just the situation Plowden had hoped to avoid. The planning function, as the Treasury saw it, had been performed too well to the detriment of its control function.

Growing criticism was once more reflected in a report by a House of Commons committee, this time the General Subcommittee of the Expenditure Committee (House of Commons, 1976) and the economic crisis of 1976 brought another set of important changes.

The 1976 changes

The changes which the Treasury introduced in this period reasserted the primacy of the control function (Wright, 1980; Else and Marshall, 1981; Thain and Wright, 1995). The first and most important change was the general introduction of *cash limits*. This was a figure of actual spending that a department must not overshoot in the coming year, no matter what happened to prices or the wages and salaries of its employees in the interim. In

translating the original constant price figure for the department
that had appeared in the public expenditure White Paper into the
new cash limit figure, the Treasury estimated the likely price and
wage increases for the year ahead. However, if these pay norms
were breached or prices rose more than expected, the level of
service would have to be cut back to meet the cash limit. In
1976–7 this is precisely what happened. Prices rose more than
expected, but even so, departments kept well inside their new
limits and the result was a cut in real spending of 2.5 per cent.
This was a much larger cut than the government had planned,
larger indeed than the announced cuts that had caused so much
controversy in 1976.

Not all departments' spending could be cash limited. Some items
of expenditure like social security, unemployment benefit or prescriptions dispensed by GPs were seen to be demand-led commitments. The DSS has a statutory duty to pay benefits of a given
level approved by Parliament regardless of the level of sickness or
unemployment that may arise in any one year. Altogether about
40 per cent of public spending was directly cash limited at that
time. Local authority spending *per se* was not included, but grants
to local authorities and their total capital spending were. Thus,
directly and indirectly, over half of public spending was covered by
cash limits.

The second innovation that flowed from the 1976 crisis was complementary to the first – a new *financial information system* (FIS).
This is a regular return of departmental spending which gives the
Treasury early warning of the possibility that a department may
overshoot its cash limit.

The third innovation was to *limit the length of the planning
cycle* – to reduce the period over which the government published spending targets, at least in any detail. That period now
only covers the year ahead and two succeeding years in broader
outline.

Cash planning

When the Conservatives returned to power in 1979 they revised
the PES system in an even more fundamental way. From 1982 the

two separate sets of targets used by the Labour government – volume and cash limits – were abolished. From that point, the figures used in the White Paper to set targets for future spending were set in 'cash terms', that is, they are the actual amount of money that government departments or health authorities, for example, are permitted to spend regardless of actual price or pay movements in the interim. Moreover, instead of these cash limits being set one year ahead they were now to cover the *whole* planning period, that is, three years ahead. The Treasury set out the advantages of cash planning in the following way:

1. Ministers discuss the cash that will actually be spent, and therefore what will have to be financed by taxation or borrowing, instead of talking about 'funny money' – numbers which could be misleadingly different from the resultant cash spent.
2. Expenditure figures can be related more readily to the revenue projection, so that 'finance [can] determine expenditure and not expenditure finance'.
3. Changes in public sector costs are brought into the discussion. The previous constant price system did not bring out the effect of, for example, the rapid relative rise in public service pay in 1979–80 resulting from the Clegg Commission and other comparability awards.
4. Previously, the 'volume' plans – that is, plans in constant prices – were regarded by spending managers as entitlements, carried forward from year to year regardless of what was happening to costs. This meant that programme managers had little incentive to adapt their expenditures in response to increasing relative costs, except in the short term in response to the annual cash limits.
5. The decisions in the annual survey, as they relate to the year ahead, can be translated directly into the cash limits and estimates presented to Parliament, without revaluation from one price basis to another (HM Treasury, 1981).

This system of 'cash planning' has remained in place ever since. The public expenditure survey that had begun as a mixture of planning and budgetary control became primarily a process of cash ceiling control. The process was to be completed in the reforms of the 1990s (see below).

Disadvantages for spending departments

Spending departments suffered a comparable set of disadvantages. For the system to work at all smoothly from their point of view, the estimates of inflation built into the Treasury's cash target for their department must be accurate. If the Treasury underestimates the level of inflation, as it has every incentive to do, departments will be forced to cut their spending further in real terms to keep within the limits. No spending department can be sure what the figures in the White Paper will mean for its capacity to pay school teachers or run hospitals. The spending targets in the White Paper thus turn out to be unhelpful for long-term planning purposes. In this way the control function finally became supreme. The rules of the game had swung the Treasury's way.

Not only is it impossible now to tell what the figures for the *future* will actually mean for the service, but even the informed observer or MP cannot tell what *has* been happening. Past cash expenditure, uncorrected for inflation, tells the interested observer nothing about whether the service has more or less resources to work with. The published figures do now show, in addition, *past* spending on each service corrected for *general* price increases. The Treasury calls this 'real terms' spending. Yet this is not what the observer interested in the health or education service wants to know. If the prices of baked beans and houses have fallen but the price of drugs has shot up, a

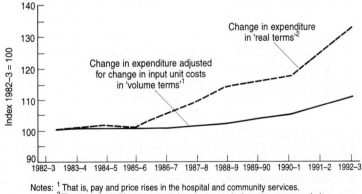

Notes: [1] That is, pay and price rises in the hospital and community services.
[2] That is, adjusted for movements in output costs in the economy as a whole, as measured by GDP deflator.

Figure 4.1 NHS spending in real and volume terms, 1982/3 to 1992/3 (Source: DoH, 1995b)

price index based on an average of prices in the whole economy will not give a good picture of how much extra the NHS can buy with its cash. The Department of Health in its reports does continue to give *both* the 'real terms' figure of health spending and the figures corrected to take account of the prices of health services – drugs, doctors' and nurses' salaries and equipment. Figure 4.1 shows the different story told by these two series.

Success and failure for the Treasury

After cash planning was introduced in 1982 the Treasury enjoyed a period of relative success in containing public spending within the cash limits and holding public spending steady as a share of Gross Domestic Product – the broad goal ever since Plowden. Indeed, for a period from 1983 to 1988 this share fell. Yet the Conservative government had set itself more ambitious targets. It had begun with the goal of reducing public expenditure in real terms (Cmnd 7746, 1979). But although cash limits restrained the rise in spending relative to the growth of the economy, they did not stop it rising in real terms. From 1978–9 to 1992–3 general government expenditure in real terms grew by 1.9 per cent per annum compared to 1.8 per cent under the previous Labour government (Thain and Wright, 1995). That was something like half the rate of growth of the Wilson and Heath years but did not match Mrs Thatcher's ambition. The Treasury thus kept revising its stated goal of reducing the share of public spending in the GDP, and then to holding it constant. Yet in the run-up to the 1992 Election the plans slipped badly again. The plans were to increase spending by 2.7 per cent a year in real terms. However, the economy plunged into a deep recession and forced unplanned expenditure on benefits, *and* the government needed tax cuts to win the election. The result was a very sharp rise in the amount the government had to borrow – the public sector borrowing requirement (PSBR). It rose to nearly 8 per cent of the GDP in 1993/4, an unsustainable level without very high interest rates. There is a limit to what systems of control can achieve if politics are against the Treasury. After the election had been safely won the Treasury tried again with another set of changes to the control system and to the budget. In their detailed account of the period Thain and Wright (1995: 439–40) conclude:

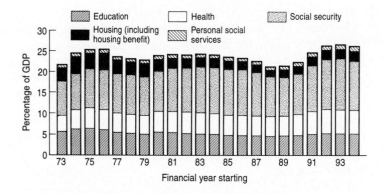

Figure 4.2 UK government welfare spending as a percentage of GDP, 1973/4 to 1994/5 (Source: HM Treasury, 1995; Hills, 1990)

> After fourteen years of ideological hostility to public spending, numerous changes to the planning and control system, and frequent modifications to policy objectives and targets, public spending is set to rise in the 1990s in real terms last experienced in the crisis years of the 1970s. The conclusion is irresistible: Conservative Governments were unable to achieve either the heroic objectives set in 1980 or the less ambitious ones which replaced them in the mid-1980s.

This is, perhaps, a somewhat harsh conclusion. Certainly since 1976 there had been a check to the underlying steady rise in the share of the GDP devoted to social welfare in the United Kingdom. The overall impact of Treasury control on welfare spending since the Plowden Report can be seen in Figure 4.2. The relaxation before the 1992 Election was profoundly worrying to the Treasury. It concluded it was time to change the rules of the game again.

A new control process, a unified budget and Treasury reform in the 1990s

Four major reforms to the process of Treasury control took place in the 1990s:

1. The creation of a new Cabinet Committee to oversee the process – EDX.

2. An accompanying reorganization of the Treasury.
3. The setting of a 'control total' at the outset of the negotiations each year, designed to limit departments' bargaining power.
4. A new 'unified budget' combining the expenditure review with the annual review of tax policy – the old budget. This was designed to sharpen spending ministers' awareness of the tax consequences of their spending claims.

The EDX Committee

It had always been Plowden's intention that the Cabinet would set a broad policy spending objective at its July meeting, leaving subsequent negotiations to take place within it. However, this had always been difficult to achieve. Certainly by the early 1990s, under Mr Major's chairmanship the Cabinet inclined to give only broad guidance, and there was a tendency for 'bilaterals' between ministers and the Chief Secretary to result in bargains being struck in which the initial total set by the Treasury for the department on the basis of last year's figure crept upwards. On some occasions the departments would appeal to an informal Star Chamber of ministers who had settled their own budgets. This also tended to result in compromises.

The intention now was to gain senior Cabinet approval to a hard spending total in June/July and to eliminate the private bilaterals subsequently. The means was to be a new top level and official Cabinet committee, chaired by the Chancellor himself and with seven senior members of Cabinet on it including the Chancellor and the Chief Secretary. This committee would brief Cabinet on setting the target for spending, taking account of the government's tax policy and the economic prognosis in June, and be responsible for all subsequent discussions with spending ministers.

The committee meets in April, one year ahead of the spending it will be discussing for the first of its budget years, to see if there are any special topics it wishes to target for the next year. Officials are sent away to do their homework. Then, in June they present the committee with papers that set out the economic prospects, likely revenue from existing tax policy and the consequent likely public sector borrowing requirement – how much government will have to borrow to cover its spending. This has become a crucial target indicator. The other indicator is the government's tax policy, and in 1995 tax cuts had become a Conservative Party necessity. The Cabinet, with Treasury advice, is then forced to set a fixed total for spending which will make these goals – economic and political – attainable, and to set spending priorities. It does this in July, leaving the summer for the work to be done in forcing each spending department's total down to meet the overall objective.

In September and October the committee's main work takes place. There are about twenty meetings at which detailed spending targets for each department, as worked on with the departments, are presented by the Chief Secretary to the Treasury at meetings chaired by the Chancellor: 'There must be cuts of x per cent and the following items are appropriate to cut.' The spending minister responds: 'This would be terrible and electorally damaging' – and then leaves. The non-Treasury members then decide the outcome – he or she had made a good point, so more might be considered on y, but that will mean being tougher on x, or on another minister, and so on. Having seen all the spending department ministers in September, the committee devotes most of October to private meetings in order to set the final figures for each department. The departments are then informed, and some very contentious issues may require further discussion. In extreme cases, an appeal to Cabinet is made, but for the most part, it seems, EDX prevails. It has the senior clout to do so. The fact that tax and spending decisions are now tied into the same budget announcement and time scale (see below) has strengthened its position. It does seem that EDX has made a difference. Drift resulting from bilateral bargains is much less in evidence so far as one can see, and some very tough expenditure rounds were carried through in 1994 and 1995.

Once the Cabinet approves the figures for each department they are written into the Red Book – the budget document. This also contains the tax changes the Chancellor announces at the end of November. Once the spending totals have been agreed he can get to work on finalizing the tax proposals in his budget. Detailed spending plans for each department are now published separately by the department concerned, and not in one big White Paper as used to be the case.

Treasury reorganization

As the principal department responsible for fiscal prudence the Treasury saw that it had to take the lead in reducing its staff, focusing more sharply on its objectives. The new control process also requires some new backing. In the past the expenditure divisions of the Treasury both shadowed each of the spending departments and ran the PES round. Under the new structure a separate group services EDX, tracks current or revenue spending trends and generally oversees the spending review. The old expenditure divisions remain. They give expert briefing on their areas of spending and oversee the departments as before, though doing so in less detail. They also have a newer responsibility to consider the broader economic efficiency issues that arise in their spending field. This could involve raising issues, like training, or promoting greater competition.

The control total

Before 1992 the Treasury tried to set a 'planning total' within which the Cabinet aimed to keep total public spending. Unlike the old early Plowden days, there was no attempt to increase the figures arrived at in last year's round to take account of *actual* price rises for that service, but a general 'uplift' was assumed in line with expected price increases in the wider economy set out in the medium-term financial strategy. From this was subtracted an 'efficiency saving' of 0.5 per cent. This, give or take various judgements, set the guideline total starting point from which the Treasury would hope to bargain spending departments down and they would hope to bargain up spending. This was a mixture of bottom-up and top-down ceiling setting in which the Treasury ministers and the spending departments usually ended up splitting the difference (see above). After 1992 the 'new control total', as its name implies, was to be set by the Treasury on a much tougher basis – top-down principles were to predominate. The starting point was the underlying growth potential of the economy measured by past trends. It was presumed to be 2 per cent per annum at that time, and to keep general public expenditure within that limit, the part of public spending that the Treasury could hope to control was to be permitted to rise by only 1.5 per cent a year in real terms. Assuming the economy over the long term did grow at this rate, public spending would remain roughly stable as a share of GDP. The logic and the method were not that different from Plowden's.

In fact, 1993–4 saw all the chickens from the pre-election spending rounds coming home to roost. The new Chancellor, Kenneth Clarke, needed to cut public spending faster than the economy was growing in order to reduce both the government's borrowing and its share of the GDP. He therefore proceeded to assume that public sector pay increases should be met out of 'efficiency gains'. In its 1995 budget the government announced that its objective was to reduce public spending to below 40 per cent of the GDP – an objective it planned to reach by 1997–8.

The Treasury not only changed the way the control total was arrived at, but it also changed its composition. The old planning total had included the whole of social security spending, for example, which goes up and down with the number of unemployed, as does debt interest with international interest rates. The Treasury could hardly be blamed for being unable to control these sums. Thus the control total now excludes cyclical social security spending, central government debt interest and accounting adjustments. It does, however, include the spending of local government, a point we discuss in the next chapter. The *Budget Report* (Red Book) for 1996–7 (HM Treasury, 1995) set out the government's expectations for the rest of this century (see Table 4.1).

In Table 4.1, the control total in the top row is the one fixed by Cabinet each year. The Treasury will try to convince Cabinet each year to keep to those figures. Clearly, a new government would want to rethink them. Cyclical social security is the sum set aside to meet the cost of benefits to the unemployed. Debt interest is the cost of government borrowing already known to be growing because of the additional borrowing the government is doing each year. With accounting adjustments, this produces the oddly named GGE(X) which the government is aiming to reduce to below 40 per cent of the gross domestic product. The revenue from selling off British Rail and other privatizations reduces the government's total net spending – general government expenditure (GGE) which appears in the National Accounts. By real growth the Treasury mean spending deflated by a general price index for the whole

Table 4.1 General government expenditure: budget plans (£bn)

	Outturn	Forecast		Projection			
	1994–95	1995–96	1996–97	1997–98	1998–99	1999–00	2000–01
Control total	248.2	255.5	260.2	268	276	283	291
Cyclical social security	14.4	14.0	13.9	14	15	15	16
Central government debt interest	17.6	20.5	22.3	24	24	24	23
Accounting adjustments	9.0	9.6	9.7	9	10	10	11
GGE(X)	**289.2**	**299.6**	**306.1**	**315**	**324**	**332**	**341**
Privatization proceeds	−6.4	−3.0	−4.0	−2½	−1½	−1	−1
Other adjustments	5.0	5.5	6.2	6	6	6	6
GGE	**287.8**	**302.1**	**308.3**	**319**	**329**	**338**	**346**
GGE(X)/GDP ratio (%)	42¾	42	40½	39¾	38¾	38	37
Real growth (%)							
Control total	1¼	¼	−1	½	½	¾	¾
GGE(X)	2¼	¾	−½	½	½	½	½

Source: HM Treasury (1995)

economy, not one that takes account of individual service spending. As can be seen, these figures assumed an almost constant level of public spending until the end of the century – an implausible goal without major policy changes in the basic social services.

The Treasury had, therefore, moved to make its target control total much more open and explicit as well as tighter in absolute terms. The markets would be able to see much more clearly if it were failing to control spending, thus imposing an external discipline on politicians. This was not its only weapon to make politicians face up to their responsibilities as the Treasury sees them. In February 1993 the government announced it would undertake in-depth reviews of all public spending – 'fundamental expenditure reviews'. They would be medium-term in focus, beyond the normal span of the public-spending cycle, and be prepared to think the unthinkable. In this respect they resembled the old PAR reviews (see above). The first in line were to be social security, health, education and the Home Office – social policy, in short. Many of the policy decisions of the mid-1990s that we shall be discussing later in the book came out of these reviews.

A unified budget

Ever since the Plowden report, *two* separate budgetary activities had been conducted by the Treasury. The first was the public *spending* review. This was usually completed by November and announced in the 'Autumn Statement'. The second was the review of taxation – the revenue side. From pure tradition this was always called the 'budget'. Budgets in other countries, like those of any firm or household, normally consist of both the income or revenue side of the accounts *and* the spending side (Armstrong Committee, 1980). In the United Kingdom, the Treasury and the spending departments sorted out the expenditure of government, announced it in November and then the Chancellor tried to find the money in his 'budget'. These tax changes were then announced in March. This had the effect of not bringing home to the spending ministers immediately or directly how a victory for them in the spending round would translate into tax increases they would all deplore when the Chancellor stood up to make his budget statement in March. Households have to consider their spending and their income together – why should not government? In a White Paper on budgetary reform (Cm 1867, 1992) the government proposed to combine the publication of the expenditure plans for the next three years, the old Autumn Statement, with tax proposals as part of a unified budget. The timing of this newer, grander budget would be just a little later than the publication of the old Autumn Statement. Thus the new budget statement comes at the end of November and then has to be approved by Parliament early in the next calendar year as the Estimates and the Finance Bill. This process bunched the work of the Treasury into a very hectic autumn, and also meant that decisions on revenue and taxes had to be made well in advance of the new financial year in April. As a result, there was some criticism of the unification of the two sides of the budget, but in truth very little new information becomes available between November and March that should affect the Chancellor's judgement fundamentally. On the other hand, the insiders' view is that the tying together of tax and spending decisions has brought home to senior ministers' minds – and those on EDX especially – the hard truth that tax cuts can only be achieved by cutting spending. In the absence of this close tie-up, politicians have a tendency to set spending targets and then hope that 'something will turn up' before budget day.

Refining the control process

The Treasury had to adapt and refine its strategy continuously through the 1980s and 1990s to remain ahead of the game (Thain and Wright, 1990).

Public sector pay and the unpredictability of pay settlements have always posed a serious threat to public expenditure control. Pay constitutes two-thirds of all current expenditure. The move towards cash planning meant that even if health service or teachers' unions succeeded in reaching a pay settlement, there was no likelihood it would be funded in full, except by the NHS or local authorities making cuts in their non-salary budgets or employing fewer staff. For the first five years of cash planning the Treasury put a 'pay factor' in its cash target. Public sector negotiators knew the consequences if they went over that limit, though in practice the Treasury might relent a little with groups like nurses and fund part of the extra settlement. The 'pay factor' was always set unrealistically low as an opening gambit by the Treasury to keep pay expectations down and to put a further squeeze on public services. Then, after five years, the Treasury tightened the rules again. They set separate cash limits for each central government department for pay and allied costs. It thus prevented settlements over the norm which could be financed by savings elsewhere. Then in September 1993 the Chancellor announced that central government would expect any pay and running cost increases in the year to be met out of 2 per cent 'efficiency savings'. Similar expectations were announced for subsequent years (see HM Treasury, 1993, 1995).

The Contingency Reserve has always existed as a cushion to meet unexpected demands for spending without breaking the overall planning target for public spending set in the White Papers. In the early years this had always been kept small but in the 1980s the Treasury increased it from the traditional 2 per cent of planned public spending in the 1976–9 period to over 6 per cent in 1990–1. This squeezed individual planned targets even more and came to be used to finance items like pay or local authority overspend, which central government knew would happen but did not want to admit to in its plans.

Local authorities have presented the Treasury with a particular problem from the outset. Though having no statutory power to control local authority spending in total, the Plowden reforms included local authority spending as part of public expenditure. It was, therefore, in theory, subject to PES overall limits. We describe in detail in the next chapter the consequent growing controls on local spending. However, in the 1990 White Paper (Cm 1021, 1990) the Treasury gave up including in the total of planned public expenditure that part of local authority expenditure which was locally financed through local taxes and charges. The logic that the Treasury could not be expected to control something that was for local councils and their electorates to decide, finally seemed to sink in, not least because the Treasury had so regularly failed to keep them to their limits. The new limit that the Treasury was trying to keep to was called the 'new planning total'. It consisted of central government's own spending, the finance of nationalized industries and public corporations, and the financial support central government gave to local authorities.

It did not last. The Treasury clearly felt uncomfortable with the notion that it could not control the self-funded spending of local councils or include this spending in the overall public expenditure accounts. In 1993 it reversed its position. It effectively took total control of local authority spending whether financed from the local council tax or not (see Chapter 5). It then included in its 'new control total' an item called 'local authority self-financed expenditure'. (For a full analysis of these different totals, see Heald, 1995.) This is the clearest statement that the Treasury does not accept that local government should have independent taxing powers, except to raise lower taxes than the limits the Treasury sets.

Cuts and controls – did they succeed?

It was the Labour government of 1976 that first broke the trend of public spending taking a higher share of total national income each year. The tight hold was maintained by the Thatcher government. As in previous economic crises capital expenditure was hit hardest but on a scale not experienced before – cut to a half or to a third of previous levels in some cases. Local authority housing expenditure suffered most. On current spending, education was essentially stabilized in real volume terms for over a decade, and the rates of growth in health and personal social services slowed down or ceased for some periods. It was social security expenditure that increased, un-cash limited and driven by unemployment. The break with the past is most clearly seen in Figure 4.2. Having risen from 15 per cent of GDP in 1966 to reach 25 per cent in 1976, welfare spending fell back to about 20 per cent in the peak of the boom years of the late 1980s to rise again to only just over 25 per cent in the years of unemployment in the early 1990s and in the post-Thatcher dash for election victory in 1992. The measures to curb the growth of spending were having their effects on the welfare share in 1994. Overall, the share of taxes taken by the government in the past two decades since the public spending system was tightened up has been remarkably stable. It is a tribute to the Treasury and the impact of their changing rules of the game that they have won as effectively as they have. Yet as we have seen, the political climate has been on their side. When, briefly, it was not, in the run-up to the 1992 election, rules did not count for much.

Some criticisms and alternatives

We have seen that the Treasury has swung the rules of the game more and more effectively in its direction since 1976 and especially since the early 1980s.

The control function

The complete dominance of the control function over the planning function in the 1980s has made service planning and efficient management extremely difficult. Cash limits are a healthy discipline for departments so long as they are realistic and are not used as a form of clandestine cuts in services. Since cash limits are set in advance of wage agreements and since wages and salaries are the largest element in social service costs, it is not easy to achieve 'realism' in the cash limits without some long-term understanding with the fairly cowed public sector unions about the scale of wage awards. If the latter is not likely to be a permanent feature, machinery for achieving some long-term pay agreements in the public sector becomes important for achieving efficient control (Heald, 1983).

The planning function

The publication of volume terms figures for past spending would make public discussion better informed. Colleagues tried to do this in Hills (1990). Some longer-term, less detailed targets and stabler financial regimes for services are as necessary as Plowden recognized them to be. The continual changing of public expenditure targets in *real* terms, and the confusing changes in grant systems have played havoc with local authorities' and services' capacity to plan.

The efficiency function

Blackstone and Plowden (1988) argue that the government was wrong to abandon CPRS and the PAR procedures, which provided the means to reassess programmes in depth from time to time. The fundamental reviews of spending begun by Michael Portillo in 1993 could be seen as a return to that tradition.

Including tax expenditure

None of these changes fully engages the central weakness of the PESC system as far as social policy is concerned – the failure to integrate tax expenditures into the system in an explicit way. It is the 'hidden face of public expenditure' (Hogwood, 1989). The consequences have been as follows:

1. The progressivity of the tax structure has been largely undermined so that the poor pay a very high price for their welfare.
2. More resources are devoted to aspects of fiscal welfare than to cash benefits or service delivery, and they are allocated in ways that pervert what individual service policies are seeking to achieve.

The decisions that the Chancellor takes, to extend or limit the tax advantages people derive from certain life styles, amount to specific social policies. They may encourage home ownership, or private health insurance, or personal pensions. They are not, however, part of the PES process. Indeed, even Cabinet ministers may not hear of them until they are told on the morning of budget day by the Chancellor. The consequences are, first, poorly debated and largely hidden. There is no capacity to discuss a trade-off of £1,000 million between tax relief on pensions and higher-cash old age pensions. Yet the tax consequences are essentially the same. Secondly, because a tax allowance reduces the total income on which a person pays tax, it has a greater value to a high-income person on a high marginal rate of tax than a low-income one who may, if he or she pays no tax, not gain at all.

During the 1980s, social policy-related tax expenditures tilted even more sharply in the direction of the non-poor. Housing expenditure on council tenants was cut, but owner-occupiers gained substantially despite the limit imposed on the value of mortgage interest that could be claimed against tax (see Chapter 13). Private pension scheme tax concessions grew as part of deliberate policy. At the other end of the income spectrum, various social security benefits that were once relieved of taxation, ceased to be so in the mid-1980s.

Despite the fact that Titmuss (1958) was one of the first commentators to appreciate the significance of tax expenditure, the United Kingdom has done little to tackle the problem until the latest revisions to the rules, and then only marginally. Departments are encouraged to include trade-offs with possible tax relief changes in their bids, but tax expenditures are still not formally part of the public expenditure accounts. Other countries have been more enterprising. In West Germany some integration of tax expenditures into the budget cycle was introduced in 1967. Budget estimates have to include their purpose and cost alongside the traditional expenditure items devoted to like functions – for example, pension tax relief alongside pension expenditure. The US Federal Budget does something similar. Canada has gone further. The Canadian Parliament since 1980 has discussed and voted on an estimates figure (an 'envelope') that includes both tax expenditures and traditional spending authorization. This forces Parliament to consider, for example, the balance between housing subsidies and housing tax allowances, and a ceiling is put on the value of the total – tax relief cannot just grow without anyone noticing. France has gone some way towards the Canadian pattern. Separate votes are required for each item of spending and tax relief, and they are published together. A reform of the PES system on the same lines is perfectly feasible. In the end, though, the control of public spending is a political issue. It will succeed or fail, be equitable or not, to the extent that politicians want it to.

Further reading

The most recent authoritative account of the public expenditure process is C. Thain and M. Wright (1995), *The Treasury and Whitehall: The planning and control of public expenditure 1976–93*, Oxford: Oxford University Press. This just stops short of the unified budget, though it is briefly discussed in prospect. Briefer accounts by the same authors include: C. Thain and M. Wright (1990), 'Coping with difficulty: the Treasury and public expenditure, 1979–89', *Policy and Politics*, **18**, no. 1, pp. 1–15; (1992a), 'Planning and controlling public expenditure in the UK – part I: the Treasury's public expenditure survey', *Public Administration*, **70**, no. 1, pp. 3–24; and (1992b), 'Planning and controlling public expenditure in the UK – part II: the effects and effectiveness of the survey', *Public Administration*, **70**, no. 2, pp. 193–224.

Other publications which also discuss the public expenditure control process and its reform in detail include the following texts: D. Heald (1995), 'Steering public expenditure with defective maps', *Public Administration*, **73**, no. 2, pp. 213–40; B. W. Hogwood (1989), 'The hidden face of public expenditure: trends in tax expenditure in Britain', *Policy and Politics*, **17**, no. 2; and A. Likierman (1988), *Public Expenditure: Who really controls it and how*, Harmondsworth: Penguin, which gives the most accessible account of the process of control, but needs updating.

Still the best and most readable account of the Whitehall process of expenditure control is H. Heclo and A. Wildavsky (1981), *The Private Government of Public Money*, 2nd edn, London: Macmillan. Though now out of date, it is still worth reading for the origins and feel of the process. However, the most detailed account of public expenditure trends in social policy and service outcomes since 1974 is J. Hills (ed.) (1990), *The State of Welfare*, Oxford: Oxford University Press.

The classic pluralist description of budgeting is provided by A. Wildavsky (1979), *The Politics of the Budgetary Process*, 3rd edn, Boston: Little, Brown.

Finally, see HM Treasury (1995), *Financial Statements and Budget Report 1996/7* (and subsequent years), London: HMSO.

CHAPTER 5

CONTAINING THE LOCALS

Political scientists and economists differ in the views they hold about the appropriate extent to which central government ought to control the activities of local government. Actual practice changed fast in the 1980s and 1990s as central government's desire to cut public spending overwhelmed all other considerations. The overall effect of these changes was largely to remove local authorities' financial independence by 1995.

Alternative theories of central–local relations

Local councils are the creatures of Parliament and they gain their powers only from Parliament. Nevertheless, historically, local authorities have had considerable independence, more at some times than others (Foster *et al.*, 1980). Rhodes (1979) distinguished four different ways of thinking about this central–local relationship that are still helpful.

The *partnership model* was the one implicit in the legislation of the 1940s. It is still to be found in the rhetoric of ministers' speeches and Departmental circulars. Central government is there to set the boundaries to local government activity, to give advice, to set minimum standards and give financial assistance, especially to poorer areas, but local authorities have a distinct responsibility to develop services in their own way, setting their own priorities. Partnership theory stresses:

1. The desirability of a plurality of political authority, especially for such services as police and education.
2. The importance of using local knowledge and reflecting local preferences.
3. That to make these virtues real, local authorities must have significant independent sources of local revenue. This point was authoritatively argued by the Layfield Committee (1976) on local government finance.
4. That there is, in practice, a large measure of consensus about the goals of social policy, so a degree of genuine independence can be tolerated by central government.

Proponents of the *agency model* argue that the partnership view is no more than rhetoric:

1. The UK is a unitary and not a federal state. Thus if central government is really serious about any policy it will get its way (Griffith, 1965).
2. Politicians are elected on party manifestos which have, increasingly since the Second World War, contained social policy commitments that must be carried out by local authorities but are often contentious. No minister can afford to fail to carry through his party's pledges even if this means forcing local authorities to comply – by creating comprehensive schools or selling council houses or imposing a National Curriculum. Hence it is appropriate that local councils are dependent on central funds.
3. Since local authorities account for a quarter of all public expenditure and since public spending and the levels of taxation are critical to economic efficiency, central government must control all public spending and hence local taxation too. The more any government wants to limit public spending, the less freedom local councils can have to raise their own revenue.

Rejecting both views as over-simple, Rhodes (1979) produced a *competitors'* model. Central and local government compete for maximum advantage and possess different resources. While central government holds some of the cards, local authorities hold others, more in some areas of responsibility than others. Statutory power and financial leverage lie with the centre, but local political legitimacy, accepted 'rules of the game', and professional knowledge, lie locally. This model accepts the virtues of plurality and local independence, and argues that a competitive local government is in the end a more efficient system; nevertheless, it does not believe consensus on policy is realistic or desirable. Again financial independence is crucial (Jones and Stewart, 1983).

The Marxist *conflict model* sees central government as the agent of capital class interests. Government seeks to cut spending by forcing local authorities to reduce services. This produces local protest and pushes more responsibilities to the centre, thus increasing government 'overload' and tight controls of local spending (Gough, 1979; Offe, 1984). This will produce a conflict with the centre which could produce constructive change or further controls.

To these four models one may add a fifth. In the 1980s the open conflict predicted by Marxists did result, but it did not end as they hoped. It was followed by a series of statutes that reduced local authorities to a *minimalist role* rather than an agency model (Glennerster *et al.*, 1991). The essence of the Conservative government's case, as it evolved, was:

1. Central government has a duty to contain local public expenditure and to determine what are the limits to any individual council's spending.
2. Only by centralizing power could the role of the state be diminished.
3. Many services do not need to be *provided* by local authorities; they could and should be put out to competitive tender to be provided by private contractors – from refuse collection to school meals provision and old people's homes.
4. Where services must continue to be run under the agency of a local authority, responsibility for day-to-day services should be in the hands of the institution – like a school – not the local authority.

Local authorities thus become regulatory agencies and little more.

Increasing financial control by the centre

The years of growth

In the period broadly spanning the years 1948 to 1975, central governments of both parties gradually extended local authorities' social service powers, or encouraged them to fulfil powers they had already been given – achieving secondary education for all, creating a national pattern of further education, developing services for the elderly, sustaining a substantial housing programme. The emphasis differed between parties but the broad expansionary thrust held. Central government not only mapped out extended statutory territory for local councils to develop, but also provided a large financial incentive for them to cultivate the new territory.

In the early postwar years, *matching* or *percentage* grants by the centre met a share of approved local spending. *Unit* grants were given for housing – so much per house built.

Even after many of the separate grants were amalgamated in 1958 into a single general grant, government continued to expand its financial support quite rapidly to make it possible for local councils to fulfil the pledges which national parties frequently gave in general elections – to replace slums or old schools, to reduce the size of classes, and much else. Indeed national politicians actually took much credit for the houses and schools built 'under the Conservatives', or 'by the Labour government'. It was in local politicians' interests to take these grants and develop services too. (For an account of this period of expansion, see Foster *et al.*, 1980, chapter 4.) Yet the growth of local services promoted by central government in this way was not accompanied by any reform of local finance. The rates continued to be, in the words of the Layfield Committee (1976), 'an inflexible and politically sensitive local tax base'. The central government thus came to fund an increasing share of local services (see Layfield Committee, 1976, chapter 5).

This expansionist financial relationship made it possible for central government ministers to talk the rhetoric of partnership, while actually bribing local authorities to act as their agents. Layfield criticized this confusion and said that the centre must make up its mind whether it wanted to adopt a centralist or localist view. It must either be accountable for the consequences of its growing financial involvement, or it must give local authorities a larger independent source of finance – a local income tax or sales tax – and give local councils genuine financial accountability.

The party's over

The financial crisis of 1976 changed all this. Central government now sought to reduce local spending as part of its general public expenditure strategy. The Treasury saw local councils as subject to that strategy just as much as spending departments in Whitehall or the nationalized industries – a very clear 'agency' view but with a negative twist. The Labour government between 1974 and 1979 took a number of steps that strengthened the centre's financial control:

1. It applied its new cash limits to approvals of local capital spending and to local grants. Instead of increasing grants during the year if prices rose or wage settlements reached were over the original target, the grant was fixed whatever happened.
2. The total share of local spending met by the centre was allowed to fall, putting more of the burden on the local ratepayer and giving local councils a financial and political incentive to economize. The share of relevant expenditure to be covered by central rate support grant fell from 66.5 per cent in 1975/6 to 61 per cent in 1979/80. The proportion of actual spending met was even lower.
3. A formal means of reaching gentlemen's agreements between central and local government was created through the agency of consultative councils on local government finance.

The new Conservative administration in 1979 wished to go further. The Local Government Planning Act of 1980 introduced major changes in the structure of the rate support grant:

1. The grant was to be distributed between authorities on the basis of a set of detailed standard expenditure figures set by central government for each service after discussion with local authorities on the consultative council.
2. Local authorities would get a *lower* rate of grant the more they let spending rise above these levels.
3. On top of this disincentive a *second* system of rougher *targets* and *penalties* was introduced, based on a council's previous spending. It aimed to fine or penalize authorities which did not actually cut their spending.

When this measure failed to force some authorities sufficiently into line, the Conservative government, in 1984, introduced a measure called *rate capping* that made it illegal for authorities designated by the Secretary of State to levy more than a certain amount in rates, their only form of independent finance.

When both the systems of targets and rate capping were enforced, a local authority would be effectively told by central government the maximum it could spend. This amounted to the most profound change in the constitutional and financial relationship between central and local government since local government was introduced in the nineteenth century.

Central government loses patience

Local authorities did not respond in the way the government had hoped. Those, mainly Conservative, councils that were spending below the standard spending levels were tempted to spend more and gain more grant; those that were spending so much that government were giving them no grant could suffer no more penalties, and all kinds of ingenious methods were used to avoid the penalties through creative accounting. There were a series of confrontations with authorities, like Liverpool, faced with threats of central government taking over direct control of services.

The government finally decided that the only solution was to introduce a form of taxation that was so unpopular to levy that it would deter local councils from raising local revenue to sustain rapidly expanding local spending and services. So the *poll tax* was born. The extraordinary history of this brief and disastrous tax is told in full by Butler *et al.* (1994). What emerges clearly is that this tax was not merely invented to provide an alternative to the rates, as Mrs Thatcher had pledged to do, but it was seen as one of a series of measures that would curb local authorities' capacity to spend and defy the government. We return to that story later, for it was to backfire badly. It was the latest in a century-long endeavour by the Treasury to contain the dangerous democratic bodies that the Victorians had created – independent, locally elected councils with tax-raising powers.

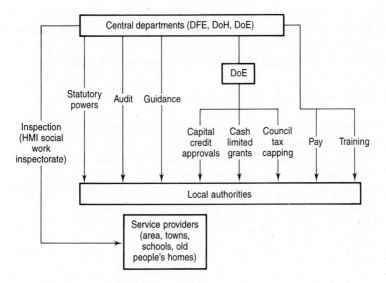

Figure 5.1 Central resource levers

The multiplying central levers of power

The legacy of decades of growing central financial control can be seen in the central levers of power that now exist (see Figure 5.1).

Statute

Local authorities can do nothing that is not expressly set out in some Act of Parliament. In this they differ from local authorities in many other countries who have power to do anything which is not forbidden by the constitution or the national law. Every action of a social worker must be justifiable under some section of an Act of Parliament. In fact, no recent government has reduced local authorities' statutory duties, only the money to perform them.

Legal action can be taken against an authority if it either goes beyond its powers – acts *ultra vires* – or does not fulfil its duties – *mandamus*. If a local authority persistently refuses to fulfil its statutory obligations, its powers can be taken over by officers of central government. This has happened in the case of civil defence powers on a number of occasions, and with the implementation of the Conservative Housing Finance Act at Clay Cross in the early 1970s. The Greater London Council was ruled by the Courts and finally by the House of Lords to be acting beyond its powers in lowering its fares in the 'Fares fair' campaign of the early 1980s.

Local authorities were not always subject to such legal control. During part of the Middle Ages, and certainly between 1688 and 1835, local boroughs and justices of the peace had considerable freedom. The strict limitation of local authorities' powers to specific parliamentary approval grew up almost by accident in the nineteenth century as a result of railway companies and other private organizations abusing their powers under private Acts of Parliament. The crucial decision, indeed, concerned the National Manure Company! (Robson, 1954). The courts ruled that such companies only had powers specifically laid upon them by Parliament, and this ruling was extended to local authorities despite the fact that they were independently elected, not mere private corporations. At various times, proposals have been made to give local authorities general enabling powers akin to continental authorities – power to do anything not forbidden them.

Audit

Auditors are normally concerned with ensuring that the accounts of a firm are an accurate record of its financial position and that employers or directors have not been absconding with the funds or 'fiddling the books'. Local authorities must have their accounts checked in the same way, but district auditors – appointed by central government – have additional functions. It has been *their* job to see that local councils do not spend money on activities which cannot be justified by statute.

The functions of the district auditor were reviewed by the Layfield Committee (1976) and revised by the Local Government Finance Act 1982. This set up an Audit Commission for local authorities in England and Wales. It appoints auditors whose powers were extended significantly. Section 15 of the Act sets out these powers. The first two incorporated existing practice, the third extended it:

1. Auditors must ensure that a local authority's spending falls within its statutory powers.
2. They must ensure that 'proper practices' are observed in drawing up their accounts.
3. They must assure themselves that the authority has made 'proper arrangements for securing economy, efficiency and effectiveness' in the use of resources. Section 26 gives the Commission power to undertake studies designed to enable it to make recommendations for improving authorities' 'economy, efficiency and effectiveness'. Such investigations have given rise to wide-ranging reports like that on community care (Audit Commission, 1986b).

Guidance by circular

Every year each government department sends a score or more of circular letters to local authorities. The contents may vary from technical advice to general policy pronouncements. For example, the Department of Education circulated local education authorities with technical scientific advice to beware of roofs containing a certain kind of cement in schools built in the 1950s.

Inspection

The Victorians invented an extremely effective system of central 'quality control' and 'information feedback'. The Poor Law inspectorate and the inspectors of schools were followed by others (Griffith, 1965). They inspected standards in schools and decided whether they were fit to receive grants. They reported in detail on the activities of local Poor Law Guardians. Later in this century, and especially in the 1950s, their functions became more concerned with giving professional advice and spreading good practice. In the 1970s, following growing public interest in the standards of education, Her Majesty's Inspectors of Schools (HMI) stepped up their activities. The old Home Office Inspectorate disappeared in 1971 when the new social service departments came into being and was replaced by a largely advisory Social Work Service. The Barclay Committee (1982) argued for the reintroduction of a formal inspectorate and the Social Work Inspectorate followed (see Chapter 11). One of its concerns, unlike its predecessor, is the *efficient* and *economic* pursuit of their duties by local social services departments. (For a description of the forms of inspection that currently exist, see Day and Klein, 1990.)

In 1991 the Conservative government proposed to privatize one of the oldest and most respected of the inspectorates – Her Majesty's Inspectors of Schools. Local schools are now free to buy in the services of private organizations to inspect their standards, but they are regulated by a government agency, OFSTED.

Capital rationing

Control of local authority borrowing began in the nineteenth century when central government was suspicious of the new local authorities and their potential to borrow money they could not repay. Thus the Treasury had to give permission for all borrowing undertaken by a local authority, not merely in total but for each project for which money was borrowed. This weapon of control was elaborated and refined, especially after the Second World War, following the example of the Ministry of Education (Griffith, 1965). Since local councils borrowed to finance virtually all their capital expenditure, permission to borrow was used by central departments to set the total capital spending limits for local authorities, determine national service priorities for capital spending, and set common design standards and cost yardsticks which ensured a tight degree of economy in capital projects.

Under the 1980 Local Government Planning and Land Act the old loan sanction procedure disappeared, and with it some of the detailed controls. A council's total net capital expenditure for the year was controlled, not its borrowing or its project-by-project spending. Money raised from selling property or land could be added. That too changed, however. Government policy swung in favour of selling council houses and other assets on a large scale and this gave councils potentially larger freedom to spend the receipts in any one year. This freedom was rapidly curtailed in the 1980s and local authorities were only allowed to spend a fraction of their receipts from sales on new building in any one year. Then in 1991 a new system of capital spending controls was introduced. Local authorities have four ways to pay for their capital expenditure:

1. From borrowing, the largest element.
2. From capital grants made by central government to cover specific types of building.
3. From 'usable' capital receipts gained by selling land or buildings like council houses or old school sites.
4. From current revenue.

Whether the receipts from the sale of property are usable or not depends on government rules. These permit a local authority to use 25 per cent of its receipts from the sale of council houses and 50 per cent of other receipts. Exceptionally, as a counterrecession policy, councils could spend virtually all receipts gained between November 1992 and December 1993. The rules were changed again to enable local authorities to enter into joint projects with the private sector from April 1995.

The annual capital guidelines
The public expenditure limits published after the autumn budget (see Chapter 4) set out target figures for local authority capital expenditure, a separate target for England, Wales and Scotland. These are set three years ahead. There is an annual capital guideline (ACG) for each main service for each local authority. Part of these totals will include a figure for capital grants made by central government for a specific purpose or project. For the most part, however, local authorities will finance their own capital spending from borrowing. The amount they can borrow for the coming year is subject to approval by central government. These annual 'credit approvals' ('net capital allocations' in Scotland) are split between what are called basic credit approvals (BCAs), which are total figures for each service, and supplementary credit approvals (SCAs), which relate to particular projects. The final element in the total annual capital guideline is the amount the local authority is presumed to spend financed out of the money received by past or current sales of property – receipts taken into account (RTIA). Central government may assign a local authority a large guideline figure for capital expenditure but also assume it will finance much of it from sales of council houses, for example, and hence give a small credit approval.

A local council can spend *more* than its total guideline if it spends more from receipts or sales than the government assume, but within its permitted limits. The ACGs for each local authority are distributed according to the measure of 'need' for capital spending determined by the central government for each block of services – education, housing, personal social services and other services. Following the 1995 Budget it was announced that part of the capital allocation to local government would from 1997 be made on a competitive bidding process. Local authorities would be encouraged to produce bids that involved using private money to help finance public projects (*Financial Times*, 14 December 1995).

Quite separate from these general services provided everywhere, the government in 1994 introduced special measures to target aid to areas in need of support to stimulate regeneration. Some of this is for capital projects reclaiming derelict or contaminated land or for work on housing estates. The total programme, 'the Single Regeneration Budget', is co-ordinated by a Cabinet subcommittee and contains multiple parts, including a process of bidding for help in launching comprehensive regeneration projects.

Controlling current spending – capping

Controlling current spending by local authorities has been central government's major headache ever since it decided in 1961 that *local government* expenditure was part of *public* expenditure and therefore should be controlled by the Treasury. I discuss the merits of this argument at the end of this chapter. Essentially, until the 1980s, central government had no final sanction over an individual local authority's decision to spend, and therefore no way, except persuasion or financial penalties, of achieving its objective. Central government tried both strategies after 1976, as we saw earlier.

Dissatisfied with its incapacity to make councils cut spending, the government adopted a final sanction – rate-capping. The 1984 Rates Act introduced a constitutional change of the utmost importance – the principle that central government could set a limit to the amount of taxation a local authority could levy. By determining a local council's grant income from the centre and setting a ceiling to a local council's revenue raising, central government acquired the capacity to set a limit on any council's spending. It did not attempt to do so for every council in the country. It set an upper range of expenditure. If a council crossed that upper threshold it ran the risk of being rate-capped. The introduction of the poll tax or community charge was meant to replace this unpleasant practice but it failed. Thatcher's government had to use community charge capping to limit some authorities' desire to levy a high poll tax – high, that is, relative to the government's somewhat ill-defined and obscure upper limit. These sanctions were usually threatened against no more than twenty councils who had to be named in Parliament and special powers taken. Smaller authorities with budgets of less than £15 million were excluded before 1991.

Capping council tax
Under the council tax which replaced the poll tax (DoE, 1991) the Conservative government kept the power to cap local tax raising. Indeed, in Scotland Westminster's power to cap councils had been less powerful. That changed. Powers to cap in Scotland were made the same as in England under the council tax. In the period after the council tax was introduced the capping limits were so tightened that virtually all councils were brought within them. To all intents and purposes total local authority budgets are now set by central government.

More from grant income

From 1976 through to the introduction of the community charge in 1990, governments had tried to curb local spending by reducing central government support. In 1975/6 central government met 66.5 per cent of local spending in England and Wales. By 1989/90 the Exchequer met only 43.4 per cent, with a further 4 per cent coming from a central grant that reimbursed authorities for part of the rate rebates that they gave to poor households. The rest, 52 per cent, was income that councils raised themselves from the property tax or *rates*. Just over half of that, or 28.3 per cent of their total income, came from non-domestic rates, a tax on the value of shops, offices and industrial property. Rather less, 24.2 per cent of their income, came from rates paid by ordinary householders.

The Local Government Finance Act 1988 changed that balance. Not only did the domestic rates disappear (see below) but the

non-domestic rates levied on shops and offices and industry became a national tax, determined by, and collected by, central government. The revenue was then returned to local councils in the
form of a grant. This effectively *increased* the share of central
grants to about three-quarters of councils' income. The community
charge had to meet the remaining quarter.

In 1990 the unpopularity of the poll tax made even that levy
politically unacceptable. In 1991/2 the community charge met only
about *14 per cent* of local expenditure. The introduction of the new
council tax has not changed much in this respect. In 1995/6 local
government spent nearly £75 billion. Only just over £12 billion was
local authority self-financed expenditure.

Deciding the level of central government grant

The outcome of the public expenditure round each year produces
the total amount of grant income local authorities are to receive.
This is called the total aggregate external finance (AEF). There is
a separate AEF for England, Scotland and Wales. This total 'envelope', as the Treasury calls it, is then made up of three different
kinds of grant, as follows:

1. The largest is the *revenue support grant* (RSG). This is allocated
   between local authorities on the basis of population and a complex assessment of needs.
2. The next largest is the payment to councils of the non-
   domestic rate income discussed above – the *national non-
   domestic rate* (NNDR). This is set at a uniform tax rate
   throughout the country, pooled and reallocated – so much per
   community charge payer in the interim, with some formula-
   based allocation thereafter.
3. Then there is a range of *specific grants* which meet a part of the
   costs of certain services that are particularly important to central government, such as the police, small items of education
   spending, the regeneration budget and National Parks.

Beyond these three basic grants were transitional measures
designed to ease the introduction of the new council tax but ceas-
ing after 1995/6.

The poll tax and the 'son of poll tax'

The accountability case

A succession of measures to curb local authorities' spending in the early 1980s failed. The government blamed this on the fact that the bulk of voters were not domestic ratepayers. Many poor households had their rates bill reduced or remitted altogether under the housing benefit scheme. The government claimed that out of 35 million voters, only 18 million actually paid rates. Voters were agreeing to high rates bills knowing that others would pay, the argument ran. This was a largely specious argument. It took the head of household – the husband usually – to be the taxpayer and assumed that wives, for example, were somehow uninterested in the tax bill or did not contribute to it. In pointing to the large element of rates paid by local industry or commerce, the government had a stronger case.

The government concluded that if local voters were to appreciate the consequences of voting for councils that wished to spend more on local services, every voter should be faced with the consequential bill – even those on low incomes. This would make local councils properly accountable to their local electorates.

Rates unpopular

Rates were unpopular. Although amounting to no more than between 3 to 4 per cent of the average household's income, the rates bill arrived on people's doormat as a single lump sum annual charge. Even if paid in instalments, it was very visible.

It was not directly related to households' capacity to pay. The more valuable the house, the higher the bill, but people's incomes do not necessarily match the value of their house. Some poor people live in houses that have become valuable through changes in the local property market. As we shall see, there may be good economic reasons to relate tax to property values, but this mismatch was perceived as unfair.

Single people living in a house on their own paid as high a rate bill as a family of four, all of whom were earning and using local services. This, too, was a popular criticism of the rates. It was used to argue that all members of the household should contribute to local revenue if they used local services. In fact, there is no reason to suppose that a household with four members is more able to pay than one with a single person, especially if three of the four are dependants. Its income is the real issue.

The unpopularity of the rates, very evident in Scotland in the mid-1980s, prompted a look for some alternative. A small task force was set up in the civil service to think unthinkable things and report back to Kenneth Baker and William Waldegrave. By January 1985 they had concluded the following:

1. That any reform must make local authorities clearly accountable to their electorates for any spending they undertook over and above government guidelines.
2. That the full effect of any such spending should fall on the local electorate.
3. That at the time many local electors did not pay rates.

The team reviewing the problem of local authority finance decided that councils should not have the power to tax local business and the business rate should become a national tax. Local councils should be reformed into unitary authorities so that the tax they charged should be clearly one council's responsibility. A poll tax should be levied as a supplementary tax because it would have the characteristic of being very overt and would hit every elector. (For a detailed account of the backroom discussions and politics of the change see Butler *et al.*, 1994.)

It rapidly became clear that to levy both rates and a poll tax would be an administrative nightmare. The poll tax became the front runner as a solution. It was introduced in Scotland first and suitably disguised under the name of the 'community charge'. The Government Finance Act was passed in 1988. The tax was introduced in Scotland in 1989 and in England and Wales in 1990. (For a sympathetic case for the change, see King, 1990.)

Poll tax revolt
The great upheaval the new system caused meant that councils had an incentive to increase their total tax levy and blame the government. The evident unfairness of charging rich and poor the same sum and the fact that this sum turned out to be very high in many areas caused the basic strategy to misfire. Instead of blaming left-wing councils for putting up their poll tax bills, the electorate blamed the government. The government had to give local

authorities a succession of higher grants to buy off opposition. The task of registering every resident and tracking their movements proved intrusive and impractical. Thus the government ended up being both unpopular *and* paying more for local government. Above all, the principle that the Duke of Westminster should pay the same tax as someone on below-average earnings, despite relief for the very poor, was simply unacceptable to a wide spectrum of the electorate. When the Conservative government came to abandon the tax after Mrs Thatcher's downfall, however, some in the Conservative Party insisted on keeping some element of the poll tax for the accountability reasons set out above. The result was the council tax.

Son of poll tax

The government proposed the outlines of a new tax (DoE, 1991) which came into operation in 1993/94. It had two elements, combining the rates and the poll tax. Like the rates the tax would be based on the value of the property. As with the old rating system the occupier, normally the head of household, would be liable to pay. Unlike the old rating system there would be no attempt to value each property in the country. Instead, properties would be placed in one of seven broad bands, each relating to a national average value. After much criticism that the top band covered far too broad a range of properties the bands were increased to eight valuation bands, A to H. A central government agency, the Inland Revenue, puts every property in the country into one of these eight bands. The local council sets a local tax rate for each band: for example, a householder may pay £400 a year council tax if he or she is living in a house in valuation band A, but £1,225 if the house is in band H.

How should the value of the property be set? There were three main contenders: the *rental value*, what the property could be rented for; a *capital value*, what it could be sold for; and *rebuilding costs*, what it would cost to replace. Only a minority of properties are rented and few at a market price. Selling prices are at a market level and more readily available. Rebuilding costs might be calculated on a rule-of-thumb basis, but the assumptions would be relatively arbitrary. The government chose the capital value – the selling price on a set date. There was much more current evidence of sales than there was evidence to fix any of the other figures.

In this respect the basis of valuation was far more solidly grounded and understandable than the old rating system had been.

It was also far simpler as it did not rely on the valuation of each house separately but only blocks of property, like whole streets, that would all be judged to fall into the same broad band. If you disagreed with this judgement you could appeal individually.

Like the poll tax the council tax would also take account of the number of adults in each household. The basic tax would assume that there were two or more in each household. If there was only one, that person could claim a discount. Poorer households could claim a council tax benefit which would reduce their tax bill.

The tax thus avoided all the main defects of both the rates and the poll tax. It was relatively easy to set, and it was as easy and cheap to collect as the rates had been. However, it avoided the criticism that the little old lady living on her own, who continually haunts these discussions, was paying the same as a family. Overall, the tax has been introduced remarkably smoothly and with little political backlash. It has also returned to a property basis of valuation, and although this is more controversial, there are sound economic principles behind a property tax.

The case for a property tax

Economic theory suggests that all forms of economic activity should be taxed as equivalently as possible to prevent distortions in the market (see Chapter 7). If one activity is not taxed and everything else is, resources tend to shift to that activity in excess of what would happen if people had free choice. With the abolition of rates, ownership and use of property became the main economic activity that was not taxed, unless it was the income of private landlords. Taken in conjunction with tax benefits that owner-occupiers receive (see Chapter 13), it can be argued that this was a significant economic distortion.

A local income tax

The case for taxing income as a form of local revenue is simply that it is most directly related to individuals' or households' capacity to pay. The Layfield Committee (1976) thought it the most feasible and equitable form of additional local revenue.

It does have serious administrative difficulties though, unless the whole income tax system is reformed and further computerized. At present, *individuals* pay tax in each of their employments and their tax is deducted by their employer. People live in *households* often in different places from their work. Adding up everyone's several sources of income and grouping it into a household income, related to where people live and the local rate, is a considerable exercise that our present income tax system is incapable of doing, at least at all easily. The introduction of a local income tax therefore requires a major reform to income tax and one that points in the opposite direction to the recent individualization of tax – with separate assessment for husbands and wives. Some move towards a local income tax remains the policy of the Liberal Democrats and would be feasible in the long term, especially if every individual or household had their own end-of-year tax assessment as happens in the United States. The Inland Revenue's agreed assessment of last year's income then forms the basis of the local tax payment.

The centralist and the localist cases

The centralist case

The Conservative government set out this case in 1983 (Cmnd 9008) and again in 1986 (Cmnd 9714). Constitutionally Britain is a unitary state – not a federation like the United States or West Germany where separate geographical units have reserved powers and can act independently within constitutional limits. Local authorities are creatures of central government. To pretend otherwise is to confuse the constitutional position. While local participation is to be encouraged, its purpose is to give local knowledge, not to be a rival to the authority of Westminster. Variations between local areas' needs can be measured and compensated for in national grants. Indeed, it can be argued that central government can draw upon and use 'superior intelligence and knowledge' (Foster *et al.*, 1980).

The government (Cmnd 9008, 1983) summarized its economic case thus:

> 1.6 Ministers are accountable to Parliament for the broad conduct of the economy. . . . For the business and for the individual it is the total level of tax that matters most, not who is imposing it.

In *Paying for Local Government* (Cmnd 9714, 1986) the government said:

> 1.13 because Governments are responsible for the overall management of the economy they have to be concerned with the amount of local authority expenditure, borrowing and taxation. Local authority borrowing has implications for the Public Sector Borrowing Requirement (PSBR), the rate of monetary growth, and interest rates.

> 1.17 The arguments against high levels of taxation apply just as much to local taxes.

These arguments are not self-evident and it may be worth spelling them out. The nature of the basic theoretical argument clearly differs depending on whether the economic analysis is neo-Keynesian or monetarist (Jackman, 1982).

Traditional *Keynesian* analysis required government to intervene in the economy to affect the total level of demand for goods and services and to ensure that this level was high enough to be consistent with full employment and not so high that inflation was generated or a balance of payments crisis precipitated. Aggregate demand comprised two basic elements, investment and consumption. It was crucial for successful demand management that central government generated or contained investment to an appropriate level. Local authority capital spending was used in this way as an economic regulator throughout the Keynesian period, 1945–76, by both Conservative and Labour governments.

For *monetarists*, control of capital spending was also important because it must be financed out of public borrowing, and that affects the money supply, interest rates and inflation. However, as we have seen, central government has always had power to control capital spending and still does.

It is over current spending that the debate centres. To neo-Keynesians it matters little what local authorities spend on revenue account. Since local authorities have no power to finance revenue spending by borrowing but must cover their expenditure from taxes, their revenue spending – on salaries, equipment and so on – would appear to produce little effect on aggregate demand in the economy. If they spend more and increase the local authority's contribution to demand, they have to take more from local rate payers, thus reducing *their* demand for goods and services. It is this last step in the logic that caused disagreement. Even some Keynesians argued that higher rates or local taxes could reduce the level of private savings, thus boosting demand above the expected levels. In fact, this is an empirical issue – are taxes paid out of private savings or current consumption? If we know the extent to which changes in local spending affect savings and if government has some indication of the level of overall local spending during the coming year, it could make the appropriate adjustments to overall policy. Moreover, the effect seems likely to be small.

Traditional monetarist theory is also dismissive of the need to control local spending. On strict orthodoxy, control of the money supply will be enough on its own. If this results in high interest rates, local authorities like other corporate bodies may reduce their capital spending as the costs of borrowing rise. That financial discipline is enough. Monetarists have been hostile to Keynesian attempts at demand management in principle, arguing that they are inflationary. Thus arguments for controlling local authorities' spending would appear to weigh even less powerfully within monetarist theory than in Keynesian arguments.

The *real* basis of the Conservative government's case then turns on the proposition that taxation is bad for the economy whoever levies it. Thus it is clearly in the wider national interest to reduce the scale of the public sector, whoever controls it, and 'where there is a clash between local and national mandates the national mandate must prevail' (Mr Heseltine, Hansard, vol. 16, no. 37).

The localist case

Those who favour local authority independence argue: 'National financial controls will lead to nationally run services and that is politically dangerous especially in the case of education' (Glennerster *et al.*, 1991). The spread of political responsibility throughout the population to local councillors, school governors and so on, informs more people about the nature of financial choices that have to be made and produces a more informed electorate. This has been a traditional argument for local and participative democracy (Pateman, 1973). The larger the scope of welfare state activities, the more force it has: 'By providing a large number of points where decisions are taken by people of different political persuasions and different backgrounds, it acts as a counterweight to the uniformity inherent in government decisions. It spreads political power' (Layfield, 1976: 53, para. 14).

Individuals and families differ considerably in what kind of education they want for their children and care for their dependants. At least the existence of a range of alternative modes of provision as between one local authority and another widens the choice available. Local independence generates alternative and innovative models of provision.

The needs of local populations, their service objectives, and the most effective ways of achieving them, differ between areas. They cannot be determined nationally; only a political and administrative system that is close to the local population, and responsive to it, can match services to this diversity of preference. In economic theory the more nearly expenditure can be matched to individual preferences, the more efficient the outcome. By analogy, the more nearly individual areas can match their populations' preferences for social spending to their expenditure, the more efficient will be the overall outcome – and the less 'coerced' local people will feel (Tiebout, 1956; Foster *et al.*, 1980). This requires the capacity to make local judgements about tax levels. Poor areas or areas with manifestly larger social problems can receive extra central help.

Those who provide and administer services must be available and open to local people's complaints and grievances. The further away the centre of power, the more difficult it is to complain. If local authority members are responsible for providing services but do not have to go to their own electorate to raise the money to pay for the services, they have less incentive to make effective use of these funds. It is always possible to blame deficiencies on central government. Proper local accountability requires a substantial source of revenue, and freedom to spend that revenue or reduce it. This was essentially the Layfield Committee's (1976) case for a localist solution. Layfield argued that the extent and complexity of central government's controls and the grant structures were such as to confuse those immediately involved and the public as to who was responsible for what. The committee concluded that comprehensibility was a necessary characteristic for democratic and accountable service administration:

> It is inevitable that arrangements may sometimes be complex and that there will be some aspects that require specialist knowledge.

But the main features of the system must be comprehensible to those Members of Parliament and councillors who are not specialists and to serious commentators and interested members of the public. The requirement of accountability cannot be met unless those who are responsible to the electorate for taking decisions are capable of answering for those decisions. (Layfield Committee, 1976: 52, para. 11)

These are arguments on which readers must make up their own minds.

Further reading

The best and most comprehensive account of the history and economics of local finance is still to be found in C. Foster, R. Jackman and M. Perlman (1980), *Local Government Finance in a Unitary State*, London: Allen & Unwin. See also the Layfield Committee (1976), *Local Government Finance*, Cmnd 6453, London: HMSO, including the 'Note of reservation' by Professor Alan Day.

The postwar history of grant and other changes up to the mid-1980s is contained in T. Travers (1986), *The Politics of Local Government Finance*, London: Allen & Unwin; and the failure of central government's attempt to control local spending by negotiation in the 1970s is covered in an interesting account in R. A. W. Rhodes (1986), '"Corporate bias" in central–local relations: a case study of the consultative council on local government finance', *Policy and Politics*, **14**, no. 2, pp. 221–45.

The full and fascinating story of the origins of the poll tax and its demise is told in D. Butler, A. Adonis and T. Travers (1994), *Failure in British Government: The politics of the poll tax*, Oxford: Oxford University Press. The Conservative government's case for the community charge is set out in a glossy and colourful publication in Cmnd 9714 (1986), *Paying for Local Government*, London: HMSO.

CHAPTER 6

SETTING THE LIMITS LOCALLY

In the light of the leverage exerted on them, how do local authorities decide what it is appropriate to spend? We look first at a number of theories about how local authorities budget.

Theories of local budgeting

Drawing on both British and American literature it is possible to distinguish a number of distinct theories about the dominant factors that affect local officials and politicians setting local budgets. Much of the literature predates the era of cuts and major central control. The most helpful studies of local budgeting in this category are Danziger (1978), Hambleton (1978), Judge (1978), Greenwood (1979), Greenwood *et al.* (1980a, 1980b) and Ferlie and Judge (1981). Cutting strategies were discussed in Glennerster (1980).

Following central guidance

One view of local budgeting is that officials are largely influenced by the advice they are given from Whitehall and that local councillors largely follow that lead, tempered only slightly by party politics. In recent years the standard spending assessments used by government to set local grant levels (see Chapter 5) have come to determine the effective ceilings for local spending because of the fierce spending caps. Since these assessments are supposed to represent what central government thinks are appropriate spending levels for each service, it is natural that they form an increasingly important part of the debate *within* local government about how much each committee shall take of the total budget. No committee is going to agree very readily to accept less than the government's implied guideline. Yet there is little money within the 'cap' left over, after that level has been agreed, to give one committee any more. Not only are local authority budget totals being driven from the centre, but so too are the allocations within the cap.

Told what to do

Central government did not seek merely to affect spending priorities but also the manner in which services were provided. This, too, was new. The Local Government Act 1988 required local councils to put out to competitive tender the provision of a wide range of local services. Only if the council's own refuse department, for example, won the contract would it be able to continue to collect refuse. This process had begun under the 1980 Local Government Planning and Land Act when councils were required to put out to tender certain housing maintenance and highways work. Under the 1988 Act the following services must be open to competitive tender if the council wishes to permit its own service departments to participate:

1. Refuse collection.
2. Building cleaning.
3. Street cleaning and other cleaning.
4. School and other catering (e.g. staff canteens).
5. Grounds maintenance.
6. Vehicle maintenance.

The Secretary of State can add to the list.

If the local authority knows that it wishes to privatize and not use local authority employees at all, it does not have to go through the compulsory tender procedure. In the first round of contracts in 1989 almost 75 per cent were won by in-house or direct service organizations (Painter, 1991).

Delegate responsibility

Not only have local authorities been told what to spend and what
to privatize, they have also been told that responsibility for
the budgets of those services they do retain must be delegated
downwards to the units that do the spending. Local authority
schools now have control of their own budgets (see Chapter
12). Some schools and all colleges have been lost to local
authorities altogether, and they are now the responsibility of
central government. Many old people's homes and other facilities have been privatized. Thus, compared to local councils in the
1970s, their modern successors have lost much budgetary
freedom.

A contest between competing departments

It is possible to view the budget battle in local authorities, such
as it remains, much like the parallel one in Whitehall, as
an interdepartmental contest. The main protagonists are the
chief officers and chairpersons of their respective committees.
The modern form of this battle was described by Greenwood
(1979). Chief officers prepare their estimates for the coming year,
setting out present spending plus price increases and what would
be necessary to meet existing commitments. Then a list of possible new schemes dear to committee members' hearts is added
and a list of possible economies and cuts, 1 per cent, 5 per cent,
or 10 per cent in total. The balance between additions and
cuts will depend on the predicted government grant that
will become known in rough form soon after the Chancellor's
Budget speech in November and will be known for certain early
in the new year ready to set the new council tax rate in February.
There then follows a 'Spanish Inquisition' procedure at which
individual cuts and new schemes are considered on a one-
off basis in private by a small group of senior politicians. The
resulting bargains are then put to the policy and resources
committee. It is in the course of this bartering procedure that
certain simple rules of battle will emerge (see below). The tough-
est chief officer, or the group with the most powerful chairperson,
will usually win.

Incrementalism, or budgeting by habit

Another view of local budgeting is that it is dominated by habit, by small additions to or subtractions from the base budget. Authors have identified considerable consistency in individual authorities' spending patterns over time despite the variation *between* authorities. In statistical terms, by far the best predictor of what an authority will spend this year is what it spent last year (Danziger, 1978). Nor is this surprising in itself. No council can hope to sack a large portion of its staff, who take the greater part of its expenditure. Many functions are mandatory. Nevertheless, over time many authorities' spending patterns do tend to be perpetuated: for example, the high spenders on education remain high spenders, and the low spenders on services for the elderly remain laggards. This reflects the traditions of an authority, or the lasting influence of a chief officer, but it may also reflect a natural desire by those involved to minimize the political conflicts that are generated when big changes are proposed in one department's budget compared with others. There used to be an in-built assumption that the rate of increase in resources available to an authority would rise year by year. Chief officers became used to submitting last year's 'base budget' corrected for price and salary rises plus an extra x per cent. This may have held good in the palmy days of the 1960s for some authorities, but even then not for many (see Danziger, 1978). Since 1976 the presumption of regular growth has been rudely shattered and has led to the emergence of new 'cutting strategies' (Glennerster, 1980).

Habits broken

In the short term, local councils responded by making a series of adjustments, some short-term, some longer-term, as follows:

1. They sold their assets – empty sites, empty schools, council houses – in the hope that this would permit them to continue to build with the money.
2. They charged for services or raised charges already in place to minimize real service cuts.
3. They cut capital expenditure before reducing current spending on staff.
4. They did not re-appoint staff or slowed the process.

5. They cut administrative and research staff.
6. They cut someone else's budget (e.g. from grants to voluntary organizations from Family Service Units to women's groups) before cutting their own staff.
7. They shifted the difficult and costly cases to other departments – often social services.

Equal pain

Unless there are good and generally agreed reasons for doing otherwise, the rule which readily minimizes conflict is simply to decrease each department's budget by the same percentage. This effectively retains their share of the total authority budget. Though this pattern is evident in some councils, especially in the less controversial services, it is by no means universal.

Your turn next

Some authorities have clearly operated a more variable rule. In some years a committee chairman and his chief officer win a particularly favourable share of the pie, perhaps because they have a popular or long-delayed major scheme to launch. Then for the next year or two they do less well, suffering a declining budget. There seems to be a feeling that having done well one year you should then take a back place in the queue.

Fundamental change

It is also clear that there have been long-term shifts in priorities as the cuts became permanent. Even relatively small preferences made year by year by the same committee add up over a decade to a significant strategic shift in budget priorities. Social service departments shifted their emphasis to community care for children and the elderly as part of an attempt to economize (Kelly, 1989). The new community care responsibilities and money after 1993 forced more fundamental changes in local authority social services departments (Lewis and Glennerster, 1996).

The demographic needs approach

One of the accepted reasons why most participants agree to such a major shift is that the population a department services has grown particularly fast. Education departments in the 1950s and 1960s, faced with rapidly rising school populations, were able to win the battle for funds locally just as the Ministry did nationally. In the

1980s, growing numbers of very elderly were a similar justification for social services departments to receive a higher share.

Corporate rationality

In the late 1960s and early 1970s a reform movement spread, dissatisfied with the apparent arbitrariness of traditional forms of budget allocation. It paralleled the growing interest in planning and public expenditure control nationally and the spread of American ideas on budget reform (Stewart, 1974; Glennerster, 1975; Hambledon, 1978). A number of Conservative councils in the late 1960s began to introduce programme budgeting or its variants under the generic title of corporate planning, often on the recommendation of management consultants, as a way of achieving greater efficiency. A number of Labour authorities did the same, believing it could help them plan service development more effectively. A national report (Bains Committee, 1972), *The New Local Authorities: Management and structure*, recommended a revised committee and officer structure for the new local authorities that would replace the old in 1974. Bains quoted with approval the critical comments of the management consultants, McKinsey and Co. Inc., on one of the authorities they had studied:

> in common with many other authorities [it] finds itself with an organisation and a system of making decisions that has changed little since the present structure of authorities was created out of the tangled web of local boards and functional administrations in the latter half of the nineteenth century. The democratic forms of the Council and committees and the rigid hierarchical structure of the service have some great strengths but in many ways are not geared to the modern task of managing thousands of people and hundreds of millions of pounds of assets. (Bains Committee, 1972, para. 4.11)

The Committee went on to recommend 'some form of overall plan towards which the authority will work and against which it can measure its achievement'. Instead of the brief annual bargaining over estimates, each year's budget would be the outcome of a longer-term planning process which set authoritywide priorities. There should be fewer, larger committees responsible for a whole range of related services – leisure, transport, education, housing, social services, for example. Most important of all, a central committee, rather like a cabinet, would be responsible for key policy and spending priorities – the policy and resources committee. Most authorities lacked such a committee before this, except in a shadow, non-statutory form within the majority party caucus. The policy and resources committee would have subcommittees looking at finance, manpower and land, and one that would review and monitor spending programmes to see that they were achieving results economically – a performance and review subcommittee. The changed committee structure was paralleled by a changed management hierarchy with a new chief executive, a managing director, at its head.

In other authorities *corporate* management was combined with a new system of *area* management. This was designed both to decentralize the delivery of services through mini town halls, and to generate local plans which would feed into an overall local authority or corporate plan spanning a four-year period. This was perhaps the height of the reform movement's optimism.

In a study of which authorities had developed the more sophisticated budget system and corporate organization, Greenwood *et al.* (1980b) tested several interesting hypotheses. They suggested that the environment within which local authorities have to work affects their organizational structure and budgeting procedures. The more complex the social problems, the more elaborate the services provided – 'differentiation'. Greater social demands for services and the interaction of these factors produce a more complex organizational response. The greater the service complexity, the larger the authority and the tighter the limits to the budget, so the greater will be the organizational need for co-ordination and priority setting – 'integration'. Hence we would expect to see, and to some extent do see, the larger urban authorities with more social problems evolving more elaborate co-ordination and planning. Whether these will be centralized or decentralized depends on local circumstances. In some areas top-down systems with powerful central corporate planning groups and chief executives will not work. Instead, authorities develop matrix forms of management – specialist study groups, collaborating on particular issues, forming and reforming. Co-ordination takes place at all levels between the departmental hierarchies.

Elsewhere, Greenwood (1979) suggested that tighter limits on spending enforced by central government encouraged more local authorities to move further away from the traditional incremental pattern of budgeting and introduce more 'rational' methods: strategic analyses of spending, attempts to forecast demands and changing needs, the introduction of zero-based budgeting. However, in the 1980s and 1990s, government's repeated and confused demands for economy and the changes in local taxation created a great deal of uncertainty which actually led some authorities to abandon what planning systems they had created. Over the 1980s the patterns of budget setting, however, changed only slowly (Skousen, 1990). Only about 30 per cent of authorities tried to undertake any medium-term financial planning in 1988 compared to 20 per cent five years earlier. By the 1990s attention was turning to ways of making politicians consider fundamental changes to their budgets as the limits tightened (Pendlebury, 1994).

On the other hand, many councils saw service decentralization, area budgeting and community councils as a move towards involving local people in the difficult decisions that cuts involved and as a way of improving their efficiency: Walsall, Islington and Tower Hamlets were all examples. Nationally, the Priority Estates Project pressed for devolved budgets and management boards to run council estates (Power, 1987a, 1987b, 1991).

Other authorities in England, and more in Scotland, have developed different variants. The authority is divided into smaller constituent parts with several wards grouped together. The administration of these services is decentralized as far as possible to conform with these areas in more accessible mini town halls. An area committee of local councillors is responsible for overseeing these local services. A local budget can be drawn up with a degree of devolved responsibility. Meetings of local electors may be held to consider area priorities and identify issues of concern to that particular area. These may be formalized in neighbourhood or community councils. There may be local meetings to discuss services for particular groups in the community such as the elderly. At an early stage in the council's budget process these issues and preferences are fed into the consideration of next year's spending plans.

A modern local budgeting cycle

All these experiments have left their mark, as has central government's heavy hand. What has now emerged in most authorities is a budget cycle that includes some or all of the following features.

A central budget constraint

The Chancellor's Autumn Budget sets financial parameters within which local authorities will have to work. So too does some guess about where the government may set a capping limit. The finance director gives committees advice on the authority's overall budget constraints for the next year. However, in many authorities, especially the larger ones, the process of thinking about next year's budget would have begun months before. What has emerged is a mirror image of the public expenditure round in Whitehall (see Chapter 4). Early in the new year, councils receive their award of grant by the Department of the Environment and the capping level, which sets a limit to council spending in all cases but parish councils. In most cases this is so near past levels of spending, often below it, that it leaves councils almost no choice in the total spending they can undertake.

The corporate function

Once one budget round is over in March, the chief executive, and the chief officers' group will prepare papers for the policy and resources committee identifying key issues for deeper analysis, possible priorities for the next financial year, and areas for major economies. The finance officers will prepare an analysis of existing spending commitments and the costs of new schemes that will be complete by next year – the costs and loan repayments on the provision of a new old people's home, for example. The finance officer will also offer advice on the revenue the authority can expect from the government and local sources on various assumptions. The policy and resources committee will then set guidelines indicating clear policy priorities that should guide the preparation of the estimates, and initiate studies that will identify areas where cuts can be made, or expansion can be concentrated. In contrast to the 'Spanish Inquisition' method, a prior decision on priorities and cuts would have been made before the hectic bargaining about detail begins. Interdepartmental reviews of policy for particular groups like the elderly or the under-5s will be a continuing feature of the corporate process going to the parent committees. Thus by the time the size of the government grant is known – about Christmas – the groundwork will have been done. A range of possible responses can be presented to members matching some overall view of priorities.

Area reviews

Area priorities are discussed and fed into the budget review process from the area organizations, if they exist.

Departmental estimates

This more traditional process continues. Detailed work on drafting the initial estimates for the next financial year by departments takes account of the prior guidelines and studies that have been undertaken. These estimates will be ready before the government grant settlement arrives and work will begin in the finance officer's department paring them down in bilateral discussions. Chief officers and chairpersons will begin the process of deciding the share of the budget that is to go to education, social services and housing, but in the light of the strategic analysis discussed above. The final decisions will be taken in January and February. After this the officers and the individual committees will be left to cut their estimates and to keep within their given targets.

The policy committee resolution

This committee will have the initial task of resolving conflicts between these four policy streams – central government constraints, the authority's or governing party's collective goals, the demands of different geographical units, and departmental interests. The final resolution will depend on the majority party group of members and the full council. It will inevitably be a political process, but it will be a more informed political judgement, so the reformers claim, than the pure bargaining process that preceded it.

In practice, the procedures adopted by local authorities differ widely, and change in response to political control and financial stress. At one extreme some authorities still follow very traditional patterns, in others a more corporate approach like that just described has been sustained. Most are a mixture of the two.

Further reading

For a description of local authorities and how they work, see T. Byrne (1995), *Local Government in Britain: Everyone's guide to how it all works*, Harmondsworth: Penguin. The following have useful chapters which discuss the local budgetary process: T. Booth (1979), *Planning for Welfare:*

Social policy and the expenditure process, Oxford: Martin Robertson and Basil Blackwell; and C. Hood and M. Wright (1981), *Big Government in Hard Times*, Oxford: Martin Robertson.

For a discussion of social service departments' early responses to the harsher financial climate of the early 1980s, see E. Ferlie and K. Judge (1981), 'Retrenchment and rationality in the personal social services', *Policy and Politics,* **9**, no. 3, pp. 333–50. For a discussion of their later, non-incrementalist responses, see A. Kelly (1989), 'An end to incrementalism: the impact of expenditure restraint on social service budgets, 1979–86', *Journal of Social Policy*, **18**, no. 2, pp. 187–210.

Increased targeting on those in special need seems to have been another response: A. Bebbington and B. Davies (1993), 'Efficient targeting of community care: the case of the home help service', *Journal of Social Policy*, **22**, pt 3, pp. 373–91. But there has also been an increase in social services unit costs and much more variability in them. Rate capping in particular does not seem to have produced a reduction or equalization of unit costs, rather a decrease in volume of service provided: A. Bebbington and A. Kelly (1995), 'Expenditure planning in the personal social services: unit costs in the 1980s', *Journal of Social Policy*, **24**, pt 3, pp. 385–411.

PART III

The sources of funds

CHAPTER 7

TAXES

Taxes form the lion's share of the revenue that pays for our publicly provided welfare services. In this chapter we begin to answer three general but basic questions: What form do taxes take? What economic effects do they have? Who bears the burden? There is a large and technical economic literature on these issues which I can only summarize here, suggesting where interested readers can continue.

The structure of taxation

Taxes are a *compulsory levy* on individuals and firms made by law and levied by government. Even with the legal penalties that exist, people go to great lengths to *avoid* paying taxes legally by finding loopholes in the tax laws; or they *evade* taxes by illegally cheating the tax authorities. One of the basic problems for any government is that the higher the level of taxation, the greater the financial incentive to avoid or evade it.

Taxes are thus to be distinguished from voluntary contributions. One particularly confusing term is used in the United Kingdom to describe one form of tax – the National Insurance or social security contribution. I shall discuss its historical origins in Chapter 14. Briefly, however, the term derives from the state's gradual absorption of voluntary sickness benefit and pension schemes. After 1948 all workers had to be members of the national scheme and pay a fixed 'contribution'. The term then became a nonsense. It bears all the characteristics of a tax and is called a social security tax in other countries.

Taxes can be levied by *different levels of government* – central or local, federal, state or municipality depending on a country's constitution. Even prior to rate-capping and the poll tax the United Kingdom had one of the most centralized revenue structures in the Western world, with the exception of France and Belgium. From 1990 it has become *the* most centralized system of tax collection anywhere. Only 3.5 per cent of total tax revenue in the United Kingdom was raised by local authorities in the form of the council tax in 1994. In France the figure for local revenue was 8 per cent but in federal nations like Canada and Switzerland it is well over 40 per cent of all revenue, in West Germany and the United States over 30 per cent, and in Sweden over 25 per cent. Those countries with most fiscal decentralization tend to expand their local service expenditures faster (Gould, 1983).

Taxes can be *earmarked* or *general*. An earmarked tax is one that is levied to cover the costs of a particular service: National Insurance contributions and social security taxes are examples. Since William Pitt's day, in the late eighteenth century, the British government recognized the absurdity of keeping multiple accounts – the King's revenue was the same from whatever source. Economists have usually held that trying to tie a government's hands to spend in line with revenue raised for particular purposes was impossible. Since *all* taxes are compulsory, earmarking is a pure fiction. More recently, however, some American authors have argued that there is a case for separate forms of tax linked to particular purposes. It enables voters to show some preference for different kinds of spending, for example by campaigning to resist or increase the education or social security tax. Earmarking, they argue, increases the amount of information and leverage voters have on tax and expenditure questions (Brennan and Buchanan, 1980). Hills (1995b) has argued that voters may be reluctant to vote for general tax increases which they see going into some big black hole of government, but *are* keen to see particular services like education and health supported – that, at least, is what they tell public opinion pollsters. It may be that they would be prepared to vote for specific taxes which they saw going to a particular service. This is something we return to at the end of the chapter.

Payment of social security contributions over a given period 'entitles' the payer to a benefit, though only until the law is changed! Payment of other taxes is not linked to any right to benefit. Social security contributions are paid into the National Insurance Fund from which non-means-tested benefits are paid (see Chapter 14). All other central government revenue is paid into the Consolidated Fund – a 'common bucket' from which remaining expenditure is financed.

The next most basic distinction is between *direct* taxes, levied on households' and enterprises' incomes, and *indirect* taxes, levied on expenditure.

Direct taxes

There are various forms *direct taxes* can take and in theory they can be levied by either central or local government.

Poll tax

The earliest and simplest form of tax was to oblige every person to pay so much each. The tax was used by the ancient Greeks. The levy of 1380 led to Wat Tyler's rebellion in the Middle Ages. It was used by Southern states in the United States to exclude black people from voting. It was discussed by the Thatcher government (DoE, 1981) as a new source of revenue for local government and initially rejected. Then, as we saw in the previous chapter, it was introduced in Scotland in 1989 and in England and Wales in 1990 but it lasted only for a very short period. The poor pay a higher proportion of their income than the rich. The share of income taken in tax falls as incomes rise. This characteristic we call 'regressive'.

Income tax

This more modern tax, dating in Britain from the Napoleonic Wars, is now the main *direct* tax on households. In 1994, personal income tax contributed 28 per cent of all tax receipts – not more, it is important to note. It is levied on all those with incomes above limits which Parliament sets each year, and the amount paid varies with a person's income above that level – their 'taxable income'. Over the long term, income tax has moved from being a tax paid only by the rich to one levied on quite poor people. The share of a person's income paid in tax could be a flat percentage. In practice, in this and in other countries, rich people pay higher rates of tax on their marginal earnings above a given level. Those with lower incomes pay, or should pay, a lower share of their income in tax. This characteristic makes income tax a 'progressive' tax. In some countries the percentage tax paid on the first slice of taxable income is quite low, say 15 per cent, and rises steadily as income rises. In the United Kingdom tax begins at 20 per cent but most people pay at the next common basic rate of tax, 24 per cent in 1996/7. Higher earners moved onto a higher rate of 40 per cent for that taxable income which topped £25,500. Most people's income is taxed directly by their employers and handed on to the Inland Revenue, an arm of central government, under a system that is called pay-as-you-earn (PAYE). In many other countries in Europe and in states and cities of America, local income taxes are levied. In 1996, the tax individuals paid on income from savings was reduced to 20 per cent to encourage saving.

Corporation tax

This tax is the equivalent of income tax on enterprises or firms. A firm pays tax on its profits but that part of the tax paid on distributed profits – that is, dividends paid to shareholders – is counted towards the individual shareholders' tax bill – a 'credit'. Profit – the company's net income – is measured as the difference between its revenue and its costs. This sounds simple enough, but defining costs, especially those of capital equipment that wears out, is a very complicated business. Historically, governments gave firms very generous allowances and permitted them to offset the costs of new capital equipment against profits, so that in practice the total revenue from corporation tax has been relatively low as a share of all revenue. In the 1980s, the Chancellor reduced the rate of corporation tax companies paid but also reduced the allowances on new investment. The main rate of corporation tax was reduced to 33 per cent in 1991/2, the lowest rate in Europe (*The Economist*, 23 March 1991), and the rate of tax for small companies was cut to 24 per cent from 1996. Total revenue from this tax was only 7 per cent of government income in 1994.

Taxes on capital

So far the taxes we have discussed (except the poll tax) have been assessed on the size of an individual's or firm's income. Another way to measure an individual's capacity to pay tax is the amount of capital assets he or she may have. Wealth, or the ownership of capital, is far more unequally distributed than income and is more unequal in this country than in many others, though wealth data in general and international comparative data in particular are deficient (Royal Commission on Income and Wealth, 1979). Hence governments interested in reducing these disparities have introduced various taxes on large wealth holders, directed in particular at reducing the extent to which large accumulations of wealth can be passed on to the next generation. A tax on inherited estates began in 1894, though death duties can be traced back much further. The modern form of death duties is the inheritance tax. If you die with assets worth more than £200,000 after April 1996 your estate pays tax. If you give your money away seven years before you die, you pay no tax. There is a sliding scale in between. Large owners of wealth with good tax advice have largely avoided paying this tax. It falls most heavily on people with very modest savings or houses, who have not taken appropriate advice. In 1994 this tax only raised £1,420 million, compared to the £68,000 million raised from income tax. Mr Clarke in his 1995 Budget proposed ending it altogether at some future point.

Capital gains tax
Here a tax is imposed when individuals part with an asset and make a capital gain on it. The gain is measured as the market price minus the price at which it was bought, indexed to take account of the general price increase in the period. There is a minimum amount of gain each year that you are allowed tax free. Owner-occupied houses are exempt. Once more people can successfully avoid the tax and the revenue is therefore comparatively small – £2,260 million in 1994.

Property tax
The old 'rates' were, and the new council tax is, the *only* form of tax revenue available to local government. The tax liability is based on the value of the property the householder is occupying. Rates developed as a tax that was meant to bear more heavily on those with means in the days before incomes could be measured as easily as they can be today. The value or size of the property a person lived in was the next best indicator. Today the value of

property is assessed in bands or groups of similarly valued property by the Inland Revenue – central government civil servants – a process which (in theory) is repeated at regular intervals. Businesses continue to pay tax on the value of their premises, but they pay national government the national business rate.

National Insurance or social security contributions

These are levied on employees, on employers and on the self-employed. They are paid into a fund specially earmarked to meet the costs of the national insurance scheme – the National Insurance Fund. We discuss this system of funding in Chapter 12.

Expenditure taxes

Some reformers (Kaldor, 1955; Meade, 1978; Pechman, 1980) have argued that instead of taxing an individual's income, it would be better to tax his or her expenditure. It would be simple. It would not, they argue, be such a disincentive to work as progressive income tax. It would be less easy to avoid and it would be an incentive to save. Other economists are less sure (Atkinson and Stiglitz, 1980: 563–6; Prest and Barr, 1985: 340–3). In many respects, taxes on purchases – indirect taxes – have a similar effect.

Indirect taxes

These taxes are levied, not on particular households or firms, but on the goods they buy or sell. They include the following.

Customs and excise duties

These are some of the earliest forms of revenue. Customs duties also perform the function of keeping out foreign produced goods. They are raised by a separate arm of government – Customs and Excise. The latter is concerned with levying tax on certain items – previously largely imported – such as tobacco, spirits, beer, and wine, and on oil, including petrol.

Vehicles

Cars and lorries are taxed before they can be driven legally on the roads. You must display the tax disc or face a fine.

Value added tax (VAT)

This is now the chief source of indirect taxation. It is essentially a sales tax levied at 17.5 per cent of the final price of the product, but is collected at each stage in the production process. The shopkeeper pays tax on his sales of all taxable goods, minus the tax paid by those who sold him the goods wholesale, and so the chain goes back to the producer. Each stage in the production process thus pays tax on the 'value they have added', hence the tax's name. Charities and small firms are exempt. Food as a product is too. Domestic heating came within its ambit in the 1990s and caused a furious political debate; such expenditure was to have carried full VAT rating, but following a defeat at the hands of his own backbenchers the Chancellor had to withdraw the second stage of this increase in December 1994.

Table 7.1 Sources of tax revenue in the United Kingdom, 1948–1994/5

Tax	Percentage of total taxes				
	1948	1964	1982	1990/91	1994/5
Income tax	31.8	32.1	26.5	27.4	25.2
Tobacco	14.3	9.7	3.3	2.8	3.0
Beer, wine, spirits	10.2	5.7	3.1	2.4	2.2
National Insurance	8.0	14.8	20.2	17.2	16.8
Local rates/council tax	7.6	9.3	11.2	5.1	3.6
Purchase tax	7.2	6.5			
Value added tax			12.8	15.2	16.7
Profits tax	6.8	4.2			
Corporation tax			5.0	10.6	7.8
Death duties and inheritance taxes	4.4	3.2	0.5	0.6	0.6
Customs duties	2.7	2.0	1.8	0.8	0.8
Stamp duty	1.4	0.8	0.8	0.8	0.7
Petrol and diesel	1.3	6.6	4.7	4.7	3.0
Vehicle licences	1.2	2.0	1.7	1.7	1.5
Entertainment tax	1.2				
Capital gains			0.6	0.9	0.4
North Sea oil			4.7	0.4	0.2
National business rate					5.1
Other	1.7	0.9	1.9	9.6	8.5

Source: The Economist, 17 December 1983; HM Treasury (1990, 1995).

Total tax shares

We can see from Table 7.1 that the structure of taxation has changed substantially since 1948. Contrary to popular belief, personal income tax and other small business income tax provides only just over a quarter of all tax revenue. That share has fallen. It is the National Insurance, or social security contributions as we now call them, that have become the second largest element with 17 per cent of the total. Tobacco has collapsed as a primary source of funds. Local government taxes once formed 11 per cent of all tax income, a share that is down to 3.6 per cent. Central government now collects the business rate and redistributes it to local government. VAT, which replaced purchase tax, has become the other main revenue raiser. In 1979, the Conservative government reduced the standard rate of income tax from 33 per cent to 30 per cent but nearly doubled the standard rate of VAT. By 1994/5, VAT was producing nearly 17 per cent of all revenue.

What effect do taxes have?

Allocative efficiency

For the government to raise large sums of money and redistribute them to purchase social services must have profound effects on the economy. These matters are the subject of a large and technical literature. The student with an interest and a good grounding in the principles of economic theory should pursue that literature beginning with a standard public finance text (Prest and Barr, 1985; Bailey, 1995). The best advanced text is still Atkinson and Stiglitz (1980). However, the issues are of central importance and can be simplified to some extent.

Classical economists begin from a model of a free market interchange of goods and services with no monopolies or imperfections in the capital market or the labour market. In such a free market, goods and services would be efficiently allocated. Everyone's preferences would be reflected in their purchases of goods and their productivity in wages paid. In economic terms, resource allocation is optimal. Economists can then theorize about what happens when we remove those assumptions one by one. The introduction of governments who tax goods and incomes in various ways is of course one of the major 'imperfections', and economic theory is concerned to show what kinds of tax would interfere least with allocations that would arise in a free market. One of the difficulties with classical theory is that there are so many other interacting 'imperfections' at work that to measure the impact of a single tax is all but impossible. Some general principles can, however, be deduced.

Direct and indirect taxes: is it better to tax incomes or goods?

Let us first compare the impact of imposing a proportional income tax – i.e. one that taxed a constant proportion of one's income, however high – and raising the same revenue as a tax on one particular product, or a narrow range of products. To take a similar proportion of everyone's income away will not affect individuals' capacities to express their preferences between goods or services, though it does bias their choices between goods and leisure. However, to raise the same revenue by concentrating all the tax on one particular product or narrow range of products would change its relative price. This, in turn, would change people's pattern of purchases *away* from that which reflected their true preferences. In theoretical terms this results in a loss of welfare for individuals.

However, this does not necessarily prove that direct taxes are more efficient in economic terms than indirect taxes, for three reasons. First, it is possible for indirect taxes to be levied at an even rate across all goods and services: for example, a sales tax with a single rate of, say, 5 per cent, or value added tax. If these taxes increase the price of all products in proportion to their original price, they distort market preferences relatively little. Secondly, a tax on a particular product may be justified on efficiency grounds if heavy 'external' costs are involved in its production or use: for example, tobacco or alcohol. The public is not faced with the true cost of these products because their use costs lives and uses public health resources. Leaded petrol, too, has pollution costs. A higher tax rate on such items can be justified if it faces consumers with the true costs, private and external, of producing and consuming the product. A tax on smoke or water-polluting production processes, a higher tax on leaded petrol, a congestion tax on vehicles in city centres, or a duty on heavy lorries that badly damage road foundations, could all be justified in these terms. A pollution tax could theoretically be set at a level that would exactly match the external costs involved. The practical difficulty lies in deciding how to value the external effects. Thirdly, an indirect tax could be justified in terms of pure allocative efficiency if a product were produced under conditions of severe imperfect competition – a monopoly, for example. In the real world it is difficult to see how such a tax could be imposed or calculated, and it would make much more practical sense to tackle the offending firm under monopolies legislation.

Taxes for the future

These arguments are not mere economic theorizing. Their logic is reflected in the kind of indirect taxes that are levied. We have seen that VAT is levied at a common standard level, with food and a few other items zero-rated. That aside, VAT does fit the rules of allocative efficiency quite well. Also, we tax tobacco and alcohol separately, and do so at a higher level in part because of the health side effects such consumption has. In the 1990s the government began to tax petrol that was leaded and environmentally damaging more heavily than non-leaded petrol. Many people have raised the possibility of extending the principle of environmental taxation even further, to face consumers with the true social costs of using carbon fuels or driving their car into crowded city centres and polluting the atmosphere.

It is becoming clear that taxation in the next century could be used as a major tool to promote a more efficient allocation of resources in society, forcing consumers to take account of the long-term implications of their actions. Taxes are not just a way of paying for welfare: they can be a way of promoting welfare too.

So far we have discussed the impact of indirect taxes on allocative efficiency. Direct taxes can also affect the 'efficient' distribution of resources. At the extreme, a 100 per cent tax will remove all financial incentives to move to the new job in a new industry that requires a particular kind of skill. At the other extreme, a poll tax that takes the same amount from everyone will keep the same absolute difference between the rewards in one job and the next. This might minimize disincentive effects but few consider such a tax fair. As so often, we have conflict between equity or fairness, and efficiency. A poll tax takes a larger proportion of poor people's pay, but does least 'damage' to the 'efficient' allocation of labour. Just how important efficiency considerations appear will depend on how far the reader accepts the basic theoretical framework. However, while it is possible to discount the efficiency consequences at low rates of tax, the higher the rate of tax, the less and less easy it becomes to do so.

Taxation and the supply of labour

The relevant economic argument that reaches the notice of even the ill-informed newspaper reader is the proposition that high taxation, or indeed any taxation at all, is undesirable because it limits the extent to which people work, produce and add to the 'wealth of the nation'. This standard economic theory refers to what is called the 'substitution effect'. It can be stated simply. Individuals could spend all their time at work or play. In practice, life is better with a mixture of work and leisure. The worker trades (or *substitutes*) one for the other until he is satisfied with the mix. At this point, the marginal pound he or she earns from an hour's work is just more than equal to the value of that hour in watching TV or pottering in the garden. Wages, in a purely competitive labour market, would reflect that trade-off (or marginal rate of substitution). When an income tax is levied, it will reduce the return or rewards for labour. At the margin, leisure will be more attractive. The individual will work less and give more hours to leisure, but this is not what he or she originally wished to do and his or her satisfaction or welfare is thus reduced.

This view visualizes workers and potential workers weighing up the pleasure gained from an hour of gardening, and balancing it against an additional hour in the office or on the production line. The focus of this theory is upon the comparison individuals are presumed to make between the *marginal* value of an extra hour of work or leisure. Clearly then, a progressive income tax which makes individuals pay a higher marginal rate of tax the more they earn will penalize work. This has serious implications for the whole economy. A low-tax economy will therefore, other things being equal, be a more efficient economy. That is the traditional conclusion from this part of the theory. Yet more advanced economic texts accept that all is not that simple (Atkinson and Stiglitz, 1980, chapter 2).

The first standard problem is that the market is not perfectly competitive. Workers are not able to choose to trade small adjustments in hours worked against take-home pay. Fixed hours and production processes, and negotiated wage rates with limited opportunity for overtime, all reduce the flexibility of the trade-off between leisure and work. Nevertheless, some workers do clearly have some freedom to earn bonus payments and undertake piecework, to vary effort with reward. Moreover, the main choices that face individuals are about what kind of job to enter. Young people may very well judge that a job in a demanding, highly paid position is not worth it because the financial rewards are taxed away. Secondly, for some people, work and leisure may not be clear alternatives. Work itself may be a pleasure and the monetary reward may be of limited importance after a minimum income is gained. Thirdly, economists often implicitly assume that more labour supply is a good thing. In a fully employed economy, this is reasonable. In the recent period of excessive unemployment and weak demand for labour, the validity of this assumption is less clear.

So much, then, for the 'substitution effect' theory. A second perspective emphasizes the 'income effect'. This postulates that people have in mind a target income they would like to receive – set by the life style of their neighbours or those just above them in the social ladder. Households will do their best, with the main earner searching for a good job, undertaking training, pursuing overtime, while the wife or second earner goes out to bring the household income up to that socially approved target. If a worker's earnings are taxed, his or her motivation to work *longer* hours, to buy the prized new car or video, is *increased*. This theory counterbalances the other. It predicts precisely the *opposite* human response to the substitution effect – higher taxes increase incentives to work. To put it another way, reducing income tax will increase people's capacity to afford more leisure. Some writers (Musgrave and Musgrave, 1980) have put the two theories together, claiming that in the *low* range of income, workers are motivated by the second effect, but later, as basic necessities have been bought and 'social' necessities too, then the trade-off between leisure and work becomes dominant and the first effect predominates. Taken to its logical conclusion, this suggests that to maximize work one would need to place high taxes on the poor and low taxes on the rich!

It is not enough, however, to argue that these two effects simply cancel one another out and we can therefore forget about them. If an individual works longer hours than he or she would wish to do in the absence of taxation, that involves a loss of welfare.

Public finance economists often stop at this point, leaving the impression that all taxation does is to introduce inefficiency. They ignore the efficiency gains that flow from providing the services which the taxation makes possible (see Chapters 2 and 3). However, in the reverse way, social policy writers tend to ignore the efficiency consequences of taxation and concentrate on the benefits of service provision. It is, therefore, important to consider both factors and to know how big the work incentive effects may be.

Evidence on the effects of taxation

Early evidence of the impact of taxation on incentives to work was reviewed by Brown (1983) and Atkinson and Stiglitz (1980). The evidence was of several kinds. There are, for example, interviews. Brown and Levin (1974) undertook an interview survey of workers to test their views about the impact of different levels of tax on their willingness to undertake overtime. The results suggested no strong association. Most workers were unclear about what their marginal tax rates were, and consequently did not have any very clearly calculated response. Low-earning workers seemed least affected, but amongst higher earners some evidence of a small disincentive was discernible.

There are also econometric studies using panel data on individuals' labour supply, wages and personal circumstances (Houseman, 1981). Overall, the results do suggest that high taxable rates do have some impact on men's working hours and quite a lot of impact on women's. Further evidence can be gained from a series of very interesting experiments undertaken in the United States in the 1960s and 1970s. They were unusual for social science research:

attempts at controlled experiments in selected communities of different kinds in different parts of America. Their aim was to see what incentive effects financial aid to poor families would produce. As a family's income rose, so the cash aid was withdrawn at different rates for different members of the sample. There was a matching sample that received no grants. The effect of withdrawing state income as earned income rises is precisely the same in economic terms as an ordinary tax on additional earnings. Moreover, a cash *supplement* to income would also be expected to lead to a fall in work effort. On both counts these experiments might be expected to show strong disincentive effects on work.

The first of these experiments was in New Jersey (Pechman and Timpane, 1975). Later experiments were undertaken in Gary (Burtless and Housman, 1978), rural areas of North Carolina and Iowa, and the western and north-western cities of Denver and Seattle (Robbins, 1982). A summary of the results is to be found in Brown (1983). All are subject to fierce statistical debates about the methods and whether the results can be extended to a national scale. Different experiments also produced somewhat different results. The earliest experiment in New Jersey suggested that the reduction in working hours produced by relatively high tax rates was small – a 0.5 per cent reduction in hours worked by men who received a cash supplement and had it withdrawn at a 50 per cent tax rate. However, wives were affected. They used their extra income gained to stay at home to look after children. The same result showed up in rural experiments. The largest experiments were the last, at Denver and Seattle. They suggested that faced with high tax rates of 50 to 80 per cent, husbands in poor families worked less – a total reduction of 5 per cent. Wives' reductions were greater – 22 per cent – while single mothers cut their hours by 11 per cent. How far it is reasonable to extrapolate these results to the non-poor is a highly debatable point.

More recently, evidence has begun to accumulate that suggests that very high rates of tax do have an effect on levels of taxable income. Whether this is because faced with high marginal tax rates, individuals manage to hide income from the tax authorities, switch into capital or do not generate as much income, is less clear. Nevertheless, a study of a sample of American taxpayers before and after significant reductions in their tax liabilities in the 1980s showed that those who had paid tax at the 49–50 per cent rate and who had enjoyed a big reduction in that rate, substantially increased their reported incomes in the following years – far more so than those on lower tax rates who had not benefited so much (Felstein, 1995). Indeed, the revealed income effect was so big that they paid *more* taxes as a result of the reduction in their marginal tax rate!

In brief

Overall, it is difficult to avoid the conclusion that high tax rates do reduce labour participation, certainly for poor households doing unpleasant jobs, for women, and for those facing very high tax rates who can affect the amount of tax they pay by changing their income and wealth-generating behaviour. But the scale of these effects at lower rates of tax, especially for those in normal jobs and with family responsibilities, is probably small. At the rates of tax currently faced by most people in the United Kingdom the disincentive effects are probably quite small. The likely large effects are those resulting from the high 'quasi tax' rates which come from the overlap of means testing and taxes that hit low-income families – the 'seven deadly traps' as Hermione Parker (1995) calls them.

None of these studies, however, deals with the issue raised earlier. How far does the knowledge that the state will tax away high salaries deter people from entering high-earning and demanding jobs? Since tax avoidance is so effective, the answer is probably, not much. However, that is not a good reason for trying to levy high tax rates that no one can enforce.

Who pays taxes?

Like so many questions about taxation, this is deceptively simple. If the government puts an extra tax on whisky, who pays it? Whisky drinkers? If the government puts a tax on employers for every worker they employ, who pays? The employers? A little more thought suggests that the interactions are more complex. What if the price of whisky is already so high that no one is prepared to buy any more if the price goes up again? In that case, shopkeepers and manufacturers might be prepared to drop their profit margins, absorb the tax and go on selling at the same price. In this extreme case, the tax would be paid by the producer or seller of whisky. In the same way, if employees and unions have already squeezed as much out of the employer as they possibly can, the employer cannot pay higher labour costs without going bankrupt. Then the effect of raising the employer's social security tax will be for the employer to pay lower wages than he or she otherwise would. These are extreme cases, but in most situations part of the cost of taxation will be passed on or 'shifted' in this way. In short, the economic incidence of taxation will not be the same as the 'statutory' incidence. By 'incidence', economists mean where the tax burden falls – who pays. Public finance theory sets out the possibilities more formally.

The theories show that the incidence question is complex and precise calculations of who pays and who benefits are very difficult to determine. One lesson seems to be that we cannot tell anything about the consequences of taxation. That would be too pessimistic. It turns out that the theoretical 'shifting' effects are less important than they seem in theory. (The relevant findings and theories are accessibly discussed in Pechman and Okner, 1974; and Pechman, 1985). Pechman's study attempts to show what difference alternative economic assumptions about the incidence of various taxes make. It illustrates the difficulty of such studies, and also suggests some broad conclusions.

The combined effect of federal, state and local taxes in the United States in 1985 fell heavily on the poorest. The share of income paid in taxes was more or less proportional to income for most families (about 20–25 per cent) and then rose for the top 10 per cent of highest income earners. The progressivity of the tax system had been reduced between 1965 and 1985. That pattern was not very different whatever theoretical assumptions were used. Remarkably similar results have been obtained by studies in the United Kingdom and other countries. Taxes do not fall more and more heavily on people the more they earn. The outcome of the political merry-go-round that sets nominal tax rates has produced a roughly *proportionate* tax structure. That finding is certainly borne out in the United Kingdom where the shift to a less progressive tax structure has had a marked effect on income distribution (Hills, 1995b).

Table 7.2 Taxes as a percentage of gross income, by income group in the United Kingdom, 1994/5, by decile

Taxes	Percentage of total income				
	Bottom	3rd	5th	8th	Top
Direct:					
Income tax	2	4	8	13	19
National Insurance	1	2	3	5	3
Council tax	–[1]	6	4	3	2
Total direct taxes	3	12	15	21	24
Indirect:					
VAT	12	8	8	7	5
Tobacco and alcohol	7	4	4	2	1
Car tax, TV, betting	6	4	4	3	2
Intermediate[2]	7	5	4	4	3
Total indirect taxes	32	21	20	16	11
Total taxes	35[3]	33	35	37	35
Average gross equivalized household income, including cash benefits (£s per annum)[4]	5,757	8,296	14,366	24,525	49,391

Notes: [1]Housing benefit meets council tax for poor families.
[2]Taxes on employers deemed to be passed on in prices.
[3]Excluding council tax from taxes and housing benefit from income.
[4]Household income is adjusted to take account of the number of people in the family, counting children as less than one.
Source: Central Statistical Office (1995d).

Findings for the United Kingdom

For many years the UK statistical service has estimated the burden of taxation and the value of benefits which households pay and receive. It is based on a national sample of households' income and expenditure. It does not attempt the economic sophistication of the American work we have described – there are no alternative sets of theoretical assumptions. In most cases it assumes that the burden of tax falls where the legal form says it falls. But intermediate taxes on production costs like the property tax, commercial vehicle licences and employers' National Insurance contributions are assumed to be passed on in consumer prices. They are treated like VAT. From households' expenditure patterns it is possible to deduce how much indirect and intermediate taxes are paid, and there is a straightforward entry of the direct taxes each family pays. There are many theoretical difficulties with the whole study (see O'Higgins, 1980), notably on the allocation of benefits (Evandrou *et al.*, 1991). However, given the nature of the overall bias, and the fact that the broad outline of the tax conclusions would probably not change dramatically under different assumptions, the results are worth examining (see Table 7.2).

Table 7.2 shows very clearly what a *proportionately* high price the poor pay for their social services through the tax system. The reasons are clear. The poorest tenth of households (the lowest decile) pay nearly a third of their income in indirect taxes if you include in that the assumption that employers pass on their taxes in higher prices. The poorest families pay 12 per cent of their income in VAT. They spend virtually all their income and pay VAT on nearly all of it except for food. Tobacco and alcohol taxes, though possibly having positive health effects, are very regressive. About 7 per cent of a poor family's income goes in such taxes, but only 1 per cent of the richest. The rich pay a total of 11 per cent of their incomes in indirect taxes, a third of the proportion for the poorest households.

Income tax, in contrast, is progressive. Poor families do pay it, but it only takes 2 per cent of their incomes. The richest households

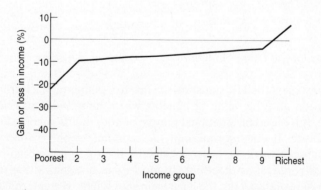

Figure 7.1 Gains or losses as a percentage of post-tax income: the consequences of tax changes, 1978/9 to 1994/5 (Source: Hills, 1995a)

pay more, but it may be a surprise to learn that it is still only 19 per cent of their incomes. This is a tribute to the way tax allowances can work for this group. National Insurance contributions rise with income but then cease to do so because of the ceiling put on them for higher earners. Council tax is difficult to express in the figures. The very poorest can, and mainly do, have it paid as part of housing benefit. The official figures show the tax as being paid by families and then the benefit is added to their income. We show council tax excluded from both income and expenditure for comparison for the poorest group.

The overall results in Table 7.2 suggest that the total tax burden faced by the households in the United Kingdom ranges between about 35 per cent of income for the very poorest back to 35 per cent for the richest tenth. The striking feature, as in the United States, is how similar is the share taken by taxes across the income range. It follows that changes in the tax structure can affect the distribution of income just as much as changes in the benefit system. The greater emphasis put on indirect taxation in the 1980s and the reduction in the top rates of tax did change the relative burden of taxation borne by rich and poor. As Figure 7.1 shows, the poorest lost about 20 per cent of their income as a result of those changes while the richest gained 10 per cent.

Taxes paid in other countries

Britons have a deep-seated belief, fostered by the popular press and some politicians, that they are more heavily taxed than anyone else in the world except perhaps the Swedes. It is true that before 1979 the marginal rates of income tax on the very rich were high (marginal tax rates are the percentage of the last pound earned taken in tax). At 40 per cent these are now in line with most highly industrialized countries. The top rate in the United States is virtually the same, for example. It is true that the rate of tax at which people begin to pay income tax is high compared to other countries. In the United States, for example, people begin to pay tax on the first slice of their taxable income at 15 per cent (1996). However, here too, the United Kingdom now has its first rate set at 20 per cent. Most Americans pay marginal Federal tax rates higher than in the United Kingdom. On top of this, many Americans will

Table 7.3 Total taxes and social security contributions
as a percentage of GDP in various countries, 1993

Country	%
Sweden	50.6
Denmark	50.0
Netherlands	48.8
Finland	46.1
Belgium	45.6
France	43.9
Austria	43.6
Italy	42.4
Germany	41.8
Greece	38.9
Canada	37.2
United Kingdom	33.1
Switzerland	32.4
United States	29.7
Japan	29.1
Australia	28.7

Source: Central Statistical Office (1995c).

pay local or state income taxes too. On the continent of Europe, social security contributions are usually higher than in the United Kingdom. Thus overall, the picture of the highly taxed UK resident is simply no longer true. Indeed, we are now one of the least taxed nations in the world. Table 7.3 sets out the international tax league table.

As we can see from Table 7.3 the share of total incomes going in tax and social security contributions takes about half of total income in Denmark and Sweden. Other European countries are not far behind. The UK population pays only a little more in taxation than those in the United States and Japan. The United States, even under Reagan, did not significantly reduce its overall tax burden in the 1980s and 1990s. Japan, with its ageing population, will surpass the United Kingdom in taxes and social security contributions before long. Australia, a younger country, has been successful in holding down its expenditure through careful targeting. We return to discuss the problems of financing the welfare state in Chapter 15.

In conclusion

Students of social policy often concentrate their attention on social benefits and social services and forget about how they are paid for. We have seen in this chapter how wrong that is. There is little point in mildly pro-poor benefits if the tax burden is heavily anti-poor. The structure of taxation matters.

During the 1980s, the level of income tax for high income groups was reduced substantially. Value added tax was increased sharply, the National Insurance contribution rose, and benefits were made less generous for some. At the same time, however, major changes were also made to the tax structure, as a result of which the poorest groups have seen their after-tax incomes fall. Tax policy is thus a crucial part of social policy – for good or ill.

Towards 2000

If we wished to pay for welfare in a way that was less burdensome on the poor and might attract support, what might be done? A programme for reform might include the following:

1. Reforming local government taxation to link the local tax to capacity to pay. In the longer term it would mean adopting a local income tax.
2. National Insurance contributions now have a ceiling. Higher earners currently pay no more than average earners. The social security tax could be levied at the same percentage right to the top of the income range.
3. The abolition of tax relief for most present purposes, including owner-occupation. This would permit a much lower marginal rate of tax and bear less heavily on the poor.
4. Introduce a tax to repay the costs of higher education for those who take courses.
5. Abolish the present inheritance tax and make recipients pay on gifts above a certain band as income.
6. Increase taxes on environmental 'bads' like driving in cities and using energy that pollutes the atmosphere.
7. Tie some taxes to services like an increase in social security contributions to pay for long-term care, with opt-outs for those

wishing to provide for themselves which would debar them from receiving state help.

Reforms of this kind would go farther towards making the welfare system more redistributive than any likely changes in the structure of services or benefits.

Further reading

The simplest and most lucid account of taxation in the UK and its impact on different income groups is: J. Hills (1988), *Changing Tax: How the tax system works and how to change it*, London: Child Poverty Action Group. It also discusses a range of reforms but it is now somewhat out of date; a new edition is expected. The best-written longer account of taxation is: J. Kay and M. King (1996), *The British Tax System*, 6th edn, Oxford: Oxford University Press. For an up-to-date discussion of recent changes and an evaluation, see S. J. Bailey (1995), *Public Sector Economics*, London: Macmillan.

CHAPTER 8

FEES AND CHARGES

Fees and charges are payments made to service providers for services rendered. The term *fee* is usually used to mean a payment that covers the full cost of the service provided. It is the market price of a professional's service – the doctor's fee, an architect's fee, school fees. In a profit-making enterprise like a private health clinic, this will include an element of profit, a return on the capital invested. If the organization is a non-profit charity, like a private school, the fees will merely cover the cost of the service minus any income the school will receive from other sources. Public sector pricing raises more complex issues, but it too is based on the idea that the price is fixed at least to cover the marginal social cost of producing the service.

The term 'charge' implies some rationale for fixing the levy other than pure pricing criteria. Charges provide the NHS with only 3 per cent of its income and the personal social services with 9 per cent. Why are they imposed? Though some economic texts suggest that the case for charging is essentially the same as that for any price mechanism, the history of charging suggests that the motivation has usually been quite different.

The history of charging

Parker (1976) summarized the reasons legislators had invoked for charging in the social services. They were as follows:

1. *Symbolism*   To express an ideological position regardless of the economic value of the charge itself.
2. *Abuse*   To reduce the cost of a service to the general taxpayer by raising the revenue from users.
3. *Deterrence*   To reduce the cost to the taxpayer by reducing demand for a service.
4. *Priorities*   To concentrate available funds on priority services and charge for less urgent facilities.

Judge and Matthews (1980) examined the history of charging in the personal social services, where many activities still carry a charge, and identified an even more varied selection of motives. It is instructive to look at some particular examples, because they show that the simple economic case for pricing turns out to be only part of the story.

To avoid stigma

In his second-reading speech on the National Assistance Bill in 1947, for example, Aneurin Bevan argued that the accommodation in a local authority old person's home should be charged for in just the same way as for a private hotel or nursing home, 'so that any old persons who wish to go may go there in exactly the same way as many well to-do people have been accustomed to go into residential hotels' (HC Debates 1947, col. 1609). This was a clear example of the phenomenon discussed by Pinker (1971). People in a capitalist or free market economy, he argued, tend to feel stigmatized when they receive something free. The prevailing value system suggests that it is only if you have paid in full for what you receive that you fully deserve to have it. Otherwise there is an element of charity and hence stigma in the exchange. Bevan seemed to be saying just that. Charges have also been advocated for precisely the opposite reason.

A symbolic deterrent

Mary Carpenter argued in 1851 that charges would be necessary in her proposed reformatory schools because otherwise unscrupulous parents would 'throw the charge of their children's bodily wants [and] those of their moral training . . . on the State' (quoted in Judge and Matthews, 1980). Though reformatory schools were later transformed into approved schools and community homes, the principle of charging never seems to have been seriously questioned. It was raised in the committee stage of the Children and Young Person's Bill of 1969 by a Conservative member who questioned whether charging should be mandatory, given the widespread variation in the levels of charging practised by different authorities. The reply by the Minister was a direct echo of Mary Carpenter: 'The principle behind this provision in the bill is that parents should be required – if their means so permit – to pay for their child's board and lodging, so that they are in no way better off as a result of the child's being in care.'

The practical effect of the charges is, however, trivial. Even in the nineteenth century the total revenue raised from parents in industrial schools only amounted to between 2.5 and 5 per cent of expenditure, while in the period 1948–69 the parental share of the costs of children in care only amounted to between 4 and 6.5 per cent. The most recent figure is 12 per cent. Most parents whose children are taken into care are extremely poor, either permanently or as a result of the crisis that has led to their being unable to look after their child. One is driven to the conclusion that here too the charge has most to do with symbolism.

A real deterrent against disapproved behaviour

There is no better example of the logical and ideological confusions into which we have fallen over the charging issue than in preschool provision. Local social service departments (formerly local health departments) provide day nurseries for some up to the age of 5. They provide care and not education – at least that is the theory. Daycare is in very limited supply. In general, only high-priority cases are able to gain a place. There also exist private daycare facilities, and child minders who provide a comparable service and who are registered and inspected by social services departments. Quite separate and distinct, so we are told by the professions concerned, are the pre-school facilities run by local education authorities – nursery classes. These take children only from the age of 3, and are staffed not by nursery nurses but by trained teachers. The schools are open for limited hours. Most children attend only part-time morning or afternoon.

Local authority nurseries charge, nursery classes do not. Why? Again we must delve back in history to understand how we reached this position. Day nursery provision by local authorities was strictly limited in the 1930s and charged for as a result of the cuts in local spending introduced as part of the National government's economy drive. But when the Second World War came and women were to be mobilized in large numbers for the war effort, the government gave local authorities a 100 per cent grant to cover the costs of day nurseries, merely charging parents for the cost of food served to the children. When the war ended, however, the policy changed. Women were no longer needed in the factories, and the traditional view, that a woman's place was properly in the home and that young children were best cared for by their mothers, reasserted itself. Government cut the grants to local authorities, arguing that nurseries were now required only for families in particular need (Ministry of Health Circular 221/45, 1945). Many were closed but local authorities began pressing government to permit them to charge and reduce the cost of providing the new nurseries that did continue. The Labour government resisted this pressure. However, the next Conservative government in the 1952 National Health Service Act obliged authorities to charge the economic cost of such provision, but to apply a means test. This further reduced demand and put state nurseries on a par with private ones, except for poor parents. Thus state day nurseries became confined very largely to the children of poor and needy parents, often single parents. Free daycare provision was, and still is, seen by many as an incentive that would attract women away from their proper caring duties. In 1993 985,000 children under 5 were receiving daycare in the United Kingdom, only 28,000 in state day nurseries (127,000 were in private nurseries and the remainder with playgroups and child minders) (Central Statistical Office, 1995a).

A way of relaxing public spending limits

Pre-school education was quite different. Legislators in the 1944 Education Act looked upon nursery education in a positive light, and indeed, laid a duty on local education authorities to provide enough to enable any parent who wanted it to send their child to a nursery school. The same Act, as we shall see later, abolished fee-paying in schools as being a barrier to equal educational opportunity – ergo, nursery education must be free. In fact, the resources, notably teachers, were not to be available after the war. There was a rapid increase in the number of primary school children, very overcrowded primary classes, and governments pushed all the available teachers and capital into primary education, limiting local authorities' right to provide nursery education even when they wished to. It was not until the 1960s that pressure began to mount on government to lift that ban and expand pre-schooling (Blackstone, 1971).

The Plowden Committee Report (DES, 1967) contains an interesting discussion on whether there was a case for introducing charges for nursery education. A minority report signed by several distinguished social scientists argued that there was. The main stumbling block to expanding nursery classes as a right, which they and the majority of the Committee favoured, was the limit on public spending. By reducing the net cost to the public purse by charging on a means-tested basis, it might prove possible to persuade the Treasury to expand provision. Without that incentive government would not implement the majority's recommendation. Moreover, they argued, very similar provision in day nurseries already carried a charge. Unless the state expanded its pre-school facilities, children would be catered for in the private sector, *increasing* class divisions. The majority of the committee did not accept these arguments. Essentially they retained the belief that nursery education should be free (even if that meant there was little of it) and that to charge for nursery classes would be a thin end of the wedge that would soon lead to charges for ordinary schooling. The teachers' unions strongly supported the majority report. Mrs Thatcher, then Education Secretary of State, in 1972 encouraged authorities to expand provision but did not accept the suggestion of charging. (Students may like to consider where they stand on this issue.)

Avoid cuts

In the 1980s many local authorities faced the opposite kind of dilemma. Faced with cuts in grant from central government, they tried to preserve services by charging users. Councils argued that rather than run down the home-help service, it was better to charge those who could afford to pay and keep the total level of service. Museum charges, and higher fees for adult and further education, were all defensive responses to the cuts as well as being supported for political reasons by some councils. Some writers have argued that there is much more scope for local authorities using their wide powers to charge in order to enhance their revenue (Blair, 1991).

To prevent abuse or reduce demand

When the National Health Service Act of 1946 was passed it was envisaged that medical care should be freely available at the point of need. Related activities provided under the Act by local authorities, like home helps and day nurseries, raised different issues, but all medical care, whether in hospital or general practice, dental care and opticians' services, was free. So too were the appliances prescribed, teeth and spectacles, or surgical appliances.

It was not long after the Health Service came into being that the economy began to go into one of its periods of crisis. The cost of the service turned out to be much higher than had been predicted. There was a particularly high demand for the dental and ophthalmic services, which had not been included in many of the pre-war insurance schemes. There was thus a very big backlog in demand from people who no longer faced a price barrier. It was this aspect of the new service that critics attacked most sharply. Popular newspapers were able to find or invent a few examples of 'frivolous' applications for dentures or spectacles. The Labour government took powers to introduce charges for dentures, spectacles and appliances, but it was not until the financial crisis of 1951 that the government finally convinced itself to introduce charges for these items in the wake of the economic crisis brought about by rearmament and the Korean war. It provoked a serious split in the Cabinet and the resignation of the Minister of Health and architect of the Health Service, Bevan, as well as Harold Wilson. The charges would prevent abuse. That, Labour Prime Minister Attlee argued, was the main reason for them (Hansard, vol. 495, col. 374).

We have seen, then, that the historical reasons for charging in the social services are diverse and often contradictory, but that does not mean that a general case cannot be made for charging on a priori grounds. I shall now set out the case for and against the extended use of charging.

The case for charges

Revealing consumer preferences

The most basic case for charging is the general case for pricing in a competitive economy (Seldon, 1977). People who wish to consume a service know what resources it uses because they are faced with a price which just covers the additional resources that are needed to provide it. If that price is too high, people will not purchase it. The pricing system thus reveals people's preferences in a realistic way. Faced with a zero price a consumer may opt to have the service just because it is free, while not really feeling very strongly about it one way or the other. Bleddyn Davies (1978) in his study of school meals charging, illustrates the force of this argument. When school meals were heavily subsidized there was little pressure to change the traditional pattern of meals, or to worry too much about quality. When the price was raised, parents and children asked whether it was really worth it, and might not sandwiches do just as well. Many authorities had to respond by modernizing their service and providing quick self-service and more popular food.

Encouraging efficiency

When a service is free it is difficult for the consumer to express dissatisfaction. If, however, they withdraw their *cash* from a particular school or college when they are not getting what they want, the teachers will have to respond or lose their jobs. There is a direct sanction the parent or student can bring to bear. (I reviewed these arguments in Chapter 3.) Instead of the public sector having the advantage of free or subsidized services, the higher the charge, the nearer it will be to the private alternative. This will put the public provider in direct and healthy competition with its private counterparts.

Social services are not different

Although some activities cannot by their very nature carry charges, there is nothing about social services that leads to such a conclusion. Most are not pure public goods and charging for them is technically possible (see Chapter 2 for a discussion of public goods). Foster *et al.* (1980) make this point to argue that there is a use for much more extensive charging for local government services.

Charging brings appreciation and self-respect

It was argued by some on the Public Schools Commission (DES, 1970), for example, that parents and children would appreciate the value of the education they received, and not simply take it for granted, if they actually had to part with some money. If they faced the full cost of schooling, parents would be very careful to ensure that their children made good use of it.

The same case has been made for social work. Free advice is largely ignored. If you pay good money to a psychiatrist or counsellor for advice you are likely to take it seriously. Moreover, as we saw earlier, it is possible to argue that to pay for a service produces an equal exchange relationship. The recipient feels no obligation, or sense of charity, in a market exchange. Pruger (1973) and Uttley (1980) argued that those who receive free services perceive themselves to be in debt in two senses. First, they are in a vague way in debt to society or the state. This induces a sense of compliance. Secondly, professionals already in a powerful position over their patients or clients because of their superior knowledge, can also induce a feeling of deference because the client has not paid for the service. If a free service builds up a high demand and a waiting list, that too increases a professional's power to humiliate or increase the client's dependency. A paying consumer at least feels he can say: 'Damn it, I am paying for this service. If I do not like it or you keep me waiting, I will take my custom elsewhere.'

The poor need not suffer

Those who favour charging reject the claim that free services are the only way of ensuring that the poor benefit from them. It is possible to adopt any of the following strategies to give the poor access:

1. To vary the charges with the income of the recipient and if the recipient is poor enough to waive the charge.
2. To enable the poor to recover the charge from an agency like the DSS.
3. To provide a voucher to everyone that can be used instead of money to purchase a minimum amount of that particular service.
4. To ensure through general redistributive tax and cash benefit policies that all families have sufficient resources to purchase these services if they wish.

All these arguments, it should be noted, make the case for *pricing*, or *fees*, at cost. What they do not do is to make the case for charging token sums to a small minority of users.

Raising revenue – the pragmatists' response

Although many politicians have not been prepared to accept the thoroughgoing case for pricing advanced above, many have, under the practical pressure of public spending constraints, been prepared to accept charging as a supplementary way of raising revenue, or to see charges increased as the only way of preserving a service.

Public expenditure bargaining in Whitehall is conducted in terms of *net* spending by the departments – that is, spending after receipts from charges have been deducted. Thus at any particular point in that debate ministers will have to weigh the merits of cutting the hospital-building programme or holding down nurses' salaries against raising the prescription charge, or reducing the number of home students compared with charging a higher fee to overseas students. The DES managed to fend off pressure to increase the size of classes and other cuts in the standard of the education service by permitting the price of school meals to rise, and then by charging overseas students the full economic fee. The DHSS defended the Health Service in the same way by being prepared to see prescription and other charges rise.

The case against charging

Social service consumers are different

The opposing view holds that social service consumers are not like consumers in an ordinary supermarket. They are not able, or are less able, to express their preferences through a market mechanism for at least three reasons (Titmuss, 1968, chapters 10 and 12).

Enforced consumers

Perhaps the extreme examples are the offenders who must make use of the probation officers' services. They are scarcely free to shop around for the officer who would give them the easiest time. Many of the social worker's functions require them to act as controlling agents, or in the interests of children against irresponsible or cruel parents, or to safeguard the community against a dangerous or disruptive mentally ill person.

The state forces children to be educated for a given period, if necessary against the parents' wishes or their indifference. The notion of giving money or quasi-money to a family to spend in a way they would not otherwise choose to do, is very far from the assumptions of a free market in which people spend their own money on something they want.

Vulnerable consumers

Many recipients of the personal social services are very old, or mentally ill or handicapped, or disabled. Moreover, these dependent people do not reach a social services department in most cases unless the family cannot care for them without help. As a consequence, such people are weak and potentially exploitable recipients of service. The model of equal bargaining partners scarcely holds. Many old people are as capable consumers as anyone else, but the very old and frail are at risk.

Second-hand consumers

Patients are not merely vulnerable. They or their relatives are not really consumers at all. The medical professional is in an overwhelmingly powerful position. The doctor is essentially the 'demander', determining whether treatment is necessary, what kind, and for how long the 'consumer' shall receive it. The phrase 'under doctor's orders' expresses a real situation that is different from a normal market. Many services like medical care are not bought in a normal commercial transaction by a user, but are bought via an intermediary or a third party, the insurance company. The consumer is often not even aware what the bill is, and if he or she is, he or she merely posts it off to the company to pay. The disciplines of the market do not apply. These are not arguments against market allocation as such, they merely suggest that the market's virtues only apply in a strictly limited range of circumstances.

Markets can be inefficient

While there is a good deal of intuitive sense in the observation that social workers and teachers respond to financial and other economic incentives like most (other) workers, it is a hypothesis rather than an empirically supported contention. We do not know that market motivation is more effective in promoting high standards of care than professional value systems, ethical standards and organizational traditions of public service, professional and peer review, inspectorates, public criticism and evaluative research. We know little about the way in which workers' motivations are affected by the creation of a powerful market test. The economic literature largely ignores the fact that the public sector has devised its own alternative modes of efficiency incentive. In many respects, these are deficient and could be extended and improved, but it is misleading to suggest that no incentives to good performance exist except market forces. There are grounds for suggesting that the market test can produce perverse incentives, as we saw in Chapter 3.

Social services can be different

While there are close affinities between education provided in a state and a private school, much of the argument does in the end turn on the belief that there is something different in the educational experience gained by a child in a local community school compared with that in a private school catering for a particular income group. These views depend on political values and preferences which we are not going to explore here, but clearly, if you believe that society as a whole will gain by children from all income groups being educated together, or children from a local community or religious group being educated together, you will prefer a system of finance that favours such provision. It is because people believe that who you are taught with is as important as what you are taught, that charging and finance are so hotly debated. Different financial incentives change the *nature* of the educational experience and are not merely alternative ways of financing the same service. Finance and provision are seen as interdependent, not independent.

Charging need not enhance consumers' view of a service

It can do the reverse. In a largely market economy, individualistic values predominate. In general, we value goods with a price, and devalue the 'free lunch', but it is possible for some institutions and professional and personal relationships to be viewed in different terms. As Hirsch (1977) points out, sexual relationships that are bought tend to be looked down on in our society compared with those that are freely chosen. Social institutions of long standing sustain their own value systems. People's attitudes to the Health Service expressed in opinion poll findings suggest that it is extremely popular in comparison with the health-care system of the 1930s. These attitudes can change if people perceive it is being neglected in comparison with private alternatives.

The poor can suffer

The process of reducing charges for low-income groups may not be effective. Precisely because 'paying your own way' is seen as the socially acceptable thing to do, where some do this and others do not, the non-payers distinguish themselves as undeserving or in receipt of special favours. Even if they are not inhibited from applying for special treatment they may suffer some loss of self-respect in receiving the service free. Evidence on this subject is extremely difficult to gather and interpret (Davies, 1978). People do not readily admit to feeling stigmatized. Probably the most decisive argument for the free personal social services is that most of their recipients are already so poor that charges bring little revenue.

In brief

There are contested arguments for and against charging for social services which resemble the more general argument about markets that we reviewed in Chapter 3. In practice, the origins of charging are diverse and often little more than symbolic. They often raise little revenue because so many of the recipients are poor. That is not true of all services, however. Services like education, which serve the richer sections of the community most, may be able to raise considerable revenue from charges or fees.

Further reading

A polemical case for charging is well advanced in A. Seldon (1977), *Charge*, London: Temple Smith; and charging, its origins and theory, as applied to the personal social services, is excellently set out in K. Judge and J. Matthews (1980), *Charging for Social Care*, London: Allen & Unwin.

The case for pricing local services is set out briefly in C. D. Foster, R. Jackman and M. Perlman (1980), *Local Government Finance in a Unitary State*, London: Allen & Unwin; while the wider use of charging for local government services is discussed in the Layfield Committee (1976), Cmnd 6453, London: HMSO.

CHAPTER 9

CHARITY AND GIVING

Giving as a form of finance

Taxes are a compulsory levy to finance services. Charges often amount to the same thing. Fees are payments made, more or less voluntarily, depending on the circumstances, for a service you buy. A gift or donation is, at its best, a payment made voluntarily so that a service may be given to others. Of course, it would be naive to claim that all gifts are made with no thought of any benefit that might accrue to the individual or to his or her family, now or at some future time, or to deny that gifts are often a reflection of gratitude for past services rendered to a member of the family or the donor themselves. Relatives may make a gift to a local hospital that has cared for a loved one. Parents or relatives often make donations to their old public school or college as some repayment for what it has done for them, or in the hope that it may give their child a better chance of entry! Many volunteers who give their time to voluntary organizations do so because it will look good on their CV or help them to be selected for a social work course! Many donors do lay down more or less stringent rules about the use of their funds, and these are legally binding on the body that receives them. They do not change as society changes and this may be an embarrassment to the organization or trust that administers such income. It is quite wrong to associate 'charity' or voluntary giving exclusively with 'voluntary' or non-profit organizations, or to assume that most of these organizations' income comes from donations. It does not. As we shall see later, National Health

Service hospitals obtain an important share of all monetary gifts and other voluntary help. But while public provision does not preclude charitable giving, the existence of the profit motive in any service usually does. It seems improbable that donors will be motivated to give time or money to a profit-making hospital or home on the grounds that it would be difficult to ensure that the patients or residents received the benefit, rather than the owner. This is a kind of market failure. The market and for-profit organizations cannot accommodate giving and voluntary action because it will always be in the interests of a profit organization to use its donations to undercut costs and increase its profit margins (Hansman, 1980, 1987). It is not surprising to find that giving is largely confined to non-profit and public organizations.

Forms of giving

Unpaid caring

It is possible to distinguish many different forms of giving in the field of welfare. First, and most important in relation to the personal social services, is *caring within the family* – services given to other members of the household, including children, or to relations outside the household. A number of points can be made about this form of giving, as follows:

1. If it were not for such giving, the burden on the formal services and on taxpayers would be far greater (Parker, 1990; Twigg, 1994).
2. Much of the most personal forms of care is done by women, but both men and women contribute a lot of time (Evandrou, 1990). Women still contribute more of the intensive care (Parker, 1992).
3. Most of the burden falls very heavily on a small number of people within the household concerned (Glendinning, 1983, 1992).
4. The motives and felt obligations that lie behind such giving are complex (Finch, 1987; Lewis and Meredith, 1988; Parker, 1993).
5. Much of this care is not voluntary, it is enforced by lack of other services, and is sometimes resented by those doing the caring. In so far as this is the case, the result is similar to a tax on the carers concerned.

Studies in the 1980s have revealed the scale of unpaid caring. The General Household Survey's special analysis of carers in 1985 (Green, 1988) suggested that: 1.7 million adults are caring for someone living with them; 1.4 million are spending at least twenty hours per week doing so; 3.4 million are bearing the main responsibility for the care of someone. Overall, about one adult in seven was caring for someone who was sick, elderly or handicapped. Although some of the early literature suggested this was a largely female responsibility a reanalysis of the General Household Survey suggests that while 15 per cent of women are caring for someone, 12 per cent of men are (Evandrou, 1990). But since women live longer when more of such caring is undertaken there are more women carers in absolute terms – 3.5 million compared to 2.5 million men and at the 'heavier' end of caring – that is, more intense, personal and time-giving (Parker, 1992).

The type of care given is gendered to some extent: 28 per cent of women are giving personal care and 19 per cent of men. Men do more physical work. As Parker (1990) points out: 'The costs to informal carers of caring for dependent people can include economic, physical, emotional and opportunity costs: loss and reduction of employment; reduced income; increased expenditure; restricted family and social life and physical and emotional strain.' Where families had a severely disabled child, mothers' participation in the labour market was lower, they worked less hours and were paid less. Fathers' employment is not as affected. The same kinds of effects can be seen in studies of families with disabled young adults (Hirst, 1984) and a disabled spouse (Martin and White, 1988).

Putting a cash figure to the loss of employment that results from caring responsibilities is far from straightforward. It is estimated that for women to give up work to look after disabled relatives cost them earnings of £8,500 if they had no children and about £7,000 if they had. Family income in families with dependent children is lower (Smyth and Robins, 1989). Evandrou (1990) showed that, nationally, the equivalent income of carers (taking account of family size) was somewhat lower than for non-carers, but the real drop in income was experienced by those caring for someone in their own household. While non-carers' individual equivalized median income was £87 in 1985, carers with a dependant in their household had a median income of only £64 a week. This drop in income can be seen as a private contribution to the cost of care by the family itself. The policy question is how far families should bear the burden them-selves and how far the state, through social security, or otherwise, should pay for the costs of disability (see Chapter 14).

It is not only care of the elderly and disabled that costs time and loss of earnings, but children above all do so. The costs of child rearing again fall predominantly on women. This has been called 'the family gap' (Machin and Waldfogel, 1993). Over the whole of the life span, women's earnings are half those of men (Evandrou and Falkingham, 1995), and most of this shortfall can be directly and indirectly accounted for by their greater caring and nurturing activities. The extent to which these activities ought to be dis-proportionately undertaken by women is more controversial. The fact is that women are paying for society's welfare on a scale that dwarfs all other forms of finance.

Giving human capital to voluntary organizations

Giving skills
Many voluntary organizations depend heavily on those with tech-nical, secretarial, accountancy, fund-raising, carpentry, building or professional skills, giving their advice free of charge.

Giving time
Volunteers who give their labour free provide an important part of work done by Citizens' Advice Bureaux, law centres, marriage guidance, youth work, and teaching English to foreigners. The Wolfenden Committee's (1978) survey of voluntary work in the social service field showed that 14 per cent of the national sample reported undertaking some work of that kind in a twelve-month period. Ten per cent, or just over two-thirds of all those giving time, worked with some identifiable voluntary organization. On average these people claimed they spent about six hours a week on such work, and this was equivalent to about 400,000 full-time workers. Later surveys of voluntary work have produced varied results. The annual survey of individual giving and volunteering by the Charities Aid Foundation suggests that 30 per cent of individ-uals volunteered their time in some way in 1988–9 in the month previous to the survey. By 1993 the figure had fallen to 21 per cent. On the other hand, the number of hours given on average may

have risen slightly (Halfpenny and Lowe, 1994; Martin, 1995). In total, something like two billion hours of time were donated in 1993. The General Household Survey in 1992 suggested that a quarter of all women and a fifth of men did some kind of voluntary work, figures consistent with the previous study quoted. It showed, however, that the time given was class-biased – the figure being about two in five men and women from professional occupations and one in ten from unskilled backgrounds (Central Statistical Office, 1995a: table 8.4).

Giving in kind

Anyone who has ever participated in a voluntary organization, youth work, or parents' association will know what a central place is taken by jumble sales and selling raffle tickets, though car boot sales seem to have taken over more recently! Unlike America, there is nothing equivalent in Britain to the 'food bank' through which gifts of food can be distributed on a communitywide basis to poor people. The most highly organized and valuable system of giving in kind is the gift of blood. Titmuss's (1970) famous book *The Gift Relationship* used the example of donating blood to raise the whole discussion about giving and social welfare onto a philosophical level of debate. He argued that there were some peculiar features of blood as a commodity that made the donating of blood efficient. Since blood could be infected and since detection was both difficult and expensive, the best guarantee of purity was the screening of donors who had no monetary incentives to lie about their past medical experience. (Titmuss's work predated AIDS, which reinforced his message.) However, Titmuss's argument was deeper and more general. Donating blood was an example of a social institution that embodied non-selfish actions by individuals without demeaning the recipient. It was important to provide an opportunity for that to happen in all welfare organizations for it sustained an unselfish motivation which was in the end necessary to sustain social institutions.

Giving cash

The only form of giving that shows up in formal accounts is cash. It comes broadly from three sources: direct giving by households and enterprises; indirect giving by taxpayers; and charitable bodies' own income from property trusts or investments.

How much does the ordinary household give in cash to charity? The Charities Aid Foundation regularly asks a national sample of individuals about their cash giving as well as volunteering (Martin, 1995). Its surveys suggest that about 80 per cent of individuals give something to charity and that figure has not changed much in the period since 1987. However, only about two in five people gave more than £1 in the previous month in 1993. The typical, or median, amount was £2.50. The arithmetic mean amount was about £10 a month, a figure boosted by a few people giving a lot. For the economy as a whole, the figure mounted to about £3 billion a year of cash giving in 1993. We are, therefore, not talking about huge sums compared to the total raised in taxes – £250 billion in 1994 – or the cost of the National Health Service – £30 billion – though the money may be important for individual organizations. The level of giving has not increased in real terms at all significantly since the late 1980s despite attempts to increase its attractiveness through various tax reliefs. Most people do not give in ways that attract tax relief, only 10 per cent do. Most give in door-to-door collections and similar ways.

Tax encouragement

Any income a charity receives is not subject to tax. Charities are also exempt from paying various taxes such as VAT. Taken together, these are a significant help and in effect constitute an indirect government subsidy. In 1990 the total value of tax concessions to the voluntary sector may have amounted to £1 billion (Kendall and Knapp, 1995b). In so far as the levels of government expenditure are fixed by general political considerations, if one group is expressly given favourable tax treatment, the value of tax revenue lost is a cost that must be financed by other taxpayers and other services. An individual can also trigger tax help by making a covenant to a charity. By undertaking to make a part of his or her income over to a charity for four years or more the tax the individual pays on that income is given by the tax authorities to the charity concerned. A similar arrangement is available for gifts made of over £250 on a regular basis from income each year. Thus the *price* of giving is reduced for taxpayers, especially higher-rate taxpayers. If I want a charity to benefit by £100 and I am paying tax at 25 per cent, I need only give £80 and let the Inland Revenue pay the rest. If I pay at 40 per cent on my top income, I only need give about £72. The higher the tax rate the more incentive there is to give to charity. The lower the tax rate the more costly it is to give to charity compared to ordinary spending. The lower marginal income tax rates of the 1980s made giving to charities relatively more expensive compared to private consumption.

In America there are more generous tax advantages for giving to charity since individuals and firms can offset any one-off gift against tax, whether in cash or kind. The inducement to give is greater, but by the same token there is a cost to the Exchequer in lost revenue. Some early work in the United States (Feldstein, 1975; Clotfelter, 1985) has suggested that the scale of charitable donations increases faster than the reduction in tax revenue and that the level of giving would increase sharply if tax reliefs were given. Some have therefore concluded that such a tax deduction system would increase the flow of revenue to charities by more than the tax loss and hence produce an increase in social service provision. There are, however, several assumptions in that argument.

It depends, first, on the assumption that the donations which would be made would go to charitable social service agencies providing for the same groups as statutory agencies. If tax relief-induced donations did not go to pay for main-line social service functions, and elected representatives still felt it necessary to continue to provide them, they would have a lower tax base on which to raise the revenue.

The second assumption is that additional tax relief will indeed increase the level of giving. During the 1980s the Conservative government took several steps to increase tax relief on gifts with this in mind. After 1980 it was possible for charities to reclaim tax paid on money covenanted to them for four years or more, not just at the standard rate of tax, but at the higher rate if individuals paid tax at the higher rate. The 1986 Finance Act introduced tax relief on regular giving to charities deducted from your pay packet. In the 1983 budget, gifts to charities were exempt from capital transfer tax. In 1990 the Gift Aid Scheme made allowance for tax relief on single cash gifts to charities. In short, a lot was done to increase the level of charitable donations from individuals in the 1980s. Does it provide a new way of paying for welfare in the 1990s?

Jones and Posnett (1990) examined the relationship between the level of covenant giving and the tax price (that is, the tax relief you gain if you give through a covenant). They were unable to find any link when other variables like prices and incomes were taken into account. They also point out that more recent American work has cast doubt on the relationship there too. More recent surveys suggest that only a very small part of giving is done in a way that attracts tax relief – perhaps only 10 per cent (Martin, 1995). In short, the latest evidence does not suggest that allowing more tax relief will promote much more giving.

Corporate giving

Companies are another source of cash aid. Again the Conservative government tried to encourage such activity by enabling companies to make one-off tax-deductible donations. The level of corporate support, however, remains low. A survey of the top 500 company donors was undertaken covering the year 1993/4 (Passey, 1995). Of those that replied, the typical or median gift by a company was for £219,000 a year in cash *and* non-cash support – non-cash giving being in terms of employees' time, training and other forms of goods and expertise. Cash income from for-profit and nationalized companies in the United Kingdom only amounted to about 4 per cent of charities' income in 1990. Companies' transfers to charities in 1994 amounted to £390 million or a mere 0.02 per cent of corporate income (Central Statistical Office, 1995b: table 5.1).

International comparisons

An international survey of voluntary sector activity and income undertaken by Johns Hopkins University in America (Salamon and Anheier, 1995) shows that private giving is only a small part of the sector's income in all countries. On average over their sample of agencies from seven countries in Europe, America and Japan, private giving only constituted 10 per cent of charities' income. Fees for service accounted for 47 per cent of income, and public sector grants and contracts for 43 per cent. The United Kingdom had a slightly higher emphasis on gifts at 12 per cent. The United

States had the highest giving share at 19 per cent but it was still the minor part. Private fee income is highest in the United States, the United Kingdom, Japan and Italy, while public sector income dominates in France and Germany. As Kendall and Knapp (1995b) argue, much depends on how you define the sectors in different countries. A broad definition of charities is dominated by educational institutions like universities and schools as well as cultural and entertainment activities. A narrower definition of welfare agencies produces a rather different picture, with many very small agencies, but the picture of low income from gifts does not change.

Wolpert (1990) compares levels of giving and voluntary sector activity in different localities in the United States. He finds that some areas are much more generous than others. Contrary to the theory that individuals are more likely give when taxes are low, he finds that areas with high propensities to give are also areas that vote for high taxes and social spending. Voluntary and state social service activity seem to be complementary, not opposites.

The limits of giving

We have seen that gifts of time, skills and even blood can be a significant component in the income of social service organizations, especially in the personal social service field. Private money is less important but still significant for some areas of voluntary non-profit social service. Giving is also qualitatively important for the giver. It is a means by which a person can express concern and gain satisfaction, especially if the gift takes the form of personal involvement. Nevertheless, there are limits to the extent that charity can be an effective form of financing social welfare.

Prejudice against giving

The Victorians were much concerned with pauperization. They feared that well-meaning people giving out money to the poor would merely encourage the 'non-deserving' poor to pursue their lazy and irresponsible ways. It was this fear, indeed, that lay behind the creation of the Charity Organization Society, whose aim was not to prevent charity but to curb its excesses and 'irresponsible' handouts. Though such fears may be associated, possibly wrongly, with Conservative values, a contrasting attitude is expressed by many on the left. They do not feel that charity is an appropriate response to poverty. The causes, they believe, are social and political and should be tackled as such. Handouts to the poor will merely reduce the pressure for such change and are particularly pernicious if they are given by the rich, who are, in effect, purchasing their own privilege at a small price. Both sets of attitudes reduce the motivation to give.

Reluctance to receive

To give usually brings status. To be a recipient is normally to put oneself in a subordinate position. It is not until that gift has been repaid and the exchange relationship put in balance again that a person will feel no sense of obligation. The more sensitive we are to the possible stigmatizing consequences of charity, the less motivation there will be for giving. The more remote the relationship between the giver and the receiver, the less these inhibitions may be. Perhaps that is why there is so much voluntary help given to local hospitals. No one supposes that because volunteers help out in the pathology laboratory, or carry tea round or give blood, that the patients will feel stigmatized. That is because giving is being undertaken within the context of a service that caters for everyone, and the gift is granted by what Titmuss (1970) called the 'unnamed stranger'. Nevertheless, such impersonal giving has its disadvantages. There are, we may postulate, different kinds of giver. Some people may be pure altruists. They merely require the knowledge that they have given to their fellows, but most people will wish to have a closer involvement. The more remote the giving, the less they will be motivated.

'Free rider' problems

If we could be sure that everyone in the community were equally generous it might be possible to finance social services by announcing how much it would cost to run the Health Service per head in the coming year and then leave it to individuals to post an appropriate sum to their local health authority. We would all act on the assumption that others were acting in a similar manner. The problem is that it would be in the self-interest of any one of us to withhold our contribution, let everyone else contribute, gain free health care *and* keep the cash. We would get the ride free, as the economists put it. (For a fuller discussion of the economic theory, see Collard, 1978.) If we know that the tax man will force compliance if our neighbour tries to gain a free ride, we may more willingly pay our taxes. By the same reasoning, it would be unlikely for individuals to donate to an activity that the state was already undertaking unless they could be sure that their gifts were not merely being used to reduce other taxpayers' liability. Arguments of this kind are very evident in discussions about how parents' associations should respond to education cuts. If parents do come in and give a computer or prevent the school library closing by providing books, may the council not simply take the opportunity to make more cuts in the hope that the parents will pay up?

The unevenness problem

If giving is specific, its spread will tend to be uneven. If a millionaire has a mentally handicapped child, services for such children in his home town may be superb, regardless of how many such children there are in that town.

The problem of fluctuating incomes

As we saw earlier, economic crisis or simple chance factors like media coverage and fashion will affect the scale and permanence of giving for particular purposes. Charities therefore face fluctuating incomes that make it difficult to offer consistent and continuous provision unless they are big and have endowment or trust income to draw upon – and even then unwise investment policy or a fall in dividends or share prices may affect the level of the service offered.

These inherent limits to voluntary or charitable giving apply most directly to basic main-line social service provision where the state accepts a clear residual responsibility. It *will* provide if no one else does. In this situation, the 'free rider' problem becomes dominant. If I wish to maximize my impact on improving human life, I can best do so by putting my effort into activities I know are unlikely to take place otherwise, and into small-scale ventures where I can actually see results for my efforts. It was for these reasons that Beveridge (1948) saw the role of voluntary activity fitting best *on top* of a sound comprehensive foundation of public social services. Voluntary action could provide innovation, experiment, specialist extra help, and the filling of gaps left by the state.

The economists' case for a third sector

Arguments about voluntarism and giving are apt to get confused with arguments about mixed economies of welfare and plurality of provision. They are, in fact, quite distinct. A non-statutory non-profit agency may well have volunteers working for it and receive donations. These factors will affect its organizational structure and ethos (Billis, 1989) but are not crucial to its essential characteristic – it is not a profit-making agency and it is not under direct political control. Why should such a third sector exist? Is it merely a remnant of the past? Weisbrod (1986), an American economist, produced a theoretical justification. He argued that since there was evidence of market failure (see Chapter 2) and public sector failure (see Chapter 3) it was logical to expect there to be room for a third kind of organization that served purposes which public and market institutions failed to do. Weisbrod defined this purpose in the following terms: 'Voluntary organisations come into existence as extra governmental providers of collective consumption goods' (Weisbrod, 1986: 30).

Governments provide only as much help for the environment, parks or other public goods as the median voter will pay for in taxes. Voluntary organizations funded by giving provide an outlet for those frustrated voters who would like more parks or public goods but find government is unprepared to pay for them. The problem with this explanation is that most voluntary organizations do not provide collective or public goods. That is especially true of welfare agencies where, in technical economic terms, the services offered are not pure public goods, as we have seen. Hansman (1980, 1987) rejected Weisbrod's argument except in limited cases and approached the question not from the point of government failure, but from that of market failure. Individuals who wish to give are not going to do so to an organization which is motivated by profit, for fear that firm will absorb their gift into its profit margins (see above). Hansman argues that 'donative organisations' are ones with which the market cannot cope. He does not deal at length with welfare-type agencies, however; as we have seen, they are not mostly financed by gifts. Here, it may be argued, the reason for the existence of voluntary organizations is to be found in their capacity to meet the needs of stigmatized and marginalized groups with whom voters do not have sympathy or about whom they know little (Billis and Glennerster, 1995).

A more cynical view is that some organizations have political leverage, and have thus persuaded governments to give them tax advantages which enable them to stay in business and earn high incomes for those running them in a way that they would be unable to do if they were forced into the unsubsidized marketplace. Salamon (1992) presents a theory of 'voluntary failure' which is a moderate version of this view.

Wolfenden's case

One more sympathetic attempt to generalize the distinct contribution of the voluntary sector was made by the Wolfenden Committee (1978) on the future of voluntary organizations. The Committee argued that the two main agents for providing social care were the state, local and national, and the 'informal' sector, families and individuals helping one another. It stated:

> Although the voluntary system, as we have shown, was once the chief form of collective action outside the Poor Law, it can now best be seen in terms of the ways in which it complements, supplements, extends and influences the informal and statutory systems. (Wolfenden Committee, 1978: 26)

The voluntary non-statutory sector was able to extend provision because it could attract the services of people who would not be prepared to work for a public authority. Not being bound by statutory rules and political control it was better able to innovate – perhaps trail blazing for local authorities to take up when the experiment was seen to work. Voluntary bodies could provide alternatives to local council or NHS provision, thus giving clients a choice of some kind. Some kinds of social need may not be met by the state because the groups involved are too small or too unpopular for politicians to be prepared to incur displeasure helping them: for example, alcoholics, drug addicts or battered women. A non-statutory body with gifts from concerned members of the public can fill such gaps.

Running through much of the public debate on voluntary organizations, and not entirely absent from the Wolfenden Report, is the confusion the reader will recognize between a non-statutory organization that provides services and can have significant or even total support from state funds, and the notion of voluntary donations of time or money, which are not exclusively given to non-statutory bodies. Many voluntary bodies became heavily dependent on grants from central government under the urban aid programme and the Manpower Services Commission schemes for unemployed young people in the 1980s. After 1993, social services departments were under a duty to spend most of their new community care money on non-statutory agencies. There are some good arguments for taxpayers' money being channelled to social service providers that are not statutory bodies. They may be freer to experiment or help unpopular clients, and the government can then disown them or cut off funds more readily if it is attacked. This kind of tactical reasoning must, however, be sharply distinguished from the argument for voluntary or charitable sources of income with which we are concerned in this chapter. By a similar slip of logic it is sometimes presumed in such discussions that voluntary bodies are the only or the main beneficiaries of voluntary help and cash aid. But much volunteer help now flows to statutory services, like hospitals and old people's homes. The NHS has more volunteers working for it than any other agency. One rationale for the non-government *sector* is that it can more readily mobilize 'voluntary' help, but this is not necessarily so. The state sector could, if it wished, make a good deal more use of voluntary help. Some of these issues were explored in a useful international study by Kramer (1981). He compared the role of voluntary organizations for the physically and mentally handicapped in Britain, the

United States, the Netherlands and Israel. Their scope and role were very different in many ways but, as he argues, there were more basic similarities than differences. The unique features he identified were rather different from those identified by Wolfenden, Beveridge and other writers, such as experimentation or innovation. These were actually relatively infrequent in the voluntary sector, which was often conservative in its approach, while the state sector could be innovative. What the voluntary sector did, which democratic government could not do, was:

1. To provide *specialist* care on a selective or *exclusive* basis: for example, for families of a particular religious denomination, or area. Governments, rightly, find it difficult to be overtly discriminatory, or to specialize in idiosyncratic ways. Voluntary organizations attract support from such narrow groups and enthusiasts precisely because their constituency of appeal is a narrow one. In a pluralistic society, this is to be welcomed.
2. To act as *advocates* or defenders of the specialist care of the group for which they are working: 'The mission of defending and articulating the interests of undeserving populations at risk takes on more importance as the social services in the welfare state become universal' (Kramer, 1981: 261).
3. To provide a vehicle for *self-help* or *consumerism*: that is, groups of families, dependants or sufferers who seek mutual support, or a means of articulating their concerns. In practice, Kramer argues, the older traditional voluntary organizations gave little or no place to the consumer. They were typically paternalistic. The newer, smaller, spontaneous groups – of parents with mentally handicapped children, for example – must be voluntary and self-help to retain their independence and to enable them to build the self-respect of their members. To achieve these purposes, such organizations must be free from government interference or control.
4. To *provide mainstream services*, not distinctively different in kind from those of state welfare; to provide supplementary services, complementary services, or services on a cost basis to agencies of government. Kramer points out (as I have done) that there may be particular advantages of wider choice or plurality in these cases, but they are the advantages of a private or mixed market, not voluntarism as such.

Kramer also adds some warnings. If voluntary organizations expand, especially if largely in receipt of public money, they tend to
take on all the disadvantages of size and age – bureaucratization or
'creeping formalization', as he calls it. Agencies can become
dependent on public finance, subservient to government or those
who give the funds, such as large corporations. In this case, they
are less able to perform their exclusive and critical functions 1–3.
They suffer from 'donor dependency'. Their very idiosyncratic and
undemocratic nature, which is part of their strength, can lead to
their rule by a narrow and self-selecting group. Since they are
subject to neither the disciplines of the market nor the ballot box
they can become *ineffectual*. He returns to this claim with more
force having looked at the way new right governments expanded
the voluntary sector in the 1980s (Kramer *et al.*, 1993). They may
be destroying the very virtues of voluntary organizations by
making them do too much and become too dependent on
public money.

We shall return to these arguments about the mixed market
for personal social services and recent government policy in
Chapter 11.

Further reading

Economics students should consult D. Collard (1978), *Altruism and Economy: A study in non-selfish economics*, Oxford: Martin Robertson. An
excellent American text is S. Rose-Ackerman (1986), *The Economics of
Non Profit Institutions*, Oxford: Oxford University Press, which contains
the Becker article and much else comprehensible by social policy students.
This could be supplemented by P. R. Jones (1983), 'Aid to charities',
International Journal of Social Economics, **10**, no. 2, pp. 3–11.

Social policy students should certainly read R. M. Titmuss (1970), *The
Gift Relationship*, London: Allen & Unwin, a classic exposition of the case
for donating blood; together with comments on his thesis, for example:
K. Pruger (1973), 'Social policy: unilateral transfer or reciprocal ex-
change', *Journal of Social Policy*, **2**, pt 4, pp. 289–302. D. Billis (1993),
Organising Public and Voluntary Agencies, London: Routledge, discusses
the relationship between government and voluntary organizations. G.
Parker (1990), *With Due Care and Attention*, 2nd edn, London: Family
Policy Studies Centre, is the best overview of research on informal care.

Two general discussions of voluntary organizations which should be read are the Wolfenden Committee (1978), *The Future of Voluntary Organisations*, London: Croom Helm; and R. Kramer (1981), *Voluntary Agencies in the Welfare State*, Berkeley: University of California Press, an international study. Discussion of the use of informal helping networks in social care is to be found in J. K. Whittaker and J. Gabarino (1983), *Social Support Networks: Informal helping in the human services*, New York: Aldine; and in J. Twigg (1994), *Carers Perceived: Policy and practice in informal care*, Milton Keynes: Open University Press.

For information on levels of giving by individuals and firms, see Charities Aid Foundation (1995), *Dimensions of the Voluntary Sector*, Tonbridge: Charities Aid Foundation, or a more recent edition of this publication.

PART IV

Financing the services

CHAPTER 10

PAYING FOR HEALTH SERVICES

The history of health care finance in the UK

It is impossible to understand why health care is financed the way it is in the United Kingdom without looking briefly at its historical origins. Moreover, they illustrate many of the theoretical points that have been raised in previous chapters.

The hospitals

By the early part of last century two kinds of hospital had emerged that set the pattern for finance and provision for the next 150 years (Abel-Smith, 1964). The *voluntary hospitals* were private charities. They ranged from ancient foundations, like St Bartholomew's and St Thomas's, to smaller local charities. Most hospitals in the provinces relied on donations or regular subscriptions to keep going. Such giving was not unconditional. Sometimes the hospital was obliged to purchase goods from the traders who were subscribers, and donors also had the right to nominate people whom they wished to receive attention. One group that were frequently excluded were the poor – those who could not be guaranteed to be able to pay their own funeral expenses. Those with infectious diseases, too, were excluded and children who were vulnerable to them. The chronic sick, the elderly and others who would need long-term care were a drain on the hospitals' budgets and of little interest for teaching purposes. So they were increasingly excluded.

It was not only gifts of cash that kept the voluntary hospitals going, but the donation by leading doctors of their services. What these men gained in return was prestige and professional recognition that came from practising at one of the teaching hospitals.

Despite these developments, charitable subscriptions supplemented by local appeals could not keep pace with rising demand and increasingly expensive treatments. One obvious way out was to charge richer patients a fee, but the hospital governors feared that this would deter charitable donations. In smaller towns where the general practitioners ran the hospitals (often called cottage hospitals), patients were already charged. So, reluctantly, the larger voluntary hospitals followed. Financially squeezed by the depression of the 1880s, they began to accept paying patients. They were treated in a quite different way and in separate wards – the forerunner to the modern pay beds. In 1895, the Royal Free appointed an official 'almoner' to ensure that patients were genuinely poor and that they contributed what they could afford to their treatment. The practice became widespread and a new profession emerged to administer the process – the precursors of the modern medical social workers. Yet payments of fees on a means-tested basis changed the nature of the voluntary sector and caused widespread resentment.

After the First World War the voluntary hospitals faced a severe and growing financial crisis. An immediate Exchequer grant was provided to tide the hospitals over the emergency. Moreover, people who covenanted money to the hospitals for over six years secured income tax relief on the sum (1922 Finance Act). Thus an indirect form of Exchequer aid began. Another new source of income was the contributory schemes, the largest being the Hospital Saving Association. In return for paying a small weekly contribution the contributor and his dependants acquired a presumption that they would be treated free without a means test – though this was never a legal right. The association usually paid the hospital a weekly flat rate. These schemes were very unpopular with the medical profession as they limited the number of private patients who would pay the doctors direct. In short, voluntary hospitals that began as charities had, by the 1930s, developed an enormous variety in their forms of income. There was also great variety in the standard of treatment they offered. Since consultants gave their time free they were more available in more wealthy urban areas which could support the private practices that provided their income. By the Second World War, many of the voluntary hospitals were still in serious financial trouble, a problem the war helped solve, at least temporarily, as the government paid large sums for the treatment of war casualties (Titmuss, 1950).

Alongside the voluntary hospitals there had gradually developed a state-provided hospital sector. Its origins lay in the Poor Law and it was never to lose that association. The Poor Law workhouses came to accommodate growing numbers of sick, elderly and infirm paupers, and a medical officer was employed, along with nursing staff, to care for these people. Under the Metropolitan Poor Act of 1867 and a Poor Law Amendment Act of the following year, Poor Law Guardians were able to create separate infirmaries – pauper hospitals. They were to be equipped like any other general hospital ward. The association with the stigma of poor relief remained, however, and to a very large extent these hospitals became the home for the long-stay patients and the elderly who were such a drain on the finances of the voluntary hospitals.

In 1929, as part of the larger reform of the Poor Law, these hospitals became the responsibility of local authorities – the county councils. They also had control of the hospitals that had been provided under other statutes to treat the mentally ill, those with infectious diseases, tuberculosis and the mentally handicapped. Moreover, several of the more ambitious authorities, like London and Middlesex, developed their own acute hospitals. During the war the Coalition government produced a plan to reorganize completely the chaotic system of hospital finance and provision. The local authorities were to be the main organizers of hospital provision, combining together in joint authorities to plan care in their areas, including the voluntary sector. They would have no direct control over such institutions except that they could pay them for particular services. It had some similarities to the Conservative reforms of 1990. Such a system would not have reduced the wide disparity in standards of care or the process of means-testing or the financial difficulties of the voluntary hospitals. When the Labour government was elected in 1945, it produced more radical proposals – nationalization of the local authority and voluntary hospitals. The 1946 National Health Service Act was the result (Webster, 1988; Glennerster, 1995b). Hospitals were to be wholly *funded* from taxation *and provided* by statutory bodies, Regional Hospital Boards and managed by hospital management committees, with nominated members. That change was carried into effect in July 1948 and remains the basis for hospital finance today.

Primary care

The finance of primary care has had a very different history (Stevens, 1956; Eckstein, 1964; Gilbert, 1966; Honnigsbaum, 1979). Medical practitioners began as individual private entrepreneurs selling their skills and medical knowledge, such as it was. But it was never a free market. The Royal College of Physicians, incorporated by Henry VIII in 1518, established a monopoly of medical practice in London by licensing registered physicians in the area. Surgery grew as a separate profession under its own Royal Charter. Both groups sold their services mainly to the rich and the upper classes, *giving* their service to the voluntary hospitals in the large cities.

It was the apothecaries who were the originators of what, today, we call the family doctor, or the general practitioner, and the dentist. They were shopkeepers who sold medicines or cures and established their right to treat the sick during the Plague. They extended their functions to holding surgeries with dispensaries and to visiting the sick at home. They became 'the doctor' for the working class, but they remained private entrepreneurs who had to make their living by charging for their services. At the same time, working people developed their own form of voluntary associations – the friendly societies – that enabled the better-off sections of the working class, at least, to receive cash benefits when the wage earner was ill, with the illness certified and treated by a doctor paid by the society (Thompson, 1980). By the beginning of the twentieth century they had about six million members. Commercial insurance companies also grew, and some doctors in poor areas ran their own sick clubs to which the poor contributed on a regular basis to obtain free treatment when they were sick. That system and the friendly societies were needed to keep doctors in business at all in the poorest areas of the industrial cities.

By the end of the nineteenth century the friendly societies were also in financial trouble. Their members were surviving longer.

Instead of dying by the age of about 40, more were living to an age at which they could not continue to work and had to be supported. It was a burden the societies' funds could not bear. Moreover, few schemes covered women or children. This threw growing numbers on the Poor Law and added to a rising poor rate. Lloyd George's attempt at a solution was to copy from Germany's social insurance scheme and create a British variant – National Health Insurance (Gilbert, 1966). This provided sickness benefit and the right to free treatment and drugs for members, together with the choice of a local doctor from those who practised in the scheme (1911 National Insurance Act). It was essentially an extension of the friendly society schemes – the societies helped to administer it – but it also covered occupational groups who had never been able to be members. It covered all manual workers and those earning up to a given sum – £430 a year by 1942. Each employee and his or her employer had to contribute so much per week to the scheme. The doctor received a per capita payment for each of those registered with him or (rarely) her. Once established there was natural pressure to extend the scheme. Excluded groups and those just above the income limit always felt aggrieved, and pressed for inclusion. Though workers were in the scheme, it excluded children, non-working wives, the self-employed, and the elderly. This illustrates the difficulty of confining provision of a sought-after service to low-income groups (Goodin and Le Grand, 1987).

Two other features of the scheme were both bitterly resented by working people. First, the flat rate contributions required were the same for each person. The incomes of similarly sized approved (friendly) societies were the same, but those which covered miners or those in more dangerous or unhealthy jobs had a high call on their benefits. White-collar societies were thus able to be much more generous, covering members of the worker's family and dental treatment, convalescent care, ophthalmic care and more. The resentment arose from the concentration of high-risk categories in particular occupations and the reluctance of insurance companies or societies to include them – a perfect example of cream skimming and adverse selection, discussed in Chapter 2. Attempts to extend the scope of risk pooling by using richer schemes' surplus funds to help poor schemes failed.

The second unpopular feature of the system arose from the different attention doctors gave to members of the state scheme compared with their private patients, often even segregated in different waiting rooms. These perceived injustices led the trade union and labour movement to campaign vigorously for an end to the insurance system and for a single universal Exchequer-funded scheme to cover all forms of primary care. This solution was to be embodied in the 1946 Act. The general practitioner, however, retained his claim to be 'an independent contractor' by receiving a sum of money from the central Exchequer for each person who signed on to the practice. The doctors in poorer areas, in particular, were substantial beneficiaries of this arrangement which gave them a secure income for the first time. They were private individuals or partnerships, paid by the state to provide a universal service free at the point of use.

The third leg of the 1948 tripartite structure to the NHS was the community health service, administered, as it always had been, by local authorities and hence financed like any other local service partly by central government grant and partly out of local revenue – the rates. The services included midwives, health visitors, district nurses and various clinics. In 1974 the structure changed and they were taken from local authorities and amalgamated within the new health authorities – first area, and then later (1982), district health authorities. The community health services then came to be financed wholly by central government. We discuss the reforms of the 1990s below but they did not change the way the NHS was financed. It remained a primarily Exchequer tax-financed service.

Expenditure on the National Health Service

From 1948, when the Health Service began, to 1995, current expenditure in real terms (excluding price increases) rose more than threefold. Total spending on the NHS represented about 4 per cent of the gross domestic product in 1948, and rose to 6.5 per cent by 1995. Compared to most other advanced economies, the United Kingdom's total spending on health, publicly and privately financed, is low (see Table 10.1). The richer the country, measured here in terms of US dollars per head of population, the more they tend to spend on health (see the first column). Our European neighbours tend to spend between 1 and 2 per cent more of their

Table 10.1 International variations in health-care spending, 1992

Country	Per capita[1] GDP (US$000)	Health expenditure as % of GDP	Public health expenditures as % of total
	Seventeen countries		
United States	23.2	14.0	45.7
Switzerland	22.3	9.3	67.9
Luxembourg	21.8	7.4	91.4[2]
Japan	19.7	7.0	71.2
Canada	19.1	10.8	72.7
Austria	18.1	8.8	65.2
Denmark	17.8	6.6	82.0
Norway	17.6	8.0	94.8
Italy	17.5	8.5	75.2
Iceland	17.1	8.0	85.2
Australia	16.8	7.9	67.6
Sweden	16.7	7.9	85.6
Finland	14.5	9.4	79.3
New Zealand	14.4	7.7	79.0
Portugal	9.8	6.0	69.8
Greece	6.3	5.4	76.1
Turkey	3.7	4.1	65.7[2]
	Seven countries[3]		
Germany	20.4	8.7	71.5
France	18.6	9.4	74.8
Belgium	18.2	7.9	88.9
Netherlands	17.0	8.6	76.6
United Kingdom	16.3	7.1	84.4
Spain	12.9	7.5	80.5
Ireland	12.4	7.1	76.1[4]

Notes: [1]Measured by purchasing power parities
[2]1990
[3]See OECD (1992)
[4]1991
Source: OECD (1994).

GDP on health than we do (see the second column). This is partly because they are richer and the costs of what they supply are higher – notably, doctors and health professionals are paid more – but it is also the case that their standards of accommodation are better and waiting times shorter. The United Kingdom also stands out as providing more of its health care financed from public expenditure than most other countries except the Scandinavians.

The United Kingdom's low spending figure is, in part, a tribute to the way the NHS has been able to keep down health costs which have increased much faster in other countries, most notably those with insurance-based systems of finance (see below). Nevertheless, strong underlying trends have been pushing up costs in Britain as they have in other countries – the increasing sophistication of medical treatment, the survival of those who would have died in an earlier decade, new and expensive drugs, the growing awareness amongst the public of potential treatments, a reluctance to merely grin and bear pain and discomfort, and above all the ageing of the population. It is ten times as expensive to provide health care for those over 85 as it is for people aged between 16 and 44 (see Figure 10.1). Nearly half the total expenditure of the hospital and community services goes on the care of people over 65.

Sixteen per cent of the budget goes on the care of the mentally ill and mentally handicapped. Neither of these categories of patient are likely to get full private insurance cover or indeed any at all.

Nearly two-thirds of the total budget is used to pay for staff. The largest part of that – nearly half – is on nursing staff. Medical and dental staff only take about one-eighth of salary costs. Drugs, dressings, X-ray and laboratory expenses take the largest share of the non-salary costs. Hospitals take the lion's share of the NHS

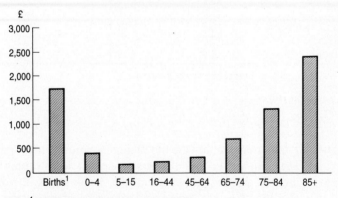

Note: [1] This figure is for all births, including stillbirths.

Figure 10.1 Hospital and community health services gross current expenditure per head by age, 1992/3 (Source: DoH, 1995)

budget. Family practitioner services take just over a fifth of total NHS spending. They comprise the services of general practitioners, opticians, dentists, and the cost of drugs dispensed by chemists.

Despite the growing demographic and other pressures on the NHS it has reduced the real costs of treating patients in the last ten years. The length of stay of in-patient treatment has fallen and the number of patients treated as day patients has increased two and a half times (1989–95). This has been made possible by new, less invasive surgery and other advances. Technology does not always prove more expensive!

The present system of finance

The main source of provision for health care in the United Kingdom is the National Health Service. Only 6 per cent of the finance of health care in the United Kingdom comes from private health insurance (Hills, 1995b). The National Health Service claims its funds from three sources: general taxation, which provided 83 per cent of the total in 1994–5; about 13 per cent came from a small addition to the weekly National Insurance contribution; and the remaining element came from charges, 3 per cent, and other receipts like land sales, 0.9 per cent (DoH, 1995). The National Health Service contribution is really a historic relic of the pre-1948 insurance-based system. Beveridge thought a small part of the new scheme's income should go to the NHS as it had under the old. Since everyone has a right to treatment, whether they have been contributors or not, it is difficult to justify.

Charges to patients are made for drugs, appliances, dentistry, spectacles and, most recently, opticians' services. Though patients were excluded from all payment under the 1946 Act, the Labour government amended that Act in 1949 to give it power to levy charges if it wished on prescriptions and appliances. Prescription charges were not actually introduced until the next Conservative government in 1951. Apart from a brief period after 1964 when prescription charges were removed, these charges have remained ever since and have been increased regularly. In 1996 the charge was raised to £5.50 per item on a prescription – that figure was 25p in 1979! The scale of dental charges has risen sharply since the 1970s and now approaches the economic cost. Those on low pay or receiving income support are exempt from all the charges. Those excluded from paying for prescriptions are: hospital in-patients, those suffering from diseases that need continuous medication, expectant mothers and those with a baby under 12 months, children under 16, or under 19 if they are in full-time education, and people over 60. Expectant mothers are exempt from dental charges, as are children at school and those on low incomes, and similar exemptions apply to sight tests, glasses or contact lenses. Young people up to 14 qualify for free treatment but not dentures. These exclusions make the charges an inefficient way to raise revenue. Over four-fifths of the prescriptions are issued free to those exempt groups we have listed.

Road traffic casualties

This is a relic of the attempts to provide an income for the voluntary hospitals in the 1930s. The Road Traffic Act of 1933 obliges motorists or their insurance company to make some contribution to the expenses of treating the victims of an accident if the driver is liable. The sums involved are very small and do not cover anything like the cost to the NHS of car accidents.

Private pay beds

One of the concessions Bevan made to the consultants in 1946 was that they could keep their separate private pay beds in NHS hospitals. Private patients can occupy separate accommodation and be treated by the specialist of their choice, in return for paying a fee. Under the 1977 Health Service Act, this is meant to be a 'full cost' fee which the Secretary of State fixes. The 1978–9 Labour government tried to phase out these beds but under the 1980 Health Service Act they were extended. It is probably not the case that the fees are fully economic. Many feel that they do not reflect the valuable backup services a modern hospital and trained staff provide.

Amenity beds

An ordinary NHS patient can ask to be given a greater degree of privacy in a separate room if it is not needed on medical grounds for other patients, and can pay for the privilege.

Overseas visitors

Under regulations introduced in 1982 any overseas visitor who falls sick and requires treatment other than in an accident or emergency will be charged for his or her treatment on a special scale of charges reflecting the 'full cost' of the care. Various visitors are exempt: students here for more than a six-month course, European Union residents and those from countries who give UK residents free treatment (reciprocal arrangement nations).

Other income

Most of the old teaching hospitals inherited from pre-NHS days have trust fund and endowment incomes that they were allowed to keep and administer. They are regularly supplemented by new gifts and bequests. Other voluntary hospitals with such funds lost them to the Exchequer, which pooled them in a central fund. In 1974 this fund was allocated out to the regional and area health authorities and in 1982 they were once again reallocated to the new district authorities. Many hospitals have a League of Friends who raise money on their behalf.

This is how the National Health Service's money is raised. How is it allocated to the hospitals and family doctors and other services?

Allocating the money

Of the total NHS budget, as we can see from Figure 10.2, a small part, about 3 per cent, is taken by the central department to provide central administration, a few specialist services and to give a few specific grants. The Department of Health, for example, manages the NHS superannuation scheme. It meets the running costs of the Public Health Laboratory Service, which gives technical assistance to local districts facing an outbreak of an infectious disease, perhaps spread from abroad or of a rare kind. It finances the Dental Practice Board, which checks approximately forty million remuneration claims made by dentists for their work. The Prescription Pricing Authority keeps a check on doctors' prescribing, feeding back detailed comparative data to each GP to help them to contain costs. The Health Education Authority does work on a contract basis, as from 1996, but is paid by central funds. The

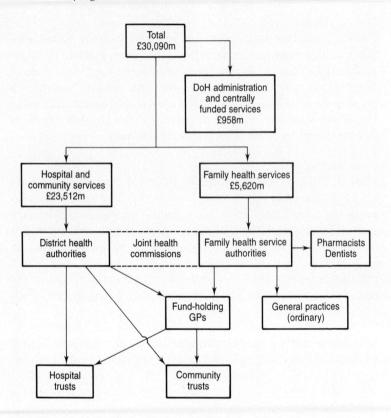

Figure 10.2 Allocating the Health Service budget in England, 1994/5

National Biological Standards Board is responsible for maintaining the high standards of substances used in vaccines, blood products, and other substances and medicines.

The rest of the budget is allocated in two parts: that which pays for the hospital and community services – four-fifths of the total – and the remainder which goes to the family practitioner services – the GP, the dentists, the opticians and the cost of drugs dispensed by GPs.

Financing hospital services

We begin with the finance of hospital and community services. In the early years of the Health Service the ordinary hospitals, the community health services and the teaching hospitals had been separately financed. Variations between the hospital regions remained wide. The reason lay in the budgeting procedures. Every year, each region's allocation was merely rolled forward, with small additions to the previous year's spending and extra to meet the current costs of new hospital premises. The spending patterns of the 1970s still reflected the inequalities of the pre-war system. The NHS had failed to produce 'a uniform standard of service for all', as Bevan put it in 1945. Variations within regions were even greater (Buxton and Klein, 1975, 1978; Jones and Masterman, 1976; Culyer, 1976).

After the 1974 reorganization, the new regional health authorities took over responsibility for all hospital and community health expenditure. The reorganization presented an opportunity to redress some of the old inequalities. The difficulty was partly political; the favoured regions, London notably, had powerful friends in the big teaching hospitals. An important first step was to include these hospitals in the budgets of the regional health authorities; their claims had to be considered alongside those of everyone else. The next step was to devise a budget allocation procedure that reflected the health needs of different areas. It was one thing to agree that this was desirable, another to agree a measure of need. A working party was appointed in 1974 to produce one. It reported in 1976 (DHSS, 1976d) giving its name to a formula that was to decide how much revenue money (i.e. not capital) each region should have in England – the Resource Allocation Working Party (RAWP) – Scotland and Wales (SCRAW) and Northern Ireland (PARR). Regions were free to allocate revenue to districts as they wished. In practice, these allocations reflected the scale of existing facilities and their resident populations. Therefore, although resources had come to be allocated more fairly between big regional areas, wide inequalities existed between districts within those regions. As part of the NHS reforms introduced by the Conservatives the formula-based allocations were taken down to the district level. Economists from York University were asked to devise a formula that took account of the relative demands different kinds of local population would put on the NHS (Carr-Hill *et al.*, 1994). They were able to make use of new information from the census on the number of old people living alone and those with long-standing illnesses, as well as new localized information on the use of hospital services by different groups. That, combined with new statistical techniques, produced one of the most sophisticated means of measuring the health needs of different areas anywhere in the world. It differentiated between acute hospital services and other services like mental health and geriatrics. It implied significant shifts from past allocations, giving much more to some districts especially those in poor inner-city areas. The government of the day took fright and damped the effects of the new allocations (Peacock and Smith, 1995). Nevertheless, this new system of local allocations is an important step forward and produces one of the more advanced ways of allocating finance according to social need that we have here or in any country.

How does the formula work? In essence, each district gets its share of the total amount of funds available on the basis of the size of the population served, weighted to take account of the use different sections of that population can be expected to make of the service. The York study demonstrated that those areas with more people in particular age or social groups used hospital services more. If a district has more old people, or those without carers, those people count for more than one because they use hospital or community services more frequently. Those areas with relatively high death rates up to the age of 74 tend to use hospital services more. Old people with poor housing and with no families or supportive neighbours fill more geriatric beds.

Purchasers and providers

Under the changes introduced by the 1990 Health Service and Community Care Act, implemented from April 1991, the district health authorities became 'purchasing authorities'. These authorities were always financed and run separately from family health service authorities which organized the GPs. Under new legislation these separate bodies can merge, forming a single local health agency or commission. They use the money they have been given to buy services from hospitals either in their own districts or elsewhere.

Most of the hospitals and community services are now run by self-governing trusts. These latter bodies are each run by a board whose chairperson is appointed by the Secretary of State, as are its members after consultation with the chairperson. The trusts have to finance their current expenditure themselves from contracts made with district health authorities, with fundholding GPs (see below), or with private insurance companies. The trusts are independent public corporations whose assets, like their buildings, are owned by and can be sold by the trust but within strict Treasury rules. They must earn a return of 6 per cent on their capital – the buildings and land and other equipment; they must break even on income and expenditure, taking one year with another; and they must keep within an external financing limit, that is, the amount they can borrow to spend on capital. The trusts have to pay for the building and land they inherited (capital charges) as a way of making them aware of the costs of holding on to too much property which could be sold for other purposes. The trusts also are expected and encouraged to use private finance to help fund their capital projects – the 'private finance initiative', and they must produce 'business plans' for three years ahead.

Fundholding

The Act also created a quite new form of purchaser of hospital and community services – the fundholding general practitioner (Glennerster, 1994). Under this scheme, groups of family doctors who originally had more than 10,000 patients could opt to become fundholders. The figure was reduced to 7,000 and then to 5,000 from April 1996. Even smaller groups can gain powers to purchase community health services like community nursing. Part of the hospital and community budget that would otherwise be allocated to the district is transferred to the general practice. The amount depended initially on the number of patients referred in the previous year multiplied by the actual cost of those referrals in the hospitals concerned. Now the allocation is partly based on a formula which reflects the age and sex of the practice population. The practice is given a management allowance to help administer the scheme. In addition, it also receives a sum to meet the costs of all the drugs it prescribes.

All these separate budgets are amalgamated and can be used for any of these purposes. If a practice economizes on its drugs bill, it can, for example, use the extra to pay for a physiotherapist to visit the practice. These doctors then make their own contracts with whatever hospitals or other providers they wish to and pay them when a patient is treated. They continue to be funded like any other GP for their own work as GPs (see below). Fundholders' budgets enable them to purchase a range of non-emergency care, surgical procedures, outpatient care and laboratory tests from whichever hospital or provider they choose. Experiments are taking place (1996) with 'total fundholding' in which groups of GPs have been given powers to purchase the whole range of hospital and community services for their patients.

Financing the family health services

The family *health* services comprise not only the cost of the family doctor service – about 27 per cent of the total – but medicine prescribed by GPs (53 per cent), dentists (18 per cent) and opticians (less than 3 per cent). These are *gross* figures. In fact, significant amounts of both the ophthalmic and dentists' costs are met from charges on patients. The cost of this sector has risen by 35 per cent in real terms from 1983/4 to 1993/4, including a 75 per cent increase for GPs' services, a 51 per cent increase for pharmaceuticals, and offset by a fall in ophthalmic costs reflecting the withdrawal of free eye tests. The system of paying the family doctor retained the pre-1948 idea of a payment per patient registered with that doctor. Gradually there was added a whole range of extra payments as financial inducements for doctors to provide adequate surgery facilities, and to encourage them to practise in unpopular industrial and inner-city areas, and in remote rural areas.

The Thatcher government sought to extend the financial incentives, encouraging doctors to undertake preventative health checks and reaching immunization and vaccination targets. It also sought to tighten up on what it required of doctors who received the basic NHS practice allowance for the upkeep of their premises. If they were to be paid this sum the doctor should in return guarantee to keep their practice open during certain convenient hours. A much fuller 'contract' was discussed with the profession. No full agreement was reached and the contract was imposed on GPs in 1990.

The notion of paying GPs to provide certain specified standards of service and undertake certain preventative health measures was a step forward, in terms of both public health accountability and *promoting better health*. The usefulness of certain of the activities, like visiting old people once a year or screening, was disputed by the medical profession. Essentially, the Conservative government said to family doctors: 'You want to remain private practitioners on contract with the NHS. So in return we shall specify in more detail what we expect from you. We expect surgeries to be open certain hours, and for you to undertake certain preventive health measures for all your patients whether they normally come to the surgery or not. If you see and screen more than a certain target number of patients you will be paid more.' These targets were more difficult for some doctors to meet in deprived areas or in practices where the population moved frequently, but the principle made sense and produced more preventive work.

Dentists

Most dentists are paid on a fee for service basis. They claim for each piece of work done and are paid according to rates laid down by the Dental Practice Board. They then receive a net sum that takes account of the sums patients pay. Dentists in health centres can be salaried.

Chemists

Chemists are paid for the costs of the drugs they dispense on an NHS doctor's prescription. On top of that a percentage is added to cover the chemist's overheads and profit. They are paid for remaining open after normal hours on a rota basis and sums are paid to keep chemists open in remote areas. From this gross total is deducted the amount they collect in prescription charges.

The private sector

About 15 per cent of the population have some form of private health insurance cover (Laing, 1995). The scale of private cover has grown. From 1971 to 1990 the number of people insured with the largest insurers, British United Provident Association (BUPA), Private Patients Plan (PPA) and the Western Provident Association (WPA), rose from 2.1 million to nearly 8 million. However, the figure had fallen back to less than 7 million by 1993 (Central Statistical Office, 1995a). This was partly related to the recession and the fact that employers were less willing to pay for such fringe benefits. There may be another reason. Research has shown that one important reason for people choosing to opt for private insurance is the length of the waiting lists in their area

(Besley *et al.*, 1996). However, the length of time people have had to wait for NHS treatment has fallen substantially since the reforms. Thus the benefit derived from private insurance has been eroded. This is not exactly what Mrs Thatcher had in mind when she set out on the reform of the NHS! In 1990 the Conservative government introduced tax relief on premiums paid by people aged 60 and over. Very few people have taken advantage of it. The cost of full cover in old age is very expensive or unattainable. The private health market is largely confined to a narrow range of relatively uncomplicated surgery for those who require speedier treatment or more attractive surroundings than an NHS hospital. About 'two dozen procedures account for 70 per cent of expenditure' (Propper and Maynard, 1990).

More private finance?

Given the constraints on tax funding for the NHS, some critics have suggested that more private finance would provide a solution. This was exactly the case advanced at the time of the last review of the NHS under Mrs Thatcher. This option largely failed to make headway for many of the basic theoretical reasons that were outlined in Chapter 2. At the time, in evidence to the review, Barr *et al.* (1988: 7–9) argued:

> Private medical insurance has efficiency problems of two kinds: gaps in coverage and incentives to excessive consumption of medical care. Gaps arise, first, because private policies generally offer incomplete (or no) coverage of chronic or pre-existing medical problems because the likelihood of treatment is too high, nor of the medical costs associated with pregnancy because this is the result of deliberate choice not a random risk. In addition the elderly, if they can obtain insurance at all, pay very high premiums. (These groups take perhaps two thirds of the cost of the NHS.)
>
> In addition to such gaps, private medical insurance can also face third party payment problems, leading to exploding costs: where doctors are paid a fee for service, and treatment is paid in full by their insurance company, both doctor and patient can act as if care were free, which encourages excessive use of expensive medical resources.
>
> The theoretical arguments receive empirical support from private systems elsewhere. It is not sufficiently appreciated that the American private medical system is buttressed by government spending on

a very substantial scale in precisely those areas where private medical insurance has gaps: Medicare (for the elderly), Medicaid (for the poor), veterans' benefits (often chronic health problems) and maternity and child welfare. Equally predictably, given the third party payment problem, the cost of those publicly funded has come close to running out of control.

Inspection of the comparative figures is both instructive and startling. The UK currently spends around £400 per person per year on medical care, about £360 via the NHS, the rest private. In the USA *public* spending on medical benefits (ignoring tax relief) is around £470 per person per year and private spending about £640, giving a total of three times the UK figure. *Public* spending in the USA is higher than in the UK; the US spends nearly one and a half times that amount *in addition* on private medical benefits, yet health outcomes in the two countries are broadly comparable.

The fear of the cost consequences of third-party health insurance no doubt worried the Treasury most. Certainly the Chancellor at the time, Nigel Lawson, not known for his left-wing credentials, seems to have been convinced by this case (see Lawson, 1993: 613). For whatever reason, the government chose to accept the case for retaining an Exchequer-financed service free at the point of use. However, they also accepted the case for major change, in particular the case for an internal or quasi-market within the NHS (see Chapter 3). Some Conservative critics from the think tanks were disappointed that consumer choice and true market solutions had not been taken further (Green, 1990).

An internal market: the case for change

In 1985 an American health economist Alan Enthoven had published an influential critical analysis of the NHS. It was also publicized in *The Economist* (22 June 1985; see also Enthoven, 1991). He argued that the NHS suffered from:

1. *Gridlock* 'It is more difficult to close an unwanted NHS hospital than an unneeded American military base.'
2. *Inefficiency* There were no incentives to run a ward or service more efficiently except persuasion. Consultants were on lifetime contracts and had no reason to change.

3. *Perverse incentives*   A consultant who treated more patients would shorten the queue and attract more patients without attracting more resources – in other words, more anxiety and no reward or means to do the job. He might have added that the more effectively he or she reduced the waiting list, the less private income the consultant would be likely to attract from patients who decided to go private.
4. *Overcentralization*   National pay settlements meant staff were difficult to attract in areas with high demand for labour – especially nurses in London, for example.
5. *Accountability*   No one knew what anything cost or whether they were keeping within their budget.
6. *Free capital*   Since central government had always paid for new building, local districts and services did not have to face the cost of using buildings and capital, and hence tended to waste space and capital assets.
7. *Customers not central*   Patients are so grateful to be treated that they do not complain and are not taken seriously.

None of these points was new, but Enthoven's solution, drawn from recent American reforms, was to introduce competition and an internal market. District health authorities should cease to have direct responsibility for managing the hospitals and units. They should become purchasing bodies, buying services from whichever hospital or unit could give the best deal.

Contracts could be with a specialist unit outside the area, which would be able to keep its facility going by attracting patients needing that care and bringing with them the cash to pay for their operation. Those contracts would be made on a competitive basis with the hospital providing the 'best buy', and would be of three main kinds:

1. *Block contracts*   These would provide accident and emergency service for everyone at a given sum per year and meet certain quality criteria.
2. *Cost and volume*   These would undertake a certain number of operations for half a million pounds. If 10 per cent more were done, payment would increase by 12 per cent, but if less than the volume target was achieved, payment would be reduced.
3. *Cost per case*   In more specialized units, each operation, episode or visit might be paid for separately.

Hospitals could lose their monopoly status

The market incentives would encourage consultants to do more, to obtain more resources, to offer a good service, and to win the contract. Information would have to improve and with it account-ability. Services would be charged for the value of the buildings they occupied in order to encourage economy. The basic idea of a *purchaser–provider* split, with the district health authority as pur-chaser, was the crux of the Enthoven plan and became the basis of the working party's plan.

How was the purchaser–provider split to be achieved? Hospitals might be privatized, or turned into voluntary hospitals, as the Con-servatives had favoured before 1946. In the end a compromise emerged under which some – eventually most or all – hospitals and community units were to be allowed to become 'independent trusts', owning their own buildings and having their own governing bodies. Those that did not survive in the marketplace would close because they could not attract the revenue to survive. The logic of the purchaser–provider split and the American model suggested that all units should be independent. For some, this had the addi-tional attraction that the hospital trusts could, at a future date, be simply floated off as private bodies.

An alternative model for the internal market

There was an alternative model on offer, advanced by an English professor of health economics, Alan Maynard (1986) of York Uni-versity. Maynard's analysis of the NHS failings was similar to Enthoven's. He too wanted to distinguish purchasers from pro-viders; the difference lay in his choice of purchaser. The district, he argued, was too distant from the consumer. The GP was nearer to the patient, knew more about the practical needs and family situa-tion, and was in a good position to act as the proxy but expert consumer. If cash followed patients in ways that reflected the pref-erences of consumers informed by their family doctor, it would be possible to combine the virtues of consumer choice and free access to health care, and to avoid the high cost of the American system of private health insurance. This view was favoured by the new Secretary of State, Kenneth Clarke, who came into office late in the discussions of the working party on the reform of the NHS. Giving the GP power to buy hospital services for his or her patient might help redress the relative loss of status and power of GPs and primary health care in general compared to the hospital consultant, and could be a strong corrective to some inefficient practices within hospitals. The consultant in the old voluntary hospitals (see above) depended for his or her income on patients referred by the GP. In the post-1948 NHS the consultant was paid a salary and could pick and choose patients from his or her waiting list, and thus the GP became a supplicant. If GPs had the purchasing power they could redress the balance again.

There were, however, serious problems with this idea: most practices were too small and had too little managerial capacity to manage a large budget; a small budget might be swallowed up with a few very expensive cases; and patients who cost a lot might be turned away by a GP. The idea, therefore, was modified: only large practices would be allowed to opt for the scheme; only cheaper procedures would be included; high-cost patients would have their higher costs met by the district, with patients who cost more than £5,000 a year having the extra met by the district initially. The result was the General Practice Fundholding Scheme (see Glennerster (1994) for a full history). There were, therefore, two competing ideas for the finance of hospitals and community services: contracts set and paid for by districts, and contracts set and paid for by GPs – one top-down funding, one bottom-up. The government went for both at once.

The merits of districts and GPs as purchasers

1. *More explicit accountability*   Hospitals and community units have to say exactly what they can do in a year, and districts and GPs can specify the quality criteria and kinds of service they want.
2. *Incentives for districts to rationalize their services*   Districts can buy what they want from a nearby district or a teaching hospital, rather than attempt to provide everything in their own areas.
3. *Districts have a clear task*   Their primary job is to measure local health needs and monitor the quality of the service. The management of the hospital or service can be left to the unit manager or chief executive of a trust.

4. *Poorly run services face sanctions*   These units will fear that they may lose their contracts and have to close. This will make them perform better.
5. *GPs may be in a better position*   Fundholding GPs have proved less afraid to switch contracts to better units or consultants, and could make more flexible contracts, demand more attention, and use their funds to encourage consultants to come to the surgery rather than rely on patients to go to outpatients in the hospital. They have a strong incentive to ensure that hospitals make efficient use of their money on behalf of their patients. The GP benefits if his or her patients are treated quickly and effectively: they are not troubling that GP any more, and also the GP becomes more attractive to patients. The district purchaser, on the other hand, has no equivalent direct motive to engage in difficult negotiations with a hospital, to threaten to take away custom. His or her salary will be paid at the end of the month come what may. Moreover, the district official has little direct information about patients' satisfaction with the service given by particular hospitals. In fact, a GP may well have more information than the district official on consumer-relevant issues such as the waiting times and the way the patient is actually treated as a human being (Glennerster, 1994).

Difficulties with districts and GPs as purchasers

These also illustrate many of the theoretical points made in Chapter 3:

1. *Costs*   Contracting and the accounting information required has been costly to obtain. Management of decentralized budgets by GPs has been costly.
2. *Outcome measures*   Measures of quality and outcome barely exist, making it difficult to make good judgements about 'the best buy'.
3. *Competition absent*   In many areas and for many services there are few real competitors. The local district general hospital is the only possibility. This leads to districts asking hospitals to continue as before, with the same money and few changes.

4. *Measures of need and priority*   These are poorly developed. Some districts are relying on minimum cost rather than good value as a result. GPs with funds and negotiating power may achieve a better deal for their patients than those with no funds.

Towards 2000

The changes to the NHS outlined above were controversial, but increasingly, commentators have concluded that on balance they have probably been beneficial, both because the output of the hospital system has improved under pressure of competition and because GP fundholders have been able to initiate new ways of delivering services that are breaking the traditional barriers between hospital and primary care (Robinson and Le Grand, 1994; Dixon and Glennerster, 1995). Others disagree (Ham *et al.*, 1995). The Labour Party, too, has been coming to accept that some of the reforms have produced real benefits, so that many of these changes may well survive any change of government.

Further reading

The financial history of voluntary and public hospitals is to be found in B. Abel-Smith (1964), *The Hospitals 1800–1948*, London: Heinemann. The best brief history of the NHS, including the Conservative reforms, is to be found in R. Klien (1995), *The Politics of the National Health Service*, London: Longman.

For an account of the recent reforms to the finance of health care in different parts of the world see the following two volumes: OECD (1992), *The Reform of Health Care Systems: A comparative analysis of seven OECD countries*, Paris: OECD; and OECD (1994), *The Reform of Health Care Systems: A review of seventeen OECD countries*, Paris: OECD. For a useful collection of views about recent similar reforms in various countries, see R. Saltman and C. von Otter (eds) (1995), *Implementing Planned Markets in Health Care*, Milton Keynes: Open University Press.

A useful review of various alternative sources of revenue for the NHS is to be found in S. J. Bailey and A. Bruce (1994), 'Funding the NHS', *Journal of Social Policy*, **23**, pt 4, pp. 489–516.

CHAPTER 11

PAYING FOR PERSONAL SOCIAL SERVICES

It is difficult to draw any clear dividing line between health care and the personal social services. This makes their separate systems of finance a problem. Again history helps us to understand how this came about.

The personal social services as a distinct category really only date back to the 1970 Local Authority Social Services Act in England and Wales and slightly earlier in Scotland. The new social services departments inherited a diverse range of powers and duties drawn from many existing Acts of Parliament previously administered by different local authority departments. They shared responsibility with the National Health Service for the care of groups like the elderly, the mentally ill and the mentally handicapped where the boundary lines of responsibility were extremely vague. In addition, non-statutory, or 'voluntary', organizations have continued to be more important providers in this field, partly because it is nearer its pioneering stage than other services, and partly because the services cater for specific categories of 'deserving', people who attract charitable help and encourage the creation of small specialist organizations. They are also services in which lay people can still play a part. Charging is widespread, for the diverse reasons I discussed in Chapter 8. The private for-profit sector provides a great deal of residential care. Changes to the social security rules in the 1980s led to an increase in social security payments to meet the costs of care in private homes. Informal care is more important than all these. Overall the services present a complex picture – the most mixed form of finance of any we shall study. To simplify matters, I shall distinguish briefly several groups of responsibilities and outline the forms of financial support that have grown up in each case.

The history of personal social service finance

Residential provision

Until recently the largest part of a social service department's budget was devoted to residential care for the elderly, children, mentally ill and handicapped people and the physically disabled. The residential bias dated back to the 1834 Poor Law Amendment Act. The Local Boards of Guardians were responsible for providing workhouse accommodation for the poor, and these included a growing number of elderly who had no independent means, children and the homeless. This responsibility passed to the welfare committees and children's departments of local authorities in 1948 and on to the social service departments in 1970. Throughout, local revenue and central government grant have been the main sources of finance, but, as we saw in Chapter 8, charges were introduced in 1948 in a deliberate attempt to break with the Poor Law tradition of free accommodation for the destitute. Today the public sector provides only about a third of all places in old people's homes. The rest are provided by charitable or private for-profit organizations. Local authorities have a duty to inspect such accommodation.

During the 1980s the number of private old people's homes and the number of places in them began to rise sharply. Some increase had been discernible from the mid-1970s when local authority spending on residential care was reduced and individual families began to pay for their own or relative's care. Then, in the early 1980s, as a by-product of changes to the social security regulations, poor residents began to be able to draw more readily on social security funds to help them pay the fees. Under regulations that governed the old supplementary benefit system, and the national assistance scheme before that, payments towards the cost of care in a private or voluntary home were extremely rare. In 1979 they amounted to only £10 million. The changes of the early 1980s extended the duty of local social security offices to meeting fees if residents had no resources of their own. This led to a rapid rise in the finance of such homes through the social security budget. By 1989 the figure had reached £1,000 million (DoH, 1989) and by 1992 it had reached £2,500 million. Central government was financing a massive increase in private residential care while encouraging local authorities to place more people in the community. The perversity of this approach was first criticized by the Audit Commission (1986b). Roy Griffith's report on community care (DoH, 1988a) proposed ending the payments by social security, placing all the responsibility for *funding* such care on local authorities. This policy was legislated in the National Health Service and Community Care Act 1990 and implemented from April 1993 (see below). By the mid-1990s, only about a quarter of local authority spending on the elderly, net of charges, was devoted to residential care.

Protection and care of children

A second source of statutory responsibility derives from the powers given to the courts at the end of the nineteenth century to prosecute parents for wilful cruelty and to commit children to the care of 'fit persons', including local authorities. Councils' powers were gradually extended so that they could take children into care if they were deprived of a normal home life because of the death or illness of parents, homelessness, or unsatisfactory home conditions that put the child at risk. This activity, too, was primarily financed from the rates with general Exchequer support, but, as we saw in Chapter 8, governments from the mid-nineteenth century onwards were anxious to deter irresponsible parents and insisted they must contribute on a sliding income scale to the cost. This did not mean that a local authority had to provide care itself. In practice, it will frequently place children in ordinary households who are paid to look after them, or it may pay a non-statutory body to take the child. The authority's task is then to inspect those arrangements to safeguard the child. The new basis of parental responsibility and the state's role in protecting children is defined in the Children Act 1989.

The Act extended local authorities' powers to help prevent family breakdown. They have a duty to 'safeguard and promote the welfare of children within their area who are in need'. That term is closely defined to mean a situation in which a child is unable to achieve or maintain a reasonable standard of health or development without services being provided by the local authority, or where the child is disabled. Local authorities must 'take reasonable steps' to identify children in need and prevent them suffering ill treatment or neglect. They must open family centres and provide daycare for children under 5 who are in need. These activities are financed, like all others in the departments, out of the general central government support for local authorities and local revenue. The claims of the elderly, the new community care responsibilities and the Children Act 1989 were in serious competition throughout the 1990s.

Meals on wheels

This service began as a voluntary activity in the Second World War run by the Women's Voluntary Service or a local Old People's Welfare Committee (Slack, 1960). For many years it was merely an activity authorities could support financially. It only became recognized as a main-line statutory function in 1962 and more fully in the 1968 Health Services and Public Health Act. Voluntary bodies had made some charge to cover their costs. Local authority grants merely covered their overheads, or any shortfall that arose from the proceeds the WVS gained from selling their meals. The practice of charging continued when local authorities began to provide the meals. Ministerial advice made it clear that even if the revenue were tiny and administrative costs high some charge should be made: '[Authorities] will no doubt bear in mind that for many elderly people it is important to pay at least in part for any such service' (DHSS Circular 5/70, 1970, *Organisation of Meals on Wheels*). Since then, pressure on local authority budgets has increased reliance on charges.

Home helps

Local authority provision of this service grew up in the 1920s and 1930s to assist mothers of young children who needed domestic help. The service carried a charge though the precise rationale was never spelt out. The issue was, however, debated when provision was included as a function of the new local authority health departments. Bevan was pressed to allow free service in line with the general principle of free health care. He resisted, using the following argument:

> It is a perfectly reasonable proposition that, where domestic help is needed and the persons concerned are able to provide it for themselves, they should do so, and where they are able to make a contribution they should make it . . . it seems to me wholly unjustifiable that we should provide a service of this sort without any payment whatever. (HC Debates, 1946, col. 1562)

What Bevan was arguing by implication, it seems, is that many people already provided themselves with an almost identical service out of their own pockets – a 'char lady' or 'domestic help'. A local authority could not simply begin providing a comparable service free without undermining the private service and landing itself with an intolerable demand for the public equivalent. Again, in the post-1976 economic climate, charges have grown to levels equivalent to costs but they are applied on a sliding scale according to income.

All charges

Taken together all forms of charging produced about 10 per cent of local social services departments' income by the mid-1990s. Since most of the departments' clients are poor there is a limit to their capacity to gain such revenue to finance their activities.

The promotion of welfare

In 1920 local authorities were given powers to promote the welfare of blind people, and in 1948 welfare authorities were given a more general duty to promote the welfare of the handicapped, a duty that was later extended to cover the deaf. Powers and duties of authorities were set out in more detail in 1970. These powers have always been used not merely to provide services, but also to fund local organizations who are in various ways providing support through social clubs, training workshops or day care.

The voluntary origins of social care

So far we have looked at the origins of particular statutory duties, but in many ways the origins of social work lie not in statute but in the activities of volunteers – 'do-gooders', some would say – who pioneered helping activities in a variety of ways. The Charity Organizational Society sought to organize and co-ordinate charitable activity and developed social case-work methods as a way of making such help more 'effective'. Residential care for children, housing management, work with offenders, prison visiting and aftercare are all examples of statutory services that had voluntary origins. In the 1970s and 1980s a new and much wider range of non-profit and non-statutory agencies developed self-help groups and began to act as advocates for many groups, from battered women and AIDS sufferers to disabled children and the mentally ill. Then the Conservative community care legislation of 1990 required local authorities to spend part of their new resources on private, including not-for-profit, organizations.

Expenditure on the personal social services

These services are small in public expenditure terms. If we take the current range of activities covered by modern social service departments, their predecessors in the late 1940s and early 1950s spent about 0.2 per cent of the GNP. Over the whole of the 1950s that total grew by about 7 per cent in real terms. Several factors accelerated that growth rate: Peter Townsend's horrifying accounts of conditions in the old workhouses that posed as old people's 'homes' (Townsend, 1962) and the growing numbers of very elderly; concern with juvenile delinquency in the late 1950s; the development of preventive social work with families; and political interest in 'community' services as an alternative to expensive hospital care. In the 1960s, spending just about doubled in real terms (Ferlie and Judge, 1981; Wistow and Webb, 1982). The new amalgamated departments were set an expansionary universal role by the Seebohm Committee (1968). The Department of Health and Social Security encouraged them to expand. During the period 1970–5, real spending doubled again. Then local government

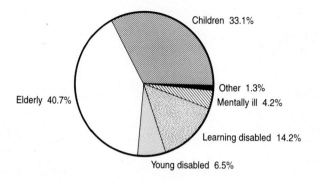

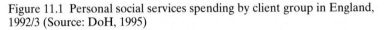

Figure 11.1 Personal social services spending by client group in England, 1992/3 (Source: DoH, 1995)

finance changed for the worse, and the pace of expansion slowed sharply, but did continue. There was 11 per cent real growth in the last five years of the 1970s.

Thus by 1979 the services took the equivalent of about 0.9 per cent of the GDP – a near fivefold increase in their share since 1950. In the 1980s that share remained more or less static (Evandrou *et al.*, 1990). Nevertheless, the demands on these services have been growing sharply too. Fewer of the mentally ill and those with learning difficulties are in long-stay hospitals, there are more families at risk, and there are more very elderly people. For many years government claimed that a 2 per cent per annum growth in the real volume spending was necessary for the personal social services to meet the needs of an elderly population. In the 1990s the figure has been put by the Department of Health at 1 per cent a year. The share of spending allocated to each of the groups of clients is broadly shown in Figure 11.1.

Then came the 1990 NHS and Community Care Act which removed the right of those receiving income support to claim help from the state in paying their private residential care bills. Those people in homes could continue to receive support but no new cash was forthcoming. Instead a sum was transferred from the social security budget to the local authorities for them to decide how best to cater for the needs of the group who would in the past have used private residential accommodation. We discuss the complex financial mechanisms below, but it did lead to a significant increase in the money available to social services departments as well as an

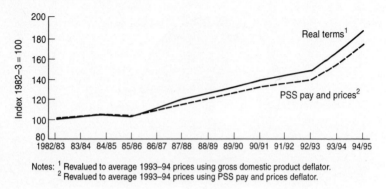

Notes: [1] Revalued to average 1993–94 prices using gross domestic product deflator.
[2] Revalued to average 1993–94 prices using PSS pay and prices deflator.

Figure 11.2 Real and volume terms spending on local authority social services, 1982/3 to 1994/5 (Source: DoH, 1995)

increase in the demand for their services (see Figure 11.2). By 1994, personal social service spending by government had risen to nearly 1.5 per cent of the GDP.

Standard setting and inspection

The central departments have inherited various powers to inspect local standards of service from the old Poor Law days. These powers were included in the 1948 National Assistance Act, the Children's Act 1948, the later Children and Young Persons Act 1969, and the Mental Health Act 1959. In 1971 a new Social Work Advisory Service was formed to take over these functions, but primarily its task was to provide professional advice on social work to local authorities and the Secretary of State. The Barclay Committee (1982) recommended that the service be transformed back into a full inspectorate, comparable to Her Majesty's Inspectors of Schools, monitoring the general standards of professional practice in the social service departments and residential establishments. The government accepted this advice and added its own gloss. The new Social Service Inspectorate was also to monitor 'the efficiency and effectiveness' of social service departments. Its most high-profile activities have been to mount investigations of various child abuse cases and instances where local authorities have come under particular investigation (DoH, 1988b; DoH, 1988c). It played an important role in advising on and monitoring the introduction of the new community care legislation after 1990. For a brief account of the Social Service Inspectorate's work, with others, see Day and Klein (1990).

A new basis for funding community care

I have already mentioned that the rapid growth in social security funding of private residential care was beginning to create a large open-ended flow of money from the central Exchequer to private homes. The Treasury was keen to put a stop to this flow. Private homes, and many families, were keen to see it continue. What agency should decide whether a family or elderly person was in need and of what services? The conclusion that it had to be local authority social services departments was one that Mrs Thatcher personally resisted for a long time. In the end, aided by the Griffiths recommendations (DoH, 1988a) the government accepted that this was the only solution (DoH, 1989).

The perversities of social security funding were not the only absurdity in the financing of community care. The care of those living in their own homes or residential accommodation falls to local authorities to finance. The alternative – care in hospital – may be more expensive in resources but not in its cost to the local authority. Since the NHS is financed by central government a local council will face a larger bill if people move out of hospital and into the community. The local council has very good reasons to oppose such moves, especially if its expenditure is capped. On the other hand, the NHS would like to reduce its spending on old people by transferring them to local authorities as soon as possible. It felt even more justified in doing so after the 1990 Act, which made local authorities explicitly responsible for community care and gave them more money. The Act was taken as justifying a running down of longer-stay geriatric wards. This not only shifted the burden onto local authorities. Since individuals have to contribute on a means-test basis for local authority care, while they receive NHS care free, it was also a shift of the costs onto private households. Individuals who had capital worth more than £8,000 were given no help with their care in nursing homes and had to contribute something if their assets were worth more than £3,000. In the 1995 Budget these limits were raised to £16,000 and £10,000 respectively.

In the mid-1970s the then Labour government recognized the perverse incentives for the two systems to offload old and mentally ill people onto each other. It gave the NHS powers to make grants to local authorities to develop community care services; this was called 'joint finance'. The sums of money involved were tiny, rising to only 5 per cent of social service departments' budgets in the mid-1980s. Moreover, the money was a *temporary* grant. Beyond a few years the local council had to take up the total cost of the new facility or service. As the screw tightened on local councils' funds after rate-capping they became reluctant to accept such long-term commitments. The 1990 National Health Service and Community Care Act was an attempt to resolve the problems. It created a new financial framework for community care, residential care and the support for those who are mentally ill, which came fully into operation only in the last half of the 1990s.

Specific grant for the mentally ill
The first part of the changes that came into effect in 1991 related to the mentally ill. It is a reflection of the level of public and political concern with this group that the government agreed to treat it as a special case. From 1991/2 a specific grant has been made to social services departments of local authorities to develop social care services for people with mental illness including dementia, whatever its cause. The Department of Health allocate a provisional sum to each local authority on the basis of a formula. Social services departments have to agree with their local district health authority what social care services should be provided with the grant. Once formal agreement is reached the regional office of the Health Service Management Executive and the Department of Health are sent the details for approval. Other forms have to be sent to the Social Services Inspectorate regional offices and to the Department claiming the grant, and returns made describing how it was spent. The funds are meant to be targeted on the severely mentally ill. This whole process is typical of the complex administration that attaches to specific grants even though the sums involved are small. If no agreement between the local authority and the NHS is possible locally, the Social Services Inspectorate seek to 'facilitate' agreement.

The grants are annual, for up to three years initially, and cover recurrent (that is, not capital) spending. In 1995/6 the government made £47.3 million available to local authorities in England for new services and £66.6 million available to fund the continuation of services previously agreed in past years. This total of just over £100 million was equivalent to about 1.5 per cent of social services departments' budgets. Local authorities have to contribute 30 per cent of the costs of any scheme from their own funds. The government said it would continue these arrangements until 'at least 1997/8'. Claims for the grant are made biannually for a March and September instalment.

Other specific grants
Various other very small PSS specific grants exist: for projects to help drug and alcohol abusers; projects for HIV/AIDS sufferers; and training grants.

The special transitional grant
When Sir Roy Griffiths proposed that social service departments should take charge of community care policy and take over the social security funds allocated to private residential care, he also said: 'central government should provide directly to social service authorities by a specific grant a substantial proportion of the total public funds it estimates are needed to meet national objectives' (DoH, 1988a: para. 5.12–13). This would have included expenditure, then financed from the social fund and joint finance. His recommendation was not initially followed, but after widespread concern that the money being transferred to the local authorities might not find its way to community care, the government relented and introduced a temporary measure. The social security transfer money and money that resulted from the end of the Independent Living Fund were to be separately accounted for as a special grant to local authorities for a temporary period, and local authorities would have to account for its use. A designated sum was transferred in each of three years: 1993/4, 1994/5 and 1995/6, which in total amounted to nearly £2,000 million. Each new tranche came as a specific grant that had to be accounted for, and 85 per cent had to be spent on services provided by the independent sector – profit or non-profit. In the next year this sum was transferred to the general support local authorities – part of the PSS standard spending

formula. Thus by 1997 the grant would be phased out and merely added on to local authorities' central government grant.

An 'enabling' not a providing department

In line with the logic that lay behind the NHS reforms in the 1990 Health Service and Community Care Act, social services departments were to see themselves as *purchasers* of community care services (DoH, 1991). They were to be responsible for identifying the needs of their populations and publishing a plan for the provision of community care services in their area. In that plan, the government argued, departments should 'promote the mixed economy of welfare' (DoH, 1991: para. 2.1.4). They should, in meeting the needs for community care, do as follows:

1. Invite tenders from private and voluntary bodies.
2. Stimulate the establishment of not-for-profit agencies.
3. Encourage new voluntary sector activity.
4. Create 'self-managed' units for services they continued to provide themselves.

The department stressed the advantages of splitting the assessment of individuals' needs and the purchase of services to meet them from direct service provision, as follows:

1. It would widen individual clients' and social workers' range of choice (e.g. in old people's homes or daycare facilities available).
2. It would help local authorities identify the true cost of service provision by making each provider unit in the local authority cover its costs and compete with external providers.
3. It would clarify budgetary responsibilities and encourage devolved management.

The government advice was also that the advantages of this approach would be greatest if 'the purchasing power is close to the client'. Care managers working with clients should have responsibility for purchasing care for their clients from a devolved budget. This follows the model evolved in Kent and evaluated and advocated by Davies and Challis (1986), though they had never combined their model with privatization and contracting.

The Audit Commission (1989) similarly advocated such devolution of financial control. It argued that where the supply of services depended on central decisions in a social services department, allocations of services to clients became too concerned with fitting clients into existing premises or services rather than matching clients' needs to a flexible range of care. The Kent Community Care Scheme's answer, exemplified in the Audit Commission's advice, was that if you put cash in social workers' hands, they would have the power to buy a flexible mix of services from wherever they wished. In practice, directors of social services have been reluctant to devolve spending power to front-line staff – 'field social workers running around with cheque books' as one director is quoted as saying (Wistow *et al.*, 1994: 76).

The United States has been taken as the model for such service contracting (Ketner and Martin, 1987). However, there is also much criticism of the results of the trend to a contract culture in personal care services in the United States (Schlesinger, 1986; Kramer and Grossman, 1987; Demone and Gibelman, 1989). It is argued that:

1. Setting and responding to such contracts is difficult, time-consuming and expensive. This tends to drive away the small and more informal organizations.
2. There are very few real competitors. Local statutory purchasers' agencies tend to build up close, 'sweetheart' relationships with local voluntary or private agencies, excluding competition.
3. Large organizations tend to move into areas where profits are to be made, undercut their rivals, drive them out and then raise their prices.
4. Getting contract compliance is very difficult to do well, as the measurement of standards and outcomes is technically difficult and expensive.
5. Contractors tend to dump the difficult cases to keep down their bids for the next round, 'adverse selection bias'.

Local authorities may find themselves in the worst of both worlds – abandoning existing direct managerial control of services without being able to achieve effective monitoring, and with no true market test because competition is limited. On the other hand, even limited competition may make rigid social service departments and services more responsive to clients.

Social service departments have found it difficult to divide themselves into purchasing arms and providing arms, especially since the government were confused about what they meant and some local authorities were reluctant to respond (Lewis and Glennerster, 1996). Other more Conservative authorities were keen to divest themselves of service-providing activities. This has left very different mixed economies of welfare in different parts of the country.

The non-statutory, non-profit sector

Non-statutory, non-profit providers were already more common in the personal social service sphere than in any other. There already was a mixed economy of care. Such organizations have long been funded by local authorities to provide specialist services on their behalf. Local authorities may have given a *general grant* in support of that organization's activities. They may have made a *specific or reciprocal* grant on the understanding that the agency accepts families for intensive case-work, for example. These quasi-contracts have now often become formalized. Many find that introducing a 'contract culture' is frustrating and limiting. The range of non-profit organizations varies widely in different areas; in some localities they are numerous, in others not. In Birmingham, on one count there were at least 860 formal social service organizations, even in the 1970s (Newton, 1976). In two wards of Glasgow there were about fifteen organizations per 10,000 population (Johnson, 1981). Hatch (1980) looked at the origins of such organizations in three towns, and found that though there was a considerable mortality rate amongst voluntary bodies – nearly 4 per cent per annum – new organizations were being formed faster than old ones were dying! The growth points appeared to be those concerned with the disabled, the playgroup movement, advice and counselling, and neighbourhood groups. Hatch and Mocroft (1983) surveyed the varied scale of support given by local authorities, looking in depth in two local areas. This variation persists.

After 1979, the Conservative government sought to increase the role of the non-statutory sector, leading up to the 1990 legislation I have discussed. Paradoxically, other policies pursued by the same government have made things harder for the non-statutory sector. Cuts in grants to local authorities, capping and even the abolition of the GLC and the metropolitan counties have harmed the sector. In any squeeze, councils tend to restrict cash grants to outside bodies.

The personal sector

The personal social services are unusual in another sense. Local authorities pay individuals and families to undertake a very important part of their functions. The most obvious example of this is the system of foster care, but the principle can be and is extended to other aspects of caring or 'tending': for example, neighbourly aid schemes, and payments to local people to help certain elderly people in their street. Of all children in local authority care, 70 per cent are boarded out with foster parents, or are under the charge of a parent, guardian, relative or friend. Numbers in these categories have increased sharply in the last twenty years. However, the biggest form of care is, as we saw in Chapter 9, unpaid caring by close kin. New legislation to extend local authority powers to give disabled people cash to buy their own care was introduced in 1996.

The private for-profit sector

Running alongside the statutory and non-profit services, there are the private for-profit providers, homes for the elderly, day nurseries for the under-5s, child minders and many more. Because the groups that are being provided for are so vulnerable, there is a real danger of exploitation, and for that reason, social service departments have considerable powers of inspection and regulation. Such facilities must be registered with the local authority and conform to minimum standards of staffing, building design and safety. During the 1980s the balance of provision for the elderly steadily shifted from local authority to private profit and non-profit organizations in response to government policy, especially the social security changes.

Towards 2000

Opinion is divided about the way forward in financing the personal social services. Some would like to see the measures taken in the 1990s developed. The costs of long-term care for the very elderly in particular are likely to grow substantially (Richards, 1996). Some argue that individuals should be given tax inducements or possibly required to prepare for their old age by investing in private long-term care insurance, possibly in combination with schemes that make use of the capital value of elderly people's homes (Laing, 1993). In practice, despite some interest from insurance companies in this country and in the United States, very little such activity has taken place. Insurance companies themselves are reluctant to offer open-ended commitments to potentially very expensive care that may last a long time. Young people do not see the need and find it difficult to see themselves in a nursing home. Thus when the premiums are cheap, the demand is low. When people do see the need in their sixties, the price is very high and for incomplete cover (Rivlin and Wiener, 1988 and Wiener *et al.*, 1994). The Conservative government has proposed a partnership with private insurers. In return for taking out private cover the state will reduce its charge on that person's assets when long-term care is provided (DoH, 1996).

Others would like to see an extension of the voucher or cash solution. This would extend the principle of the attendance allowance and would enable elderly people deemed to be in need to receive cash from the state in order to purchase care of their own choosing. This model was advocated by President Chirac in his election campaign in 1995, building on the French equivalent which combines cash giving with advice to old people on how to get what kind of help. Still others believe that the German solution of adding the finance of long-term care to the social security system should be explored – though its cost led the Conservatives to abandon this idea in 1993. Some argue that the 1971 split between health care and social care is the fundamental problem and that the funding and administration of community care should be amalgamated in the hands of a new agency.

The open-ended requirements of groups like the long-term sick and disabled and the mentally ill mean that the full financial responsibility is never likely to be assumed by the private insurance sector. The question for the wider community is how should the costs be shared?

Further reading

The best overall discussion of the history of charging is in K. Judge and J. Matthews (1980), *Charging for Social Care*, London: Allen & Unwin.

An account of changes in government policy on finance and spending since 1974 is to be found in M. Evandrou, J. Falkingham and H. Glennerster (1990), in J. Hills (ed.), *The State of Welfare*, Oxford: Oxford University Press. The early response to the community care legislation of 1990 and an analysis of the new mixed economy is contained in G. Wistow, M. Knapp, B. Hardy and C. Allen (1994), *Social Care in a Mixed Economy*, Milton Keynes: Open University Press. A more recent detailed account of changes in five local authorities is to be found in J. Lewis and H. Glennerster (1996), *Implementing the New Community Care*, Milton Keynes: Open University Press. The origins of the most recent changes in the finance of the personal social services are to be found in: Audit Commission (1986b), *Making a Reality of Community Care*, London: HMSO; and in DoH (1988a), *Community Care: Agenda for action*, London: HMSO.

For an American survey of contracting experience, see H. W. Demone and M. Gibelman (eds) (1989), *Services for Sale: Purchasing health and human services*, New Brunswick, NJ, and London: Rutgers University Press.

CHAPTER 12

PAYING FOR EDUCATION

The history of education finance

Pre-1870

With the exception of very limited activities like regimental, workhouse and prison schools, the state in England was not involved in actually providing education until after the 1870 Education Act and then only on a residual basis, filling in where the churches and private bodies had left gaps. State *provision* thus came later in England than in most other countries in Europe and North America. That did not mean, however, that the state played no part. Ever since the seventeenth century in Scotland, grants from the local rates had been made to support parish schools, and in 1833, in the wake of the newly reformed Parliament, a very small grant was made to support the work of the National Society which promoted Church of England schools and the British and Foreign Schools Society that promoted Nonconformist ones. The grant amounted to only £20,000 and had to be matched by local voluntary donations. Parliament was in fact extremely reluctant to give assistance on a large scale, not merely because of the cost, but also because it was felt that if the state were to contribute generously this would merely reduce charitable or voluntary activity. As late as 1861 the Newcastle Commission argued that there was no case for state provision or compulsion to attend school. The Commission's report argued that with more generous financial help the voluntary sector could meet the rising demand for education. Nevertheless, aid grew significantly from 1833 to 1870. Its purposes were extended from school building to the building of teacher training colleges and teachers' houses, the provision of furniture and equipment, and the costs of training teachers, and of their salaries and pensions.

The very complexity of this system, with its detailed checking of particular items of expenditure, put an intolerable burden on the Education Department of the Privy Council. In order to ease the problem officials proposed that these grants should be replaced by a 'system of simply testing by examination and paying by results'. The Newcastle Commission broadly accepted this recommendation and the government consolidated the various specific grants into a single unit grant per child who attended school regularly and passed the examinations set by Her Majesty's Inspector of Schools. The result was to concentrate most of a school's activities on the task of passing these exams. This became increasingly restrictive and unpopular and was abandoned in 1895.

Alongside this general system of finance for elementary education, there grew up a secondary source of state funds designed to encourage the creation of separate schools of science, art and design, and to promote classes in such subjects in other schools, including elementary schools. This multiple system of finance lasted in a modified form to the end of the century, applying to both the voluntary and the new board schools.

This early history is important because it illustrates a basic lesson. State funding of private or voluntary provision does not necessarily bring greater freedom for those institutions. The extent of central control over the content of education was far greater in the voluntary schools of the last part of the nineteenth century than in the state-provided schools of today.

The first major step to state provision of schooling came in 1870. The effective pressure came not from socialists or those who favoured state schools as such, but from Nonconformists, better represented by the extended franchise, who resented their children being educated in Church of England schools because there were no Nonconformist institutions in the area. Others argued that the old voluntary system was not capable of providing sufficient schools in the poorer urban areas. In short, it exemplified some of the classic problems of charitable provision that were discussed in Chapter 9.

1870–1918

Under the 1870 Act, schools could be provided for the first time by locally elected school boards, but only where the voluntary societies were judged incapable of providing for all the children in an area. The boards funded the building of new schools out of the rates, but they charged fees, up to 9d a week, just like the church schools. Poor children could have their fees paid for them out of the education rate whether they attended church or board schools. This was very unpopular with the Nonconformists who objected to 'church schools on the rates', and in 1876 the Poor Law Guardians took over this responsibility, but that caused more problems. Some local boards of education, and finally all, required children's attendance. Many parents said they could not pay the fees, while the Poor Law Guardians said they could. This led to interminable rows between the two statutory bodies, and the Conservative administration of Lord Salisbury in 1891 finally accepted the logic that compulsory attendance required free provision (Sutherland, 1973).

This period also illustrates another theoretical issue. West (1975) has argued that the evidence for the failings of the private system before 1870 were exaggerated by public sector bureaucrats anxious to see their power enhanced. Sutherland (1973), on the other hand, from a detailed study of the public records of the time, concludes that the initiatives that led, first, to compulsory and then to free education in 1891, came from external pressures transmitted by the politicians, not the civil servants. Yet West is surely correct in drawing attention to the way in which, once established, the state sector, drawing on its power to tax, gradually grew at the expense of the private sector. Such growth worried the Tories and the Church of England and in 1902 the separate boards of education were abolished. Education powers were vested in local education committees of the new county and county borough councils. Grants were paid to these education authorities, not directly to the schools. The unified grant was based partly on the poverty of the area and its population, and partly on school attendance. Voluntary secondary (grammar) schools received a per capita grant if they recruited a minimum number of pupils from the public elementary schools. This 'direct grant' system was to last until 1976.

The period has another curiosity. The Technical Instruction Act of 1889 gave county authorities the power to provide technical education and the 1890 Finance Act assigned the revenues raised from the new excise duties on wines and spirits to that purpose. Whatever that tax raised had to be passed on to the local authorities for technical education. It is one of the very few examples of assigned revenue we have had in public finance.

1918–58

From the outset, then, local authorities had received a specific education grant, or grants. The origins of these grants lay in the period before there were education authorities or public provision, and the education lobby liked them. It is much easier to exert effective pressure if it is directed towards increasing a grant for a particular educational purpose than urging government to be generous to local government at large in the hope that that will benefit education. The Board of Education also liked the arrangement. But by the same token a specific education grant was unpopular with the Treasury. Even more unpopular with the Treasury was the percentage grant system introduced by the 1918 Education Act – one grant for elementary and one grant for higher (including secondary) education, which replaced the plethora of specific grants. The elementary grant was based on three elements: an authority's actual expenditure on teachers' salaries (60 per cent); special services like medical and school meals (50 per cent); and the rest related to the number of children attending school. Poorer authorities gained more, but the total grant never fell below half the expenditure of an education authority. The formula for secondary and higher education was simple. The government met half of whatever the authority spent. It was a clear and intended inducement to expand such education facilities and it incurred the wrath of the Geddes Committee (1922), which was set up to find ways of reducing public expenditure. 'The vice of the percentage grant system is that the local authority which alone can really practice economy in these services loses much of its incentive to reduce expenditure' (Geddes Committee, 1922: para. 4). It proved no easy task to wrest this highly advantageous grant from the hands of the Education Department. It was to take the Treasury forty years!

After the Conservative victory in the previous year, the Chancellor, Churchill, sought to achieve substantial reductions in public spending in 1925 and as a way of complying, Lord Eustace Percy produced his famous Circular 1371 proposing a block grant for all education spending fixed at a set level – 1 per cent below the previous spending level. This aroused so much opposition that it was finally dropped and education escaped amalgamation with other grants in the 1929 block grant system. A revised percentage grant system for education and other services emerged after the Second World War and it was not until 1958 that the Treasury, deploying arguments very similar to those in the Geddes Report, finally had its way. A single new grant – the forerunner of the revenue support grant – was for a wide range of local services, including education. The finance of local education, which had managed to stand apart for 125 years, finally succumbed.

Education spending

After nearly two decades of rapid growth, from the mid-1950s to the mid-1970s, public expenditure on education as a share of national economic activity stabilized after the economic crisis of 1976 and then fell back for nearly a decade and a half, until

Table 12.1 Public expenditure on education as a percentage of GDP (at factor cost) in the United Kingdom, 1950–94

Year	% GDP
1950	3.3
1955	3.3
1960	4.1
1965	5.1
1970	5.8
1975	6.7
1980	6.3
1985	5.6
1990	5.5
1994	6.2

Source: Central Statistical Office (1995a).

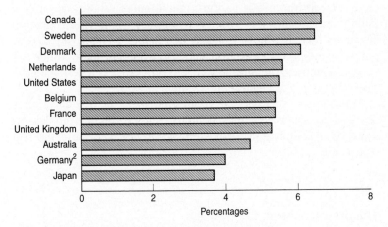

Notes: [1] Includes loan charge expenditure and subsidies to the private sector.
[2] The former Federal Republic.

Figure 12.1 International comparisons of public expenditure[1] on education as a percentage of GDP, 1991 (Source: Central Statistical Office, 1995a)

Table 12.2 Public expenditure on education by level, 1993/4 (£m)

	Current expenditure[1]	Capital	Total
Schools:			
Under-5s	1,279		
Primary	5,880		
Secondary	7,430		
Other[2]	1,520		
Sub total	16,109	841	16,950
Further education	2,628	163	2,791
Higher education	4,066	319	4,385
Other	–	38	38
Student support	1,567	–	1,567
Administration and inspection	1,330	–	1,330
Total			27,061

Notes: [1]Expenditure per pupil per annum:

	£
Nursery/primary	1,638
Secondary	2,250
Further (1992/3)	2,970

[2]Meals, transport, fees at private schools, child guidance.
Source: DFE (1995).

recovering in the 1990s as the population of school age ceased falling, staying-on rates rose, and numbers in higher education began to increase more quickly (see Table 12.1). Even so UK public spending on education had fallen behind many other advanced countries, though the range of difference is less than in the case of health care (see Figure 12.1).

Approximately 60 per cent of all state spending on education is devoted to schools, with secondary schools taking the largest share. Universities and further education colleges share the rest (see Table 12.2).

The present system of finance

Overall, the central Exchequer meets about three-quarters of all education expenditure in the United Kingdom. The local council tax meets only 9 per cent while payments by private households for their own education and that of their children amounts to 11 per cent. Tax rebates for private schools make up 2 per cent (see Figure 12.2).

The means by which state schools, colleges and universities actually receive their funds is complex. There are several quite different systems of finance at work. I shall describe each in turn.

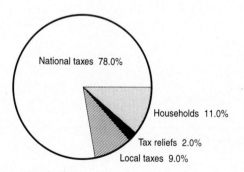

Figure 12.2 Sources of funds for education in the United Kingdom, 1993/4 (Source: Hills, 1995b)

Specific grants

In the 1980s the DES managed to return to the principle of specific grants on a very small scale. It slices off a small part of the local education authorities' education element in the local authority grant allocation and uses it to part-fund projects it approves – grants for educational support and training (GEST). Central government usually meets 60 per cent of the cost of these schemes. The total programme amounts to only 1.5 per cent of local authority expenditure. These have included computers in schools, training to implement the local management of schools, advisory teachers in maths and primary science and drugs and health education. In 1995/6 the grants included training for teachers in bilingual teaching, child protection, careers education, drug prevention and special schooling. These grants give the Secretary of State some belief that he or she can do something direct to affect what happens inside schools in addition to the National Curriculum, but their overall significance is small.

State schools

Most state schools get their money from their local education authority (LEA). The 1988 Education Reform Act significantly changed the way money reaches schools. Until that point, LEA schools were allocated a certain number of teaching posts and the teachers were paid by the LEA. The buildings were maintained by the local authority and caretaking staff were employed by the local authority and assigned to a school. Schools were given sums of money to spend on equipment and books, though in some places they were required to purchase them through the local authority. Other facilities and services like careers centres and officers, educational psychologists and teaching advisers and teaching centres were provided by the LEA. Some local authorities, like Hertfordshire, had always delegated some financial independence to school heads. The Inner London Education Authority (ILEA) in the 1970s began to give its schools more untied money, and to allocate extra to schools in areas of disadvantage with more pupils facing particular difficulties. Cambridgeshire began a more radical experiment with a major devolution of budget responsibility, giving individual schools a delegated budget to cover staff and most of their activities. This system proved popular with schools, and other local authorities were also following suit and devolving budgetary responsibility. The 1988 Act took the idea further. Two quite distinct innovations were introduced, the first controversial, the second less so: 'opted out' status, and the local management of schools.

Opting out

A governing body of an LEA school can decide to ballot parents to ask whether they wish the school to opt out of LEA administrative control. Indeed, a governing body of a local authority school *must* by law discuss *each* year whether it wishes to follow this path. If it goes to a vote of parents they can, on a simple majority, decide to take the school into what is called 'grant-maintained status' with the approval of the Secretary of State. The school is then run by an independent governing body; this body will include five parent governors and up to two teachers plus the head, but the other governors will outnumber them and are essentially self-selecting and drawn from the local area. The property and staff are transferred from the LEA to this new body.

A grant-maintained school receives money from central government through the Funding Agency for Schools. The size of the annual grant to cover a school's running expenses – its annual maintenance grant – is set by how much the local authority in that area spends on its schools. However, on top of this the government pays the grant-maintained schools a sum equal to the value of services the LEA provides centrally for its own schools. The opted-out school can use this money as it wishes. It may buy services from the LEA, buy them elsewhere, employ someone themselves (for example, to teach English as a second language), or not spend the money on these purposes at all. The higher the share of resources the LEA keeps back to allocate centrally, the more central government gives the opted-out schools on top of the base grant. From April 1995 schools in areas that have a lot of GMC schools (30 per cent of secondary pupils) will be funded by a national formula called the 'common funding formula', which is meant to have some relation to the LEA standard spending assessment. Central government meets 100 per cent of the approved capital expenditure of the schools, and local authorities maintain that GM schools have received preferential treatment in the allocation of capital spending.

By 1995 over 1,000 schools had opted for grant-maintained status. The total potential – all secondary and primary schools – amounted to well over 25,000. The Conservative government in 1996 were seeking ways to encourage more schools to opt out. One of the reasons this had not proved a popular course was the success of the second strategy in the 1988 Act – the local management of schools, which gave schools virtually the same financial independence without cutting them off from the local authority and its common services altogether.

Local management of schools
The scheme was introduced in April 1990 – later in London. It first applied to all secondary and larger primary schools, but in 1991 the government required local management arrangements to be

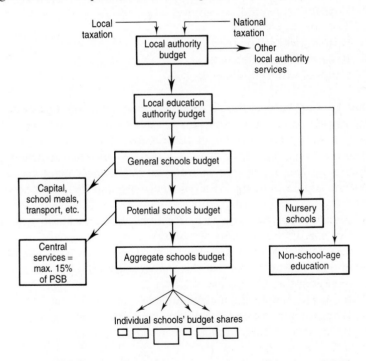

Figure 12.3 The operation of the local management of schools (LMS) (Source: adapted from Lee, 1990)

applied to all schools by 1994. It gives the school's governing body complete control of its own budget. How big that budget shall be is determined in a number of stages. Clearly, the first and crucial step is taken by central government in setting the level of general grant support that it will give the local authority, and, within that, what the authority decides to spend on education. LEAs must then decide how much they will spend on their ordinary primary and secondary schools, excluding nursery schools and special schools for disabled children. This constitutes their 'general schools budget'. They will spend part on minor capital works such as bicycle sheds, school transport and school meals. The remaining sum is called the 'potential schools budget' or PSB (see Figure 12.3).

The Conservative government decreed that by 1993 at least 85 per cent of the PSB must go direct to schools. Items that the authority might want to hold back include the following:

1. Educational psychology service.
2. Teacher supply cover.
3. Peripatetic teachers (e.g. music).
4. Repairs and maintenance.
5. Children with special needs.

The Labour Party has said it would increase the amount delegated to schools. It is still possible for schools to decide they *want* to spend money buying common services from their local authority. The remaining 'aggregate schools budget' is allocated to schools. LEAs can choose their own formula, but it must meet certain criteria laid down by the DES (Circulars 7/88 and 7/91), as follows:

1. It must not be based on past allocations but on a school's 'objective needs', the principle of 'equity'.
2. The 'central determinant of need' must be based on the number of pupils in the school, but this can be weighted to take account of various factors like age.
3. It must be simple and understandable.
4. It must reflect the costs of children with special needs.
5. It may take account of other special social factors.

Eighty per cent of the aggregate schools budget had to be allocated according to 'pupil lead factors', by which the government meant pupil numbers weighted by age. Within that figure 5 per cent can be devoted to the special needs of pupils. In addition, authorities can include elements that take account of factors like a split site or a small school.

LEAs, however, have adopted rather different approaches despite the restrictions (Lee, 1990, 1992a, 1992b, 1995; Sammons, 1991).

The formula, based on average costs per pupil, worked to the disadvantage of schools that had a low turnover of staff and a high proportion of staff at the top of their salary scales. They had to cut their staff numbers in order to pay for the more costly teachers. These might be well-run schools or schools in relatively attractive middle-class suburbs which had done rather well under the old system. In the long run the system will be fairer, as long as full account can be taken of the different pressures schools are under and the differential needs of their pupils are understood.

Free schooling?

Although local authority schools may not charge fees under the 1944 Education Act, that does not mean that schooling is free. David Bull's (1980) pioneering study for the Child Poverty Action Group showed how many calls are made upon a parent's purse that are almost impossible to avoid without causing the child distress – essential clothing, uniform, sports kit, materials for domestic science lessons, and, increasingly, textbooks. School clothing grants are discretionary. They vary widely in generosity (Smith and Noble, 1995). Travel costs up to a statutory 'walking distance' (two miles for under-8s and three miles for older children) fall on parents. As schools sought to make up for cuts in allocations from the LEA, payments for certain extra lessons came to carry a charge. Parents took LEAs to court in the 1980s and won, but the 1988 Education Reform Act permitted charges to be made for individual music tuition and for some education provided outside school hours. A survey conducted by the National Confederation of Parent–Teacher Associations in 1990 suggested that parents were contributing £55 million to schools, about 27 per cent of the normal capitation allowance to primary schools and 7 per cent of that to secondary schools (quoted in Smith and Noble, 1995).

State support to private schools

Direct support

As we saw earlier, some secondary grammar schools that were non-profit institutions had received a direct grant from central government since the 1902 Education Act. In return they provided places for children nominated by local education authorities as well as taking fee-paying pupils. (For an account of these direct grant schools, see DES, 1970; Glennerster and Wilson, 1970). The Labour government abolished this category of school in 1976, giving them the option of becoming LEA schools or relying purely on fees. LEAs continued to have the power to pay fees at independent or private schools for particular categories of children for whom their own schools could not cater, like disabled children or those needing a boarding education. The Foreign Service and Defence Department also pay for places in boarding schools for staff serving overseas.

The Conservative government reversed the decision of the previous Labour government and introduced a scheme that replaced the direct grant system in a different form. This was called the assisted places scheme. It began in a small way in 1981 and built up to pay for 35,000 places by the late 1980s, remaining at about that figure through to 1995. Selected private schools could offer places to a certain number of children, and charge reduced fees related to the income of the parent. The difference was then recovered from the government. About 40 per cent of pupils gained full remission. In the 1995 Budget, the government stated that it hoped to double the number of places taken up in an extended list of schools. The age at which pupils could qualify for state support was to fall from 11 to 5. The Labour Party has said it will abolish this scheme.

Indirect state support

Families can arrange their finances in such a way as to attract tax relief on money set aside to pay for their children's education. Private schools often have charitable status; all the big public schools do, though less than half the smaller schools (Possnett and Chase, 1985). This entitles them to a range of tax reliefs – exemption from VAT on the fees charged, and from income tax, corporation tax and capital transfer tax, for example. The total size of these reliefs could be a little over 15 per cent of the school's income, or much less if the VAT element were excluded. (For a more extended account, see Glennerster and Low, 1990; Robson and Walford, 1989.)

Private spending on private education

As state spending on education failed to keep pace with rising family income and rising expectations, families began to spend more themselves. Taking private and state school expenditure together in 1951/2, nearly a fifth was spent in private schools, but as the state sector improved, their share dropped below 10 per cent by 1979. During the 1980s, as the state sector was allowed to stagnate, the share of the schools' budget spent in the private sector rose again to about 14 per cent (Glennerster and Low, 1990). In the 1990s the share of the total school population going to private schools has declined slightly. However, including all forms of private spending on education, the total rose from 0.3 per cent of GDP in 1973 to 0.9 per cent in 1994. This was nearly a fifth of state spending on education.

Financing further education

The Conservative government removed further education, including sixth-form colleges, from LEAs' administration in 1993 and transferred their finance to the Further Education Funding Council. The colleges thus followed the pattern of the polytechnics. Created by the 1964–70 Labour government, polytechnics used to be administered by their local authorities, who received funds from a pool contributed to by all local authorities in the country. The 1988 Education Reform Act transferred their funding to a Polytechnics and Colleges Funding Council which already funded higher-level courses taking place in LEA colleges. (In Wales the polytechnic was excluded from these arrangements and in Scotland the central institutions and colleges of education were already financed directly by the Secretary of State for Scotland.) The Funding Council was modelled on the way universities had been financed for many years. The Conservative government (DES, 1991) then changed the system once again, this time amalgamating the Polytechnics and Colleges Funding Council with the

Universities Funding Council into new Higher Education Funding Councils (HEFC) for England, Scotland and Wales.

Financing universities

Before the 1988 Education Reform Act's provisions, universities had been funded by the University Grants Committee (UGC). Prior to 1919, various specific grants were made directly by the Treasury to different universities. Then the Treasury amalgamated the grants into a single global sum and made this over to a committee largely composed of senior academics to judge the merits of different institutions and disperse the money. This system lasted until the mid-1960s, by which time higher education had become a major element in the education budget. The Department of Education became responsible for making the grant to the UGC, and assumed overall responsibility for planning. The UGC continued to perform its 'buffer' role, but became increasingly subject to government intervention (Kogan and Kogan, 1983). Until the mid-1970s universities charged low fees which did not discriminate between types of student or their origins. Then universities were told, first, that they must charge higher fees to overseas students (after 1976), and then the full cost (in 1980). For home students, universities received what was effectively a grant for each student varying according to subject and level, calculated on the assumption that a certain fee was charged by the university, albeit a very low one.

The 1988 Act took this process of increasing central control to its logical conclusion. Protests and revolts by the House of Lords forced some toning down of the statute but the powers were not greatly altered (Glennerster *et al.*, 1991). Section 131 (6) of the Act stated that the Council 'shall have power to make grants [to universities] subject to such terms and conditions as they think fit.' Late in 1991, new legislation was to give the new combined funding councils even wider powers of intervention.

A new framework?

The Conservative government's proposals (DES, 1991) changed the grant-giving structure fundamentally, and it remains largely unchanged in the mid-1990s. The separate funding of polytechnics and universities and their separate status – the binary divide – disappeared. The second break with the past was the separate funding of teaching and research. The old UGC paid universities and their staff to do a mixture of teaching and research. These staff could get extra funds to mount particular research projects but the generality of research was financed as a joint product with teaching. This had the disadvantage, from the government's point of view, that if it wanted to fund universities to take more history students, it also had to buy more research by history dons. Given its wish to expand higher education more cheaply, the government decided to separate the finance of teaching and research. The new funding councils have paid the new and the old universities to teach students on the same basis. A history or science undergraduate will attract the same grant to whatever institution so long as it has been inspected and its courses approved as of 'satisfactory' quality by assessors from the funding councils. Universities also receive a fee for each student they take. If they are home or European Community students a fee is set by government which local authorities pay on students' behalf if they hold an award from that authority. Home and European students not holding an award will have to pay the fee themselves or find someone else to do so. The fee plus the funding council grant will cover only the teaching costs, including libraries and laboratories. For a short period in the early 1990s universities were able to accept any number of home students. This led, however, to a rapid increase in the number of home students accepted and an unexpected call on the budgets of local authorities to pay their fees. As a result, the central government had to repay local councils nearly all the increase, as indeed it was obliged to do under the terms of the local grant system. The Higher Education Funding Council had therefore to step in again and reimpose limits to the number of home students each university could accept.

HEFC does, however, differentiate in the amount it gives for research. It grades universities on the basis of their research rating. Those departments rated highly are given more money per member of staff in the grant the institution receives. Research councils also finance specific research projects as do other grant-giving bodies.

There has never been any control on the number of places offered at institutions of higher education to overseas students.

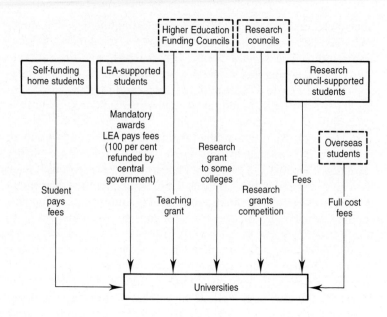

Figure 12.4 The sources of funds for higher education in the United Kingdom

They continue to pay the full cost of their education in fees. For the whole pattern of sources of funds for higher education, see Figure 12.4.

Financing students

From the 1944 Education Act onwards, undergraduate students at universities were given awards by local education authorities which both paid their fees, and gave them a subsistence allowance to cover their living expenses and residential costs. These more generous grants, and rights to them, dated from 1962. The actual sums given depended on the income of a student's parents, unless they were older students. In the 1970s these grants were not maintained in line with inflation and the means-test level of income was lowered so that more and more families and students came within the band of reduced maintenance allowances. The reduction in the real level of grant was sharpest between 1980 and 1986 (DES,

1988). Then, in the social security changes of the mid-1980s, housing benefit was withdrawn for students (see Chapter 14). All these changes made it much more costly to be a student.

Loans

Government argued that since public expenditure was inevitably going to be constrained it should be spent on teaching and research in higher education and not on maintaining students. Hence grants should continue to be phased out and 'topped up' by loans to students, which they would have to repay when their incomes were higher. Those on very low incomes in any year could claim exemption. Gradually loans would replace grants as the means by which students' living expenses would be supported by government. The level of repayment would rise as inflation rose.

This system has proved very costly in administrative terms. The scheme also seems unfair to many. Lower-income earners do not lose their liability to repay, it is merely deferred up to twenty-five years. The payments are relatively heavy early in life when incomes are low. Students are forgiven payment in any year when their earnings are less than 85 per cent of national average earnings. The government lent £316 million in 1993/4 but its repayments amounted to only £20 million. This 'mortgage type' loan scheme differs from an income-contingent loan scheme or a 'graduate tax', which calculates a former student's liability as a percentage of his or her income over a long period. A graduate tax makes graduates subject to a higher rate of tax in return for the extra use they have made of the higher education system and the higher earnings they may get as a result. Low earners or non-earners do not have a given repayment sum hanging over them. (A possible scheme using the social security system to collect repayments and minimize default was proposed and tested by Glennerster *et al.* (1995) and is discussed below.)

Manpower and training

Employers – or enterprises, as we have called them – are major funders of training. They provide training for their own employees and they pay for them to attend courses in local further education colleges. These not only receive funding from the Funding Council

mentioned above but also charge fees for courses which local employers may purchase. From April 1995 individuals of 16 and 17
not in full-time education may receive training credits – which are
vouchers that entitle them to receive approved employer-based
training or training from an approved provider aimed at NVQ
level II or its academic equivalent. Local Training and Enterprise
Councils (TECs) are funded by central government to help pay for
apprenticeships and youth training. Part of this funding will go to
pay for courses run by local colleges. The Department of Employment, which provided the training money, was amalgamated with
the Department of Education in 1995 to make the Department for
Education and Employment, thus rationalizing the funding a little.

Towards 2000

A specific grant for education?

The education world and some Secretaries of State for Education
look nostalgically back to the time when education had its own
specific grant. For ministers, it gave them the opportunity to ensure
that money won in the PESC round for a particular purpose actually
brought results in local authority spending. As it is, money gained
for education in the block grant may be spent on old people's
homes. Mrs Shirley Williams expressed her frustration in the
mid-1970s when she won money for the rate support grant to pay for
nursery education and post-experience courses for teachers, only to
find many local authorities ignoring those purposes.

In its Green Paper on the alternatives to domestic rates (Cmnd
8449, 1981), the Conservative government included an appendix
outlining some ways in which the funding of the education service
could be changed to reduce the burden on the rates. They were as
follows:

1. Removing financial responsibility from local authorities
   altogether.
2. Central government could take over complete responsibility for
   teachers' salaries.

3. Central government could pay an education block grant, rather like the education element in the present revenue support grant but going to education authorities only.

The case against change largely turns on the fear of central political control over the education service.

Abolish LEAs?

Some argue that opting out and LMS should be taken to their logical conclusion. Why not fund all state schools direct from central government like the old direct grant schools? The LEA would then be redundant (*The Independent*, 1991). The arguments for and against are a direct reflection of the issues we reviewed in Chapter 3.

Efficiency

Advocates of full competition between schools have always argued that the case for state involvement in education only extends to its responsibility to empower parents to buy education. Schools are no different from other service providers (Friedman, 1962; West, 1965; Maynard, 1975). Under the UK school market now emerging, the government will ensure that an acceptable standard of common education is provided by means of the National Curriculum, assessment tests and local inspections regulated by Her Majesty's Inspectors of Schools. With information on school performance, parents and pupils will be able to judge in an informed way between the services offered by competing schools. The most efficient will gain pupils and resources, the others will decline. This is the traditional form of efficiency competition of a free market, but as we saw in Chapter 3 it is not the only competition in which schools will engage.

Selectivity

Just as it is critically important for any health-care provider to exclude high-cost, high-risk patients, so it is true of schools. Work by Rutter *et al.* (1979) produced elaborate and effective measures of what constituted 'good' secondary schools. Yet it was still true that, when taken in conjunction with information on pupils' basic abilities and parental background, what went on in the school only explained about 5 per cent of the variance in pupil achievements. An even more detailed longitudinal study of the differential effectiveness of primary schools in London was able to explain 9 per cent of the variance in pupils' reading achievements and 11 per cent of maths attainments by reference to schools' effects (Mortimore *et al.*, 1988). Any school entrepreneur acting rationally would seek to exclude pupils who would drag down the overall performance score of the school. Any non-selective system of schooling would then be in unstable equilibrium. A process of adjustment would follow, moving towards an equilibrium in which schools would cater for children in different bands of ability, and from different social backgrounds. Some would welcome that result, others would not. What economic theory suggests is that a pure internal market between schools based on unadjusted scores would not produce a neutral outcome.

In so far as LEAs did succeed in obtaining a mixed entry to the schools in their area, parents would be able to judge the relative merits of schools' performance starting from a level, as opposed to a staggered, start. It would be necessary, in any system offering choice, for the LEA to produce studies of the relative performance of schools in value-added terms, taking account of the social and other characteristics of individual schools as the Inner London Education Authority (ILEA) did before it was abolished. The Audit Commission (1991) argued that crude league tables of exam results would be misleading, but that measures of one year's exam results compared with previous years in the same school would give a value-added measure. It would do so only if the results of the same children were compared or if the social and ability mix did not change. Most researchers in the field agree that pupil-based analysis that measures how far individuals have improved relative to their starting point on entering the school, is the only fair way to compare school performance (Thomas *et al.*, 1994).

The case so far has been that schooling can be reconciled with an element of market discipline only with a number of safeguards. These require the local education authority to play a significant role, as follows:

1. To choose a pattern of education provision, selective or non-selective, in line with local parents' collective choice.

2. To plan a structure of schools in the area. This would take account of expected demographic change and the preferences being revealed in parents' choice of school.
3. To support schools with a good inspection and advisory service, which can diagnose those schools in trouble and give them special and early support to prevent a long terminal illness, ending in closure.
4. To provide other services on demand at a market price.

Finance parents not schools?

These proposals would extend state support to private schools as well. State cash would go direct to parents. In Britain, most of the advocates of vouchers are on the political right. That is not the case in other countries, most notably the United States, where vouchers are seen as a way of enabling minority groups to opt out of traditional state school education. The arguments for the changes are as follows:

1. Minimum state involvement in the provision of education is desirable to reduce the risks of political indoctrination of children, to create diversity of practice and view, and to reduce the number of state employees. Private provision is necessary to sustain political freedom (Friedman, 1962).
2. Parents are the best judges of their children's educational needs. The case is forcefully argued by Sugarman (1980) and at greater length by Coons and Sugarman (1978). There is no consensus, they argue, over what are the proper goals and means of education. Some parents want strict discipline, others lax, some more play, others none, some want a classical 'three Rs' syllabus, others a more creative one, some want denominational teaching, others none. Thus parental choice must be paramount: 'The family is the best decision maker. Typical families listen to the child, care about the child and know more about aspects of the child's personality than any possible official choosers' (Sugarman, 1980).
3. Education and schools are like any other market. Inefficient schools will be avoided by parents. Under a voucher scheme,

inefficient schools would improve or go bankrupt (see the previous section).
4. There are inevitably some households or taxpayers who have high preferences for education spending; others have low or medium preferences. Electoral bartering produces a compromise level of spending, too high for some, too low for others. If parents were given the present value of state spending on the average child (through a voucher), they could add their own marginal extras and pay fees at a school matching their higher preference (Stubblebine, 1965). This would go some way to equate preferences with educational provision and would result in a higher overall level of education spending.

Different kinds of voucher scheme are advocated by those who lay different emphasis on the above arguments. Friedman (1962) stresses the importance of expanding the private sector of education and the case for encouraging parents who wish to spend more. Coons and Sugarman (1978) want more choice, but they also want equality of opportunity. Jencks (1971) wanted better provision for the poor and to foster choice within the state sector. These differences give rise to three fundamentally different kinds of voucher schemes, as follows:

1. Vouchers limited to state schools versus vouchers 'cashable' at any school, public or private.
2. Vouchers that cannot be 'topped up' from parental means versus vouchers that can be added to.
3. A flat-rate voucher, the same for every child, versus one that was higher for poor children and lower for children of rich parents.

These three possibilities can be combined in different ways to produce a wide range of options.

Those who oppose this move argue:

1. State interference by a totalitarian government in the curriculum will not be inhibited by financial or accounting methods. As we saw at the beginning of the chapter, the extent of central government control of the curriculum was greatest in the period when schools were privately run and state financed.

2. The practical problems of ensuring minimum educational standards in thousands of private schools are enormous. We are not dealing with an ordinary market. Parents are being compelled to purchase a service by law with the taxpayer's money. The dangers of exploitation and profiteering at the taxpayer's expense must be great.

3. Given the wide variation in parental experience of education and the rapid changes in educational practice in the past twenty years, together with children's own rights and feelings on the matter, parents may not be the best judges. Choices between subjects are more important to children than choice between schools, and the two objectives conflict with each other for geographical reasons. To ensure viable classes in a wide range of subjects at GCSE and A level, a school must be quite large. In most areas outside big towns, choice involves travelling long distances. The smaller the schools, the larger the choice *between* schools, but the *narrower* the choice between subjects in any one of them.

4. Schools are not like the corner grocer's shop. They cannot readily go bankrupt and be replaced by new entrants to the market. The consequences of run down and closure for children are serious.

5. The argument that total education spending will be increased is based on a set of assumptions that are questionable. It presumes that the electorate would be prepared to vote education as much money with a voucher scheme as under the present system. That cannot be proved and can be doubted (Glennerster and Wilson, 1970). Where many, if not most, parents were in the private sector, richer voters might well prefer to vote for lower taxes and lower vouchers.

In 1995 the Conservative government announced that it would introduce a scheme of vouchers for nursery provision in 1997, with an experimental scheme in 1996/7. Only four authorities agreed to participate. The aim was to give parents a voucher worth £1,100 which could be cashed at either a local authority pre-school nursery class or at a private establishment which would be inspected by OFSTED. Local authorities, and therefore local authority schools, would get no support from central government unless children turned up at their schools with vouchers that would have to be collected and returned to some pre-school funding agency, which in turn would be funded by central government. Parents would not be able to top up state school vouchers, but could pay private nurseries more on top of the voucher to cover their fees. The voucher will only meet about a half to a third of private school fees, so parents who have no state school to go to but cannot afford to add the extra to pay for a place in a private school, will not be able to cash their voucher.

This scheme seems tailor-made to direct public money to parents who can now afford private provision or who might do so with the help of this voucher. In this sense it will help extend the private sector of pre-school provision in line with Friedman's advocacy, but it will not target help on those parents and children who most need pre-school facilities. The scheme might have been used to encourage state schools to be more flexible and provide facilities for children throughout the working day. However, the low level of the voucher, the fact that it cannot be topped up in local authority schools, and the fact that it is confined to 4 year-olds, minimizes the impact that it might have made in this respect. State schools have been slow to respond to the needs of working parents; putting purchasing power in the hands of parents could have encouraged state schools to respond to those needs if the scheme had been differently designed (Glennerster, 1995a).

Abolish private education?

The countercase is that advanced by those who would either make the private provision of education illegal or severely restrict it. They argue that if the ideal goal is to achieve equal opportunity or an equal start in life for all children, then it cannot be right to permit some children to acquire a superior education to others. Not only do private schools permit this, they also have links with colleges at Oxford and Cambridge and sustain a network of social contacts that give those whose parents can afford private education a striking advantage in career terms and in entry to elite positions. Moreover, they foster the social segregation of children of different classes (Crosland, 1956, 1962).

Opponents argue that the right to send your child to a school that holds your beliefs as a parent, and provides what you think is an appropriate education, is a fundamental human liberty. Even if equality of opportunity is a good objective, liberty must take priority. A monopoly of education by the state, with no power to withdraw your child from its instruction, is a dangerous step to totalitarianism. Some argue that at least the state should not subsidize private education directly or indirectly unless the schools provide for all classes without privilege. This case was argued by the Public Schools Commission (DES, 1968).

Extend or abolish loans to students?

Students should, some argue, repay the *whole* cost of their education, not just the maintenance element.

The case for loans

On general efficiency grounds, economists argue that students should be faced with the true costs of the resources they are using. This argues for going further and charging students a full cost fee, and getting them to repay it when they begin earning. On equity grounds the present system is unfair. It largely benefits children of higher-income group parents who then go on to earn high incomes themselves. About four times as much public money is spent on the higher education of the richest 10 per cent of the population compared to the poorest 10 per cent (Glennerster *et al.*, 1995). Loans repaid as an addition to the normal National Insurance contribution would be fairer and spread over a longer period of the student's later life (for details of such a scheme, see Barr *et al.*, 1994).

The case against loans

In practice, loans bring no immediate gains to the Exchequer; they can do the reverse in the short run. No scheme in this or other countries actually exacts a full market rate of interest. To avoid the criticisms often levelled at such schemes that they are unfair on those graduates who do not earn high salaries or do not earn at all, the United Kingdom and other countries have fairly generous exclusions, which again reduces the potential revenue.

Far from seeing loans as fairer to lower-income groups, many, like the Robbins Committee (1963), believe that the prospect of a large loan debt would only put off more working-class young people whose parents could not cushion them. This would have efficiency consequences for the economy as well as equity. Even income-contingent loans or a graduate tax, it is argued, could have such an effect. Woodhall (1982, 1989) suggests that the evidence of other countries does not support this.

A graduate tax

To ease the problem of a loan being a disincentive to poorer students with little family experience of higher education or a mortgage, a 'graduate tax' alternative was proposed many years ago (Prest, 1966; Glennerster *et al.*, 1968). A version was introduced in Australia in 1989 under the title of a 'tertiary tax'. Graduates who receive full higher education also undertake to pay a subsequently higher rate of tax. This links repayment to ability to pay and means that those with low incomes or no incomes do not have to pay at all and *do not* retain the obligation to pay if their incomes *remain* low. Barr (1989) modified the proposal, suggesting that a higher National Insurance contribution would be a good way to collect the tax and that once a student's loan had been paid off, his or her payments should cease. There is no case for students to subsidize other students. If poorer ex-students are to receive help, the burden should be shared by all taxpayers.

A lifetime entitlement

At the other extreme, a way of achieving equity in post-school education would be to give everyone the right to receive a certain financial entitlement to post-school education or training at some time in their life – a kind of educational bank account (Schuller and Walker, 1990). This can be combined with ideas about educational leave from work. Many European countries have partial elements of such schemes (Glennerster, 1981a). A limited scheme of this kind was proposed in Britain by the Advisory Council for Adult and Continuing Education (1982). The Social Justice Commission (1994) proposed a similar if more elaborate model of a lifetime 'learning bank'. It would give each individual a capital sum that could be drawn down to pay for approved education or training.

Further reading

For a discussion of LMS, see: T. Lee (1992), *Local Management of Schools*, Milton Keynes: Open University Press.

Voucher schemes are compared and the case for experiment expounded in A. Maynard (1975), *Experiment with Choice in Education*, London: Institute of Economic Affairs; and propounded powerfully by two American liberals, J. Coons and S. Sugarman (1978), *Education by Choice*, Berkeley: University of California Press. The difficulties with markets for schooling are discussed in H. Glennerster (1991), 'Quasi-markets for education?', *Economic Journal*, **101**, no. 408, pp. 1256–67.

The pros and cons of different forms of student finance are reviewed in M. Woodhall (1989), *Financial Support for Students: Grants, loans or graduate tax?*, London: Kogan Page. A critique of the 'top up loan' introduced in the United Kingdom in 1990 is criticized and an alternative proposed by N. A. Barr (1989), *Student Loans: The next step*, Aberdeen: Aberdeen University, and elaborated on in H. Glennerster, J. Falkingham and N. Barr (1995), 'Education funding, equity and the life cycle', in J. Falkingham and J. Hills (eds), *The Dynamic of Welfare*, Hemel Hempstead: Harvester.

CHAPTER 13

PAYING FOR HOUSING

Nowhere is it more important to distinguish the provision of a service from its finance than in housing, nor to distinguish the effect of direct public spending from tax expenditures. Much of the chaos into which housing finance has fallen is a direct result of failing to distinguish the interrelated consequences of each form of state intervention. We can only understand the present confusion by looking at its historical origins. Over the past century the state has come to be involved in the housing market in at least six distinct ways, as follows:

1. By regulating the standard of houses built and permitted to remain in occupation.
2. By controlling the level of rents charged by private landlords and giving security of tenure to certain tenants.
3. By building, owning and managing houses itself.
4. By subsidizing the housing costs of its own tenants and tenants of private landlords and housing associations.
5. By subsidizing the improvement of property by public and private owners.
6. By subsidizing house purchase through the tax system.

I shall try to trace briefly the sequence of events that led the state down this long and confusing route.

The history of housing finance

State regulation, provision and subsidy

In the nineteenth century, the private speculative builder and land-lord responded to the rapidly changing housing demands created by industrialization. In many ways they did so remarkably effectively, providing houses that were better than most in Europe at a price affordable by many of the new industrial working class. However, even they could not provide tolerable accommodation for the poorest classes. The costs of building even the meanest housing with an adequate rate of return on capital were too high for the poor. Overcrowding grew worse throughout the century. Housing and health standards declined in the poorest parts of the large cities and came to pose several kinds of threat to the wider society – contagious disease, and a threat to public order and to accepted social values. 'Slums' presented such a disturbing element that Victorians sought drastic remedies (Steadman-Jones, 1971; Gauldie, 1974). The early remedies either made things worse or made little difference. Public health legislation, notably in 1848 and 1875, enforced sanitation and set minimum standards for housing in terms of ventilation, light, water, space. It also gave powers to local authorities to close and demolish slums and to prohibit overcrowding. This both increased the minimum cost of housing and reduced its supply, hence pushing it further out of the reach of poor families.

Left to itself the housing market will clear, there will be supply of a sort for the poorest, even if it is self-built corrugated iron shacks on the outskirts of large cities that one can see in some parts of the world today, or the 'rookeries' of Victorian London. However, if society is not prepared to accept that outcome, then government must find a way of creating a supply of a minimum standard of housing at a price low-income families can afford, or it must subsidize the incomes of poor households to ensure they meet these housing costs. The Victorian response was to use the voluntary sector to supply low-cost housing. They hoped that with efficient building at low interest and stern housing management the market could still work though on a philanthropic rather than pure capitalist model. To some extent this did work with a limited social group, but it did not solve the real problem. (Only 100,000 such dwellings were built in London up to 1914.) In other countries, however, this response was much more effective since government or employers stepped in to subsidize such provision, either directly or through low-interest-rate loans (Power, 1992).

Local authorities, under the 1890 Housing the Working Classes Act, had the power to build, but did not receive subsidies. Hence they were also unable to provide housing at minimum standards for the poorest without some dubious accounting that only a few authorities indulged in. On the other hand, paying money directly to poor families in order to help them pay rent for better accommodation conflicted with sound Poor Law principles. Increasingly, reformers turned to the only solution they could identify as politically feasible – central government subsidies to local authorities.

The First World War produced the first major precedent for the later pattern of finance that was to be reinforced by the experience of the Second World War (Bowley, 1945; Wilding, 1972; Merrett, 1979). The war worsened the housing shortage. The new Prime Minister, Lloyd George, had committed the postwar government to a massive building programme, and in response to unrest and rent strikes the government controlled rents. In those circumstances the only agencies who could deliver such a programme seemed to be the local authorities, but early returns showed that they were most reluctant to do so if the costs fell on the rates. Thus the 1919 Housing Town and Planning Act (the Addision Act) gave local authorities the power to build and charge low rents. If there were a deficit they had to spend up to a 1d rate subsidizing it, but the whole of the remaining deficit would be borne by the Exchequer. This form of financial carrot, and the presumptions of low rents for council tenants, remained, at least until recently. (For the complex but interesting early history of Exchequer housing subsidies, see Nevitt, 1966; Merrett, 1979; Donnison and Ungerson, 1982; Holmans, 1987; Malpass, 1990.)

In the aftermath of the Second World War and an even greater housing shortage, councils were given the primary role in meeting the shortage fast. They were given priority in the allocation of scarce building materials – building three-quarters of all new houses in the 1940s. Subsequently, their role reverted to redevelopment on a massive scale in the 1960s, to specialist housing and to granting subsidies on improvements to older housing. Each change of policy produced a new subsidy – so much per year for the life of the loan raised to build each new house. The result was a peculiar museum of bits and pieces of central government subsidy accumulated over the decades by councils, who were increasingly pressed by central government to concentrate that subsidy on poorer tenants by charging differential or income-related rents (Parker, 1967).

The 1972 Housing Finance Act swept these old subsidies away and introduced a new system. Government grants to support councils' housing costs were to be based on each council's *current* financial and housing needs. More important, low-income tenants, both public *and* private, who were wage earners, could apply to the local authority for help. Local authority tenants received a rent rebate, private tenants a rent allowance. This was the basis of the modern system of housing benefit (see below).

Following the economic crisis in 1976, local authority house building was cut drastically. The Conservative government in the 1980s switched its priority to funding housing associations as the main new providers of low-cost housing to rent. Thereafter housing finance policy remained unchanged until the mid-1990s.

Penalties on the private landlord

As we saw, the private landlord had been the dominant provider of housing in the nineteenth century; at the end of that century, over 90 per cent of houses were rented to tenants by private owners. Throughout the twentieth century, however, a number of factors have combined to erode this position steadily, so that in 1994 only 4 per cent of households in the United Kingdom were tenants of private landlords. The First World War began their decline. Rent control, introduced in 1915, was gradually relaxed and then re-introduced in the Second World War, and relaxed again in stages. Rent control on new property was ended by the 1988 Housing Act. It is often condemned as the main reason for the demise of the private sector by limiting the profitability of the landlord's housing stock. Undoubtedly it played its part, but, as the experience of the 1957 Rent Act showed, even when rent controls were removed from a large part of the market for a period, its decline continued. Nevitt's (1966) analysis shows why. The tax laws continued to treat a new house as a permanent asset, not as a piece of investment that depreciates and can be set against tax to reduce the investor's tax liability. If a business invests in new machinery, it can offset the costs against tax. Thus, Nevitt argued, private housing was badly treated by the tax laws. Far more important, the tax treatment of owner-occupiers was so generous as to make owning your own house always preferable to renting in sheer financial terms, reducing the demand for private tenancies. The modern tax situation is set out by Hills (1991a). It is, indeed, this tax treatment of owner-occupiers that has become the decisive factor in housing finance, yet it also came about as something of an accident.

Bonus for the owner-occupier

Owner-occupation began to expand in the nineteenth century because of the invention of building societies. They were originally self-help groups of artisans who formed a club, contributing regularly to a fund out of which they would buy or build houses for themselves. Its job done, the society was wound up. Then people realized the society could continue on a longer-term basis as a 'permanent society', borrowing from local savers and lending to local people to buy houses. Strictly hedged with legislation after various scandals, the local building society became the normal means of collecting small savings and financing house purchase. In the low-interest-rate, low-housing-cost period between the wars, owner-occupation boomed in the better-off areas of the South and the Midlands. The societies were given relatively favourable tax treatment compared to other financial institutions, but the real tax bonus did not begin until the 1960s.

Originally, owner-occupiers were of marginal importance and the tax system simply applied the existing rules. They were treated as if they were their own private landlord. They were assumed to be paying themselves a rent – the level of rent other people living in a similar house would pay – and they were taxed on that notional rent, just as a private landlord would be. It made good economic sense, and was a system followed in many other countries. The owner-occupier's real income *was* higher since he or she paid no rent, while his or her neighbour paid the rentman each week. Both the owner-occupier and the private landlord could offset interest and other costs against gross income, just like any business. Thus the owner-occupier received tax relief on the interest he or she paid to buy a house – just as a private landlord or other business would, on the necessary cost of investment. This system lasted until 1963, but it was gradually being eroded. Not having the benefit of weekly economics classes, owner-occupiers could not see the logic of paying income tax on income they never saw. This notional income was set in 1936 values and never changed after the war, so its real value fell, and therefore so did the real value of the revenue the Treasury received. As the number of owner-occupiers grew, the pressure to abolish the tax grew. In 1963 the Conservative Chancellor did abolish it. Because there had been no revaluations of houses the revenue was small, administratively cumbersome to collect, and unpopular to boot. The Labour Party did not object.

So far so good, but what about the other side of the equity balance – the right to set off the interest paid on mortgages against tax? That remained in place. At that time all interest payments could be set against tax, even for consumption purposes. When that relief was finally abolished in 1974/5, loans for house purchase were again exempt. The combined effect of these incremental moves was a growing tax subsidy to owner-occupation, the economic case for which has totally disappeared and which did in fact have wide and serious economic consequences I shall discuss later (Atkinson and King, 1982).

Another major subsidy also arose by accident. The Labour government introduced a capital gains tax in 1965. It was a tax on the difference between the purchase price of a capital asset and its selling price. Owner-occupied housing was exempt. There was some justification for this. If house prices are rising, and you need to buy a new house when you sell your old one, you use the money you gained from your sale. However, it has also encouraged people to 'trade up' – to buy as expensive a house as they can, and then sell and buy a larger and more expensive house as their incomes rise. This both reduces their tax burden and enables them to reap a capital gain on retirement when they move into a smaller house or into other forms of tenure.

House purchase thus became a combined form of pension, life assurance and tax avoidance. The higher the income of the house owner, the greater the gains. The more expensive the house bought and the interest set off against tax, the greater the benefits. More-over, the higher the marginal rate of tax, the greater was the tax relief. Those on very high marginal rates of tax were effectively getting almost interest-free loans. The Labour government in 1976 took the first steps to put some limits to the system. Tax relief was only available on mortgages up to £25,000. The next Conservative government raised the limit to £30,000 in 1983, but it has not been increased since and its real value has steadily declined. In 1983 most houses came within the £30,000 limit. That sum was the equivalent of a £100,000 house in the mid-1990s, by which time, therefore, most mortgage holders were receiving tax relief on only a small part of their mortgage payments. Then, in the first post-Thatcher Budget in 1991, the relief for higher-rate tax payers was withdrawn. A 40 per cent tax payer could not, effectively, have two-fifths of his or her mortgage costs paid by the Exchequer, but only 25 per cent. In subsequent budgets, the value of the relief that could be claimed was confined first to tax payers at an assumed tax rate of 20 per cent, which was then reduced in stages to 15 per cent in 1995/6. The Conservative government in the 1990s had thus steadily reduced the scale of this tax subsidy. By the mid-1990s this relief was more targeted on lower-income taxpayers buying cheap houses.

Aid from social security

Since the days of the Poor Law, assistance payments covered rent, at least in part. The Supplementary Benefits Commission, which inherited these powers, was in effect one of the largest providers of cash help towards housing costs, about £900 million compared to the total housing subsidy and tax allowance bill of £2,600 million in 1979 (Kilroy, 1982). This form of support to poor householders overlapped with rent rebate schemes run by local authorities for their tenants. Poor tenants were caught in the midst of this tangle and the Supplementary Benefits Commission wanted to rid itself of involvement in determining 'reasonable' rents. In 1983 the gov-ernment introduced the housing benefit scheme that was intended to concentrate all cash assistance to poor families in one scheme administered by local authorities. It was this scheme that was over-hauled during the social security review of the mid-1980s (see Chapter 14 and below).

Comprehensive reform

A major review of the whole system of housing finance was carried out by the Labour government in the mid-1970s. The result (DoE, 1977) produced a mass of valuable information and analysis but no significant political action. It was the Conservative administrations of the 1980s that produced some decisive changes in housing finance which we discuss below.

Expenditure on housing

Figure 13.1 shows how the state's involvement in housing finance has changed since the economic crisis of 1976 and a decade and a half of Conservative government. In 1976/7, net capital expenditure by local councils and housing associations – that is, excluding building financed from sales of property – amounted to the largest element in the state's spending on housing. By 1989/90 the level of net capital spending by both local authorities and housing associations had fallen to about £1 billion. That total was shared almost equally by local authorities and housing associations. On top of that, local authorities were presumed to be able to spend nearly as much again on self-financed capital from their sales. Throughout the 1990s the level of local authority permitted spending

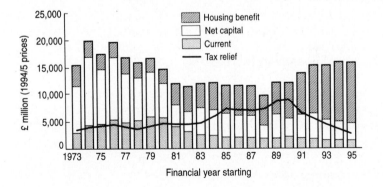

Figure 13.1 Public expenditure on housing, 1973/4 to 1995/6 (Source: Hills, 1993 updated)

fluctuated, rising in the early period at the time of the General Election but falling back by 1996/7 to the levels of the late 1980s. Between 1990 and 1993 only 10,000 public sector houses a year were added to the stock; in the 1960s this figure had been about 150,000 a year.

The next big change was in the form of Exchequer support for local authorities' current spending and the extent to which tenants' rents were subsidized. In 1976 a large general subsidy was made to local authorities' housing revenue accounts. This subsidy was used to lower the general level of rents that had to be charged to make those accounts balance. On top of this there were cash benefits to particular tenants to relieve the burden of rent. In 1976 the total level of spending on means-tested housing benefits to both council and private tenants was less than half the cost of the general subsidy to councils' housing costs. By 1989/90 the whole balance had shifted, and general subsidies to local authorities' housing revenue accounts had all but disappeared. Moreover, the great bulk of public expenditure was by then in the form of housing benefit to poor households rather than general subsidies to local councils or housing associations. Coincident with these changes was an increase in the support given to owner-occupiers. This support nearly doubled in the period between 1976 and 1990 but, for reasons described above and because interest rates fell in the mid-1990s, the value of tax relief fell back sharply (see Figure 13.1). Housing benefit is now the largest state subsidy to housing. In nearly two decades the finance of housing has been transformed.

Forms of finance in the 1990s

Overall, individuals pay for most housing costs through mortgage payments and rent; tax relief is significant too (see Figure 13.2). Here we concentrate on the direct forms of public subsidy to housing.

Local housing authorities

Unlike the rest of their finances, local authorities must keep a separate housing revenue account (HRA) into which goes all the

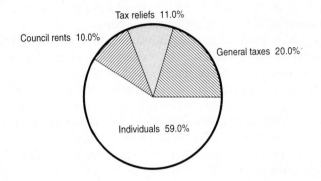

Figure 13.2 Sources of funds for housing, 1993/4 (Source: Hills, 1995b)

income and expenditure that relates to their own housing stock. Other aspects of their housing service, like house improvement grants or bed and breakfast for homeless people, come out of the council's general funds like all other services. The exact content of the HRA is carefully defined. The latest version of the definition is in the 1989 Local Government and Housing Act. In brief, it comprises the following:

1. Gross income from rent.
2. Charges for services like heating.
3. Central government subsidy.
4. Interest on capital sums gained from the sale of its property to council tenants (capital which remains in the bank because the government has not given permission for it to be spent).

Expenditure includes the following:

1. Repairs.
2. Maintenance and management of the stock.
3. Small-scale capital expenditure from income.
4. Rent rebates paid to tenants to help them pay their rents.
5. Loan charges on borrowing to build or repair the stock.

The same Act introduced the latest in the line of subsidies to local housing authorities. The key step was to 'ring-fence' the HRA. In the past it had been possible for local authorities to use their

general funds to subsidize the HRA and hence reduce rents overall. From 1990/1 this has not been permitted.

The old general housing subsidy from the central government
has disappeared and with it the practice of paying the housing
benefit to which council tenants were entitled. Central government
had forced local authorities to raise rents and was consequently
being forced to pay higher housing benefit to council tenants, who
then paid the council. It was a rising indirect subsidy from social
security funds to local councils. Under the 1989 Act, councils were
forced to raise their rents each year according to guidelines set by
central government.

The subsidy from the central government to the HRA is divided
into two elements: that which pays for the housing benefit entitlements of local authority tenants, and the housing element. The
second element is designed to meet a deficit on the HRA which
can be justified in the government's terms. The local authority is
assumed to be raising a certain sum in rent from its tenants. It is
also assumed to have legitimate maintenance costs on the property
it owns and loan charges on its debt. The subsidy is to meet the
difference between those outgoings and the recommended rent
levels. It is calculated as follows:

Approved costs:

(a)	management and maintenance allowance ($£x$ × number of dwellings)	£6 million
(b)	the interest on past loans	£5 million
(c)	cost of rent rebates	<u>£4 million</u>
		£15 million

Less

(d)	Gross rent guideline (recommended rent levels R × number of dwellings, where R is a guideline set annually by central government)	£14 million
	Subsidy	£1 million

Clearly, the higher the government sets the rent guideline, the
lower will be the subsidy local authorities receive. In the above

example, if the guideline rent were raised, the expected income would rise to £15 million. Assuming nothing else changed, that would eliminate the government subsidy. It would leave the cost of supporting the rents of poorer tenants to be borne by the income raised from the rents of other tenants. Nationally, the total of *surpluses* run by local authorities on their HRAs has grown in the 1990s. Local authorities are building very few houses and their loan charges are therefore declining, but the rents they are being encouraged to charge are rising. Nevertheless, some authorities are still in potential deficit and therefore receive subsidy.

The government has steadily pushed up the national guideline rent since 1990. The local guideline rent is fixed in relation to the valuation put on council houses that tenants have bought in that area. If they have had to pay twice the national average value of council houses, the target rent will be twice the national guideline. In 1990 the average guideline rent in most regions outside London was just over £20 a week (£29 in London). The increase in many regions up to 1994/5 was of the order of £10, but in London and the South-East the increases were £18 and £15 respectively.

A future Labour government might wish to base its guidelines on different principles. It might want to encourage local authorities to build more houses, which would increase the expenditure side of the HRA as the much higher costs of loan repayment began to fall on the account. That would begin to require rents to rise. Central government would then have to decide whether to increase its subsidy and whether to 'un-ring-fence' the HRAs by allowing councils to subsidize rents of tenants from general council revenue. The pattern evolved in the 1980s does, however, have advantages that are likely to remain. One is that clear target sums are indicated for spending on management and maintenance of property, which local authorities have, at times in the past, neglected.

Transferring the stock

The 1980 Housing Act gave council tenants the right to buy the property they inhabited from the council at a discount: that is, below the valuation made by the local valuer of the property. The extent of the discount depended on the length of time the applicant had been a tenant. The reduction in the value at which the tenant could buy was another form of capital subsidy to owner-occupiers. Poorer tenants would also lose their right to housing benefit. Better-off tenants would not have received such benefits. For them, the net gains were considerable. Between 1979 and 1995 about a million-and-a-half council dwellings were sold to tenants and the number of council dwellings as a proportion of all dwellings fell from about a third to a fifth.

As the number of tenants able to buy, even at a discount, began to dry up, the Conservative government devised another way of reducing the stock of council-owned properties. In 1988 the Housing Act gave private landlords or housing associations the right to acquire blocks of council houses or whole estates as long as tenants approved in a rather odd voting system. Few compulsory transfers have taken place, but an increasing number of large-scale voluntary ones have. By 1995 thirty-five local authorities, with the support of their tenants, have transferred their stock to housing associations. The total number of properties involved was nearly 160,000.

In addition, the government took powers to create housing action trusts. These can be used to take bad estates compulsorily out of the hands of local authorities and place them in the hands of a trust, which will improve the estate and hand it on to a private or housing association owner. This, however, has proved an almost complete dead letter, with tenants opposing nearly all of the few schemes proposed.

A longer period of Conservative government would almost certainly see most of the housing stock of local authorities sold to or taken over by housing associations or other non-governmental agencies. A trend towards more tenant ownership of estates and devolved responsibility for them is probable under any administration.

Housing associations

Both the 1974 Labour government that set up the Housing Corporation and extended the system of support for housing associations, and the Conservative government of the 1980s and 1990s, were anxious to diversify the range of landlords available to poorer tenants. If the private market had virtually ceased to exist for this group of tenants, some variety, choice and exit was needed rather than reliance on a vast single public landlord. In 1967 the Labour government extended to housing associations the right to receive government subsidies like local authorities. However, the local authority had to act as the channel and many were reluctant to do so, since it meant spending resources they would have preferred to use themselves.

In 1974 a separate housing association grant was introduced based on an entirely new principle. It involved giving associations a *capital* sum at the beginning of a new scheme sufficient to reduce the loan repayment charges to such a point that poorer tenants could pay the rent. The local rent officer would set a reasonable rent for that new property. The newly created Housing Corporation would set a sum that it expected to be spent on management and maintenance of the property. It also set cost limits to the building or renovation of the property. The total capital cost was, therefore, tightly controlled; so, too, were the other regular expenditures. It was possible to work out how high rents would have to be to cover the interest payments and the other regular expenditure. A capital sum was then given to the association sufficient to reduce its debt, and therefore its interest payments, to a point where the weekly costs of the association equalled the rent set by the rent officer. The grant was called the housing association grant (HAG).

As it turned out, the system had a fatal flaw. It assumed that the fair rent fixed at the outset would hold for the life of the project, or at least it would only be raised sufficiently to meet rising management and maintenance costs. In the long run, this meant that housing association rents would fall behind fair rents generally. If rents were raised in line with other prices and rents in the economy, the housing association would be making a surplus on that property. This led to various attempts to recover the surplus or redirect it. Other experiments in attracting private capital were tried in the 1980s.

The next significant change to the system came in the Housing Act 1988, which applied to new schemes after 1989. It reversed the old procedure: grants are now fixed as a proportion of the total capital cost, and private loans are meant to cover the rest. Government has assumed that private loans form an increasing share of the total. Rents are fixed not by a local rent officer, but by the housing association itself, taking into account the costs it has to face, which include the costs of repaying its loans.

Associations are grouped into three kinds:

1. Tariff associations, that agree a programme of development with the Housing Corporation.
2. Non-tariff associations, smaller and more specialist, that need support from the Housing Corporation for some risks.
3. Very small or new associations.

Tariff associations

The Housing Corporation sets total cost indicators, which are cost limits for building or renovation work. They vary by type of dwelling and purpose (e.g. sheltered housing). A programme of work is agreed with the Housing Corporation. A total spending figure for the programme is also agreed. A proportion of that figure is then given as a grant, while the rest of the capital cost has to be raised on the private market. If the costs of the scheme overshoot, there is no more government help. Rents are fixed to cover the costs of the loan charges and management and maintenance.

Non-tariff associations

These receive a separately negotiated 'appropriate' percentage of the actual capital cost in grant as long as the cost is not more than 130 per cent of the total cost indicator.

Other associations

Since these might find it difficult to raise private capital they can be given loans from the Corporation itself or from local authorities to make up the difference between grant and capital cost.

Rents fixed by housing associations have to cover loan repayments plus a recommended level of management and maintenance spending. The Housing Corporation advises local associations that 'the overriding requirement is that rents remain within the reach of people in low paid employment'. As Hills (1991a) points out, the problem is that the Housing Corporation and the government gave no advice on what constituted 'within the reach of', 'low paid' or 'affordable'.

The grants I have just described apply to new developments in the 1990s. Old grants on old property continue. Thus housing association finance is in a rather comparable situation to local authority housing finance in the period before 1972. It is equally ripe for reform.

Private landlords

The reasons for the decline in private landlords have been described. Rent control and the 1988 Housing Act enabled landlords to charge a market rent for new lettings. (For more detail, see Hills, 1991a.)

Improvement grants

Dating from the period after the Second World War, government has given grants to private landlords, owner-occupiers and other owners of property to improve the standards of the accommodation. This could mean installing basic amenities, or turning an old property into new dwellings. Later grants were associated with a local strategy to improve a whole area. The economic logic behind this approach is that while it may not be in the interests of any one owner to improve a property in a run-down area, if every owner is encouraged to do so, the area as a whole would increase in value and attractiveness. A public-good gain is being created. Again a change in the system was introduced in the late 1980s. A single grant replaces the old complexity. Since 1990 grants have been mandatory: that is, the council must give one if a property is thereby brought up to a given standard. Though the grants are mandatory they are subject to a means test – only poor landlords should receive them. Expenditure by local authorities on renovation grants, slum clearance and group repair of property attracts a 60 per cent subsidy from government.

Cash aid to tenants

We saw earlier that the emphasis of government funding has moved from subsidizing rents generally to giving cash aid to poor tenants. The housing benefit system underwent a series of changes in the 1980s. Following the social security review, which we discuss in the next chapter, a new pattern of benefit was introduced in 1988. Under it, tenants on income support received 100 per cent of their rent. For others, housing benefit was scaled in relation to income. The higher a household's income above an 'applicable amount', the less the benefit. Benefit was reduced by 0.65p in the pound of any income above that point. Coming on top of other means-tested benefits, housing benefit has produced a continuing serious poverty trap (see next chapter).

Homelessness

The problem of street homelessness has grown through the 1990s. It is a reflection of wider changes such as the withdrawal of social security from young people, the closure of many hostels that used to exist in places like London, and the closure of long-stay mental hospitals. Central government does give small grants to voluntary agencies for advice and emergency help. Through the 1990s until 1995/6 the government financed temporary hostel places and gave grants to housing associations working to help the street homeless in London. This 'Rough Sleepers Initiative' amounted to £182 million over six years.

Towards 2000

The fundamental reform of housing finance has been on the political agenda since the early 1970s. The reasons should already be clear. To many in all political parties the present 'system' seems both inefficient and inequitable. On the other hand, to tamper with it would both upset a great many voters, and cause unfairness of a different kind to people who have invested their life's savings in a particular form of ownership on the expectation that its advantages were guaranteed.

The efficiency case against general subsidies

1. The case for full cost pricing, outlined in Chapter 8, applies with particular force to housing. It is a matter of individual taste best

accommodated by the matching of price to consumer preference. Beyond the minimum public health standards there are few convincing public good or externality arguments against the market. Individuals can judge between houses. Competitive markets in technical advice are available.

2. General public subsidies spread the limited amount of public money thinly over households who do and do not need help to purchase an adequate standard of accommodation. There is less available to help the poorest.

3. Collective subsidized *provision* for the poor has been associated with creating social class ghettos – council housing estates which are unduly expensive, badly built, and poorly managed (Gray, 1968; Webster, 1981; Dunleavy, 1983; Power, 1987, 1992).

4. The heavy subsidy to those who borrow money for housing encourages a high demand for building society loans. It means that a disproportionate share of the limited supply of savings in the economy is attracted to house purchase. The result, it is argued, has been to lower industrial investment (Atkinson and King, 1982).

5. General subsidies to both council tenants and owner-occupiers undermine forms of private rented provision, and are also an inefficient form of help to tenants because many who do not need help get it to the detriment of other poorer tenants – in the private or public sectors. They also trap people in particular areas, encouraging limited labour mobility and hence high unemployment (Minford *et al.*, 1987).

6. Indirect subsidies to private tenants through rent control reduce housing supply and are unfair to landlords, many of whom are not wealthy themselves.

7. To argue against general subsidies does not deny the need to make it possible for poorer households to pay for the minimum standards of housing that the state insists are necessary on public health, citizenship or other grounds.

Proposed reforms

Nevitt's (1966) 'fundamental objectives' for housing reform remain the basis of many later proposals. The objectives are as follows:

1. Families with average and above average incomes should pay for their own accommodation without subsidy; those with below average incomes should receive a carefully scaled subsidy relating to their housing need.
2. The introduction of a single system of subsidies that did not distinguish between tenure.
3. A system of taxation that did not distinguish types of owner.
4. Control of the total flow of capital for housing investment irrespective of sector.

Others have argued against income-related housing allowances because of the effect they have on the accumulation of means-tested benefits that together form the poverty trap. They argue for a universal housing allowance. I mention some of the proposals beginning with the most radical. Interested students are advised to pursue the original versions. A useful overview is given by Hills (1991a).

A universal flat-rate housing allowance
Lansley (1982) proposed a need – size of family – based allowance which would vary, for example, by region. This could take the form of a tax credit – an absolute sum by which the Inland Revenue would reduce tax payment or give as a cash payment. It would be crude and would cause difficulties for those on supplementary and housing benefit who now receive their whole rent. The other main difficulty is that housing costs vary a lot from one area to another, which would make a single level of benefit inadequate in many areas. It would also be very costly and go to owner-occupiers who have paid for their house. These objections could be met in theory but would pose administrative problems.

A comprehensive means-tested housing benefit
This would effectively extend the present housing benefit system to owner-occupiers and remove other forms of support. It would avoid some of the problems a universal flat-rate scheme would entail (Grey *et al.*, 1981; Donnison and Ungerson, 1982). Objections are that an owner-occupied house is a capital asset which owners can sell to enhance their income later in life. Why should the state enhance individuals' future income just because they choose this form of tenure? There would be a temptation for

households to overinvest in housing, increase their aid from the state and then reap the benefits of taxpayer help later in life.

Abolish tax relief on mortgage interest payments
Sudden abolition overnight would affect the capital value of owner-occupied houses. In fact, as we have seen, the Conservative government has been steadily running down this subsidy. Phasing it out would be a logical next step, but other ways would need to be found to help moderate- to low-income families who now benefit disproportionately from what remains of the system.

The case for subsidized owner-occupation

The case against any of these strategies comes from both the political left and right, but above all from those who currently benefit. They argue as follows:

1. Tax relief is not a subsidy. This was argued by the building societies in their evidence to the Housing Policy Review (DoE, 1977), but is difficult to sustain in economic theory without rejecting the whole concept of tax expenditures. In any case the argument for treating all rental income and capital gains equivalently remains.
2. Changes in the tax laws would be unfair to present owners. People have made important financial decisions on the basis of the present tax law. The present value of houses reflects that part of the present tax subsidies which have been 'capitalized'. To remove them would produce a rapid fall in property values and destroy many people's lifetime savings. (This ignores the fact that house prices are affected by other changes in economic and tax policy on a regular basis.) Nevertheless, it is true that the steady removal of the tax concessions to owner-occupiers in the 1990s has been one factor depressing house prices in that period.
3. Owner-occupation has considerable public benefits beyond the fact that most people prefer it as a form of tenure. It makes people feel they have a stake in the society. It also gives people an inducement to ensure a high level of maintenance and repair and invest their own time and money in their homes. This

sustains the standard of housing for later generations. It is thus of general 'public' benefit, and should in principle be subsidized.

4. Large-scale public ownership is a bad thing in itself, giving too much power to local councils and preventing the market working. It should therefore be sold off to those who want to buy.

5. The right policy to follow is to remove all forms of subsidy and let market prices and market rents apply. Minford *et al.* (1987) propounded such a policy. This would be accompanied by some form of support for the very poorest in any tenure. It would entail removing all remaining rent controls on existing tenancies, raising local authority and housing association rents to market levels, and giving housing benefit at 100 per cent of rent to all those who were on benefits other than unemployment and sickness benefit. Those temporarily out of the labour market would have their benefit cut off when it reached 70 per cent of previous salary.

The case for public provision

1. Housing is a joint product – an appreciating asset and a consumption good. Where ownership is split between tenant and owner, their interests diverge. A private landlord especially has an interest in selling for gain, the tenant wants security. This contractual relationship of landlord and tenant cannot be properly monitored. Thus either owner-occupation, or public or non-profit ownership of rented property with social duties laid on the public or non-profit landlord, are the only fair forms of tenure that overcome this problem (Whitehead, 1984). This may justify public provision but not general subsidies.

2. If society wishes to see people occupy minimum standard accommodation, for the reasons discussed, over and above what some could afford, it should pay this cost.

3. Those who defend public provision of housing do so on grounds of efficiency. A local authority is able to acquire and develop large sites, and can reap economies of scale in improvement schemes. Many elderly owner-occupiers cannot cope with repairs and maintenance and let their properties decay. The public sector has the least underoccupation. The way we finance owner-occupation ensures that older owner-occupiers whose

families have grown up are often no longer paying for their mortgage or paying only a low figure and have little inducement to move to a smaller house and free the accommodation for a family. Lower-income families and many other social groups will never be able to afford a home of their own, and many do not want one.

The case for diverse social provision

Many accept the case above, in part, but argue that monopoly landlords are especially bad for poor tenants who have little power and that a diversity of tenures for the least advantaged is essential. It is possible to improve the management of housing estates by devolving management responsibilities to an estate level with some success (Power, 1987, 1991; Glennerster and Turner, 1993), but ideally, full control and choice by tenants depends on their owning their own estates or blocks of flats co-operatively, or being tenants of small-scale housing associations with tenant representation. Some kinds of need can only be met by private landlords and a small market of this kind should be encouraged (Glennerster *et al.*, 1991).

All in all, housing finance is probably the most unsatisfactory of all the systems we have discussed, but it is the most difficult to reform.

Further reading

The fullest account of housing finance and taxation is to be found in J. Hills (1991a), *Unravelling Housing Finance*, Oxford: Oxford University Press. Another set of proposals is to be found in P. Malpass (1990), *Reshaping Housing Policy: Subsidies, rents and residualisation*, London: Routledge.

An influential report of a committee chaired by the Duke of Edinburgh was first published in 1985 by the NFHA; see National Federation of Housing Associations (1991), *Inquiry into British Housing*, Second Report, London: NFHA.

CHAPTER 14

PAYING FOR SOCIAL SECURITY

The history of social security finance

The state has become involved in maintaining, or supplementing the income of its citizens in six distinct ways, as follows:

1. Providing last resort assistance to those in extreme financial distress regardless of the category of employment they may or may not have had.
2. Sustaining, if at a reduced level, the incomes of those who are, or have been, part of the labour force, but whose earnings have been temporarily interrupted by sickness or unemployment, or who have retired.
3. Supplementing family income during the period when there are dependent children to look after – a period when family income is reduced but outgoings are high.
4. Varying tax liabilities to encourage people to provide for their own retirement, sickness or widowhood.
5. Enforcing benefit provisions on employers for their employees' sickness or redundancy.
6. Regulating occupational and private pension schemes.

Each one of these distinct systems of income maintenance has developed its own form of finance.

258

Public assistance

This was the earliest form of state-provided relief. In Tudor times parishes were given powers to supplement private alms-giving by imposing a tax to relieve the poor. A series of Acts was consolidated in 1601. Public assistance was to remain locally administered and financed until the depression of the 1930s, despite growing central regulation. For more than three centuries, poor relief was financed by a tax on local property values – the poor rate or its successors. The tax base gradually moved from the boundaries of the local parish, to combinations of parishes or 'unions' in 1834, to larger local authorities after 1929.

Two factors brought the end of this system in the 1930s. The first was the heavy concentration of unemployment in certain areas of the country. The central government had to step in to finance means-tested benefits for the longer-term unemployed whose right to unemployment benefit had lapsed. The second was that central government feared that generous benefits would have a potential disincentive effect on workers. This led first to clashes with Labour-controlled Boards of Guardians, and then with some local authorities who were administering poor relief after 1929. Both factors came together in the 1930s and unemployment assistance became an Exchequer-funded and centrally administered system under the Unemployment Act of 1934.

The relief of poor old people was taken over by a reconstituted Assistance Board in 1942. They were to be treated in a less stigmatizing way than by the local Public Assistance committees, and the Exchequer was to meet the bill. In 1948 all public assistance became the responsibility of the National Assistance Board, and Parliament set the national minimum scales that determined what benefits should be paid by local offices and voted the funds out of general taxation. This system of support was renamed the 'supplementary benefit system' in the mid-1960s and became 'income support' in the 1986 Social Security Act. Though the pattern of benefits has changed over this long period and more people have been drawn into the means-tested net, the essence of the scheme and above all its Exchequer-funded nature, have not changed. For an appraisal of the impact of the Beveridge Report (1942) and subsequent developments in social security, see Hills *et al.* (1994).

In a relatively small and homogenous economy with much geographical mobility, different standards of basic benefit are difficult to sustain. Higher than average benefits attract those who have no work and their dependants to those areas providing generous benefits. In a largely urbanized society with labour mobility between jobs and similar costs of living, where a national sense of citizenship can be *politically* articulated, different local standards of income maintenance become difficult to sustain. As Europe's economy moves towards greater interdependence and labour mobility, the same pressures for a common basic level of income support will grow. That is already evident in the European Social Chapter and the debate upon it which will develop as the year 2000 approaches.

Social insurance

Forms of mutual support, or group insurance, by working people to keep them and their families off poor relief, spread in nineteenth-century Britain. The trade unions, friendly societies and private insurance companies came to be powerful vested-interest groups capable of exerting considerable political pressure. The idea of mutual aid by workers earning future benefit rights seemed consistent with the dominant values of thrift and the work ethic in British and American society. The idea appealed to paternalistic and socialist value systems alike (Rimlinger, 1971). On the continent of Europe different institutional legacies, the influence of the Catholic church, labour unions, social democratic parties and the fascist movements of the 1930s, have all left their mark (Esping-Andersen, 1990). The origins of income maintenance in the Scandinavian countries lie in a period when agricultural interests were dominant (Baldwin, 1990). The form social security has taken in different societies reflects the balance of interests, especially in periods when key changes took place. Yet all modern economies have had to find some way of evening out incomes from periods of labour market activity to those of non-activity or dependence (Falkingham and Hills, 1995).

There was, however, a third motive, which the early history in Britain illustrates well (Thane, 1982). The poverty of the elderly posed a financial problem, not least as a growing burden on the poor rate in the late nineteenth century. The trade union and labour movement, and radical liberals and social scientists like Booth, were pressing for some form of state pension. Some favoured finance from a regular weekly payment by workers, others funding out of general taxation. The unions opposed contributions from already low-paid workers, and so did the Treasury, on grounds that it would mean a complicated and expensive machinery to collect, duplicating the ordinary tax system. Added to these, Asquith, as a traditional Liberal, did not see state pensions as a long-term necessity, merely as a temporary expedient reflecting the particular difficulties that that generation had faced. He argued against a duplicate and complex contributory system. Hence when state pensions were introduced in 1908, they were financed out of ordinary taxation.

Yet that, too, had its problems, as Lloyd George found out during the passage of the legislation and afterwards. Universal pensions at 65 were very costly. The Treasury opposed spending anything like the sum required and in order to implement the scheme at all the Cabinet had to agree to a limited and restricted scheme beginning at 70 for those below a certain income. The pressure not to undermine the existing voluntary contributory schemes, and the fear of adding to the income tax paid by the middle class, led Lloyd George to turn to weekly contributions as the means of financing the new sickness and unemployment scheme of 1911. The effect was to limit contributions to those who were in the schemes – workers earning less than a set income (£160 per annum in 1911). The lower-paid workers and their employers would largely pay for the scheme. When pressure grew, in the 1920s, to lower the age of entitlement for old age pensions to 65, that extension was limited to and financed by those in the existing National Health Insurance scheme. The Beveridge proposals legislated after the Second World War extended membership of the National Insurance scheme to the whole working population and created a single national scheme administered by central government rather than a vast array of local societies, but the contribution principle remained. A flat-rate sum would be levied from all employees and employers, which would buy a stamp actually stuck onto a card to be held by the employer, and then passed on to a person's next employer. These contributions earned the right to benefits from the national scheme. The money was to go into quite separate National Insurance Funds held by the central government and supplemented by the Exchequer from ordinary tax revenue.

Beveridge had originally argued that every member should pay the same contribution and receive the same benefit. This put severe constraints on the scheme. Benefit levels were tied to the contributions that the poorest could afford. Other countries had not adopted this model; they had linked both contributions and benefits to earnings. From 1959 onwards, governments of both parties moved further in that direction. Contributions were raised and became a percentage of earnings. However, the old Beveridge notion, that they were entitlements to benefit and not just a tax, remained. Thus contributions rose with earnings but only up to a certain point – one-and-a-half times average earnings. Beyond that point people pay no more. The Labour Party has proposed abolishing that limit. Contributions would then become a social security tax in all but name.

In the 1960s and 1970s benefits were split into two. On top of the Beveridge basic flat-rate pension, for example, was built the state earnings-related pension (SERPS) in 1975. The Conservatives proposed abolishing it in the review of social security in the mid-1980s but, in a less generous form, it survived.

Beveridge (Cmd 6404, 1942) had argued that a clear link between contributions paid in and benefits 'earned' was necessary to distinguish insurance-based benefits received as a 'right' from Exchequer-based means-tested assistance that would continue to carry some stigma, and rightly so in his view: 'National assistance must be felt to be something less desirable than insurance benefit. Otherwise insured persons get nothing for their contributions' (Cmd 6404, 1942: para. 369). This distinction has always been a fiction to economists and the changes of the 1980s and 1990s have blurred the distinction even more. Benefits to which people had been contributing for many years were abolished. The wage-related sickness and unemployment benefits begun in the mid-1960s were abolished by the Thatcher government in the early 1980s, and the right to invalidity benefit was translated into access to a more restricted incapacity benefit in 1995. On official estimates, perhaps 240,000 people who would have qualified under the old rules will not under the new scheme (CPAG, 1995). The old unemployment benefit that had existed since 1948 was to be abolished in 1996 and replaced by a 'job seekers' allowance'. These benefits will assist those who qualify in periods of interrupted earnings but the nature of the 'contract' changes as government policy changes.

Child benefits

Probably the first proponent of cash allowances to families was Tom Paine, author of *Rights of Man* in 1791 (Penguin edition, 1969). Poverty among the working poor was, he argued, the result of the fact that their wages were not enough to support their children. Families with children should be excused the payment of taxes and paid £4 a year to bring up their children and send them to school. He was the true originator of the modern negative income tax as well as the education voucher! Much later, and never more lucidly, Eleanor Rathbone (1924, 1940) made essentially the same case. Early in the life cycle, and when children were growing up, a family's minimum needs might well be met even on a low wage, especially if there were two earners, but when children were born the spending needs of the family rose sharply and usually the family's income fell as the wife left work. A negotiated or statutory minimum wage which the trade unions advocated could never be set high enough to meet the needs of the largest families. There was no such thing as a static family living wage. Minimum needs varied with the number and age of children in a family. Incomes must reflect the extra needs of children. The only way to do that, she argued, was to link incomes to the number of children in the family. But who should pay? In Australia and New Zealand, where family allowances had been introduced after pressure for a minimum wage on precisely these grounds in the 1920s, the cost was met out of General Exchequer funds. (The allowances were income-related, tapering off as income rose.)

In Europe, family allowances had grown up first in France before the First World War, as a form of occupational welfare – paid by firms as part of the wage. After the war the practice spread, but to counteract the obvious incentive for employers not to take on men with families, allowances were paid out of 'equalization funds'. A levy on local employers who belonged to the scheme was paid into a common fund and then drawn upon by individual firms to pay the child allowance. In other countries the new schemes were financed out of contributions from employees, employers and the state. In Britain, during the Second World War, servicemen's incomes included a children's allowance; thus the state began to pay family-related incomes to a large part of its 'workforce' almost by accident (Hall *et al.*, 1975).

What proved decisive in Britain, however, was the desire to limit wage increases at the beginning of the Second World War and the introduction of a comprehensive system of national insurance benefits for those not in work. These benefits were related to the number of dependants a worker had – a wife and children. If these were to be reasonably generous, there was a severe danger that many workers would be better off out of work than in work. Beveridge (Cmd 6404, 1942: paras 4.11, 4.12) argued that this would be unfair and economically perverse. Thus the state must ensure that incomes for those with larger families are supported when they were both *in* work and out of it. This view was upheld in Cabinet and by the Treasury (Macnicol, 1980). The cost was to be met out of general taxation, which has applied ever since. Internationally, family allowances or child benefits continue to be financed in a variety of ways. The best review of the diverse ways in which families are supported internationally is still to be found in the study by Bradshaw and Piachaud (1980); see also Kamerman and Kahn (1983); Rainwater *et al.* (1986); and Lewis (1993).

Supplementing family income

Just because universal cash benefits paid out of taxation are so expensive, it has been difficult for governments to raise child benefit to a level that would raise all families above the poverty line. In 1971 after an election campaign in which family poverty had featured as a significant issue, the Conservative government introduced an additional means-tested benefit for poor families where a member of the household was in work but earning so little that they fell below the poverty line. It was called 'family income supplement'. Under this scheme, families on low incomes could apply to the DHSS to have their incomes supplemented. The scheme was financed out of general taxation. It applied to very few people. It had a low take-up and hence cost relatively little. The family was paid half the difference between their assessed income and a target figure set in relation to the family's size. In the 1986 Fowler reforms the scheme was renamed 'family credit' and the definition of income changed. It was to be calculated after deducting taxes and insurance contributions. This eased the harshness of the poverty trap on these families a little (see below). It was still paid out of general taxation.

Fiscal support

Tax relief on private pension schemes and various life assurance arrangements dated back a long way (Titmuss, 1962). Relief on life assurance premiums is as old as income tax itself. It is to be found in Pitt's 1789 Tax Act. It later disappeared, to be reintroduced by Gladstone in 1853 to enable people who were dependent on earned income to save for their retirement. This was, of course, half a century before the state provided any cash benefits to retired people. As higher tax rates were introduced, this form of saving became increasingly attractive to higher-income groups. However, it lost the Exchequer large sums of money. These reliefs were gradually withdrawn in the 1980s. A wide range of other reliefs and encouragements to save, especially through share ownership, were introduced in Conservative budgets in the 1980s and 1990s. Tax relief on private pensions of various kinds still exists (see below).

Regulated and statutory employer benefits

In the 1970s and 1980s, the state took over a new and important role in social security provision. It essentially made employers responsible for administering benefits within a standard set by the state. The 1975 Social Security Pensions Act provided for a new wage-related pension on top of the basic National Insurance pension. If employers wished to contract out of this scheme, they could, as long as they provided at least an equivalent pension. The principle was taken even further by the 1979 Conservative government in their statutory sick pay scheme. From April 1983 employers have been obliged to pay a set level of sickness benefit – statutory sick pay – if an employee (not on a short-term contract of less than three months) is incapable of work. The costs are recovered from the government by the employers who subtract their expenditure on such benefits from the National Insurance contributions the firm pays to government. The 1986 Social Security Act applied the same principle to statutory maternity pay. Statutory and occupational welfare have become closely intertwined.

Expenditure today

Social security spending in 1994 was equivalent to 17 per cent of the gross domestic product or £98 billion. The rate of spending rose especially fast during the unemployment crisis of the early 1980s and 1990s. Just over a tenth of all benefit spending went to the unemployed in 1994/5. Nearly half of the total (45 per cent) was spent on benefits for the elderly – pensions, housing benefit and income support combined. The next largest element is the cost of benefits received by the sick and long-term disabled, nearly a quarter of the total. Support to families of all kinds constitutes nearly a fifth of the bill (see Figure 14.1).

The scale of social security spending has grown more than any other major category of public expenditure since 1951. At that stage it amounted to a third of the total welfare state budget. By 1994 it was taking just over half if you include housing benefit and just under half if you do not. Benefits until 1982 rose to keep pace with real incomes in the rest of the economy. The elderly population grew and the scale of unemployment did too. In the 1990s spending on the elderly has stabilized in real terms and has taken a

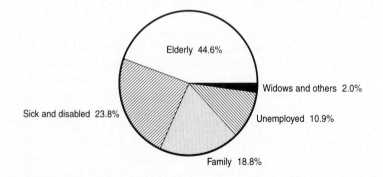

Figure 14.1 Benefit expenditure by group (Source: Cm 2813, 1995)

declining share of the total social security budget. The reasons are twofold. First, the increase in the size of the population over 65 has levelled off. Secondly, and more importantly, the Conservative government broke the link between the annual benefit increase and the rise in the earnings of the employed labour force. Benefits were only raised in line with prices. Benefits thus fell behind average earnings, becoming a smaller and smaller percentage of previous or average earnings year by year. In 1983 the basic pension was equivalent to 46 per cent of average personal disposable income: that is, the average income each individual has after direct taxes had been taken off. By 1994/5 this benefit was worth only about a third of average disposable income. An even sharper fall was evident for those on unemployment benefit (Hills, 1995a). This was equivalent to nearly 40 per cent of average personal disposable income in 1977 but the figure had fallen to not much more than a quarter in 1994/5.

Despite its significance, social security expenditure in the United Kingdom is still lower than in most other advanced industrialized countries. Table 14.1 compares the level of spending on social protection benefits in European countries expressed in terms of spending per head, standardizing for the purchasing power of

Table 14.1 Relative levels of social protection benefits in Europe, 1992

Country	Current expenditure per head[1]
Sweden	150
Luxembourg	149
Germany	129
Netherlands	129
France	121
Denmark	121
Belgium	112
Italy	105
UK	**100**
Spain	64
Ireland	60
Portugal	42

Note: [1]Expressed relative to UK = 100 spending power.
Source: Eurostat (1994).

Table 14.2 Average income of pensioners by source, 1979 and 1992

Income source	Average income (% share)	
	1979	1992
Earnings	12	6
State benefits	61	50
Investment income	11	20
Occupational pensions	16	24
Total gross income (%)	100	100
Per week at 1992 prices (£)	111.8	168.1

Source: Cm 2813 (1995).

money in each country. It shows that the level of benefit spending in Sweden is about half as much again as it is in the United Kingdom. Many other countries spend about 20 per cent more, and only the really poor countries spend less.

The large changes in state spending on social security have been matched by compensating changes in the incomes of the retired. As the state has withdrawn, those in a position to be able to do so have developed their own sources of retirement income (see Table 14.2).

Earnings have provided a declining source of income for the elderly. There has been a steady fall in the number of men working beyond the age of 60 and most are now out of the labour market well before the age of 65. There has been a small increase in real benefit incomes of pensioners since 1979 but a large increase in income from occupational pensions and investment income. State benefits constituted 60 per cent of pensioners' income at the beginning of

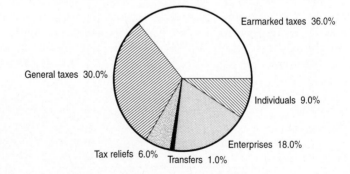

Figure 14.2 Sources of funds for social security, 1993/4

Mrs Thatcher's term; by 1992 the figure was 50 per cent. Private sources of finance for retirement will have become the dominant feature in the next century. They are much more unequally distributed, however. The sources of funds for income transfers overall in the economy are shown in Figure 14.2.

Financing social security today

The National Insurance Fund

Prior to 1948 there were no fewer than fifteen separate social insurance funds administering different benefits. To sustain the notion that the new benefits would be 'earned as of right', Beveridge proposed unification into a single scheme. Three funds, a basic fund, a reserve fund and an industrial injuries fund, were created, into which National Insurance contributions were paid and from which benefits were paid out. In 1975 the separate funds were amalgamated. To quote from the Comptroller and Auditor-General's prelude to his report on the Accounts for 1989/90:

> The national insurance scheme is financed on a pay-as-you-go basis from contributions, which are mainly earnings-related, and income from the investments of the National Insurance Fund. The rates of contributions for any year are fixed at a level which will enable the Fund to meet the expected expenditure in that year on benefits and administration and retain a working balance. (National Insurance Fund Account 1989/90, HC 617, 1989/90)

The balance sheet of the combined National Insurance Fund for 1993/4 is summarized in Table 14.3. From that we can see that total receipts, made up of contributions from employees and employers and self-employed people, came to nearly £35 billion in 1993/4. Parliament then voted income to meet the loss of contributions from firms deducting the costs of paying for their employees' sickness and maternity leave under the statutory schemes we discussed above. There were other odds and ends of receipts that came, for example, from recoveries made from firms who had gone bankrupt and not paid their employees' redundancy pay to which they are entitled by law. The state pays these and then recovers the costs if it can through the courts. Finally, the surplus on the fund and its working balances it has to keep are invested. This gained the fund investment income of nearly £470 million. In this year the total of receipts outweighed the costs of the benefits by over a billion pounds and added to a balance in the bank of £3.5 billion put away for more difficult times.

What is noticeable by its absence is a line in the accounts which used to appear from 1948 right through to 1988 – the 'Consolidated Fund Supplement'. This was a general subsidy to the fund from general taxation. Beveridge had assumed this would be a large element and for many years it amounted to about 18 per cent of

Table 14.3 National Insurance Fund, 1993/4

Receipts and payments	£000s
Receipts	
Contributions	34,941,546
Grants made by Parliament to keep a reasonable working balance and compensate the fund for loss of income from statutory sick and maternity schemes	8,711,000
State scheme premiums	148,205
Income from investments	469,809
Other receipts	64,576
Total receipts	44,335,136
Less **Payments**	
Benefits	38,463,795
Personal pensions	2,859,527
Transfers to Northern Ireland	40,000
Administration	1,555,387
Redundancy payments	268,974
Other	35,045
Total payments	43,222,728
Excess of receipts over payments	1,112,408
Balance	
Balance at beginning of year	3,436,244
Excess of receipts over payments	1,112,408
Balance at the end of the year	4,548,652

Source: House of Commons (1995).

the income of the Fund. Then the Conservative government began reducing it. It formed only 13.4 per cent of the total receipts in 1982/3, and continued to fall gradually until it was formally abolished in 1988/9. Social security benefits were to be entirely financed by contributions and the ordinary taxpayer relieved of the burden. That was one reason why the Government in the 1980s was able to reduce the standard rate of income tax but had to raise the social security contribution to match the reduction.

Employee contributions

These depend on earnings and whether you are opted into the state earnings-related pension scheme. In 1995/6 workers paid 2 per cent of their earnings up to £58 a week, the lower earnings limit, and 10 per cent on earnings between that and £440 a week. These lower and upper limits are changed every year. The effect of this upper earnings limit is that higher earners pay a lower percentage of their earnings in contributions than average earners. The justification is that these are 'contributions' not taxes and higher earners above this level do not get higher pensions.

For those contracted out of SERPS the lower rate contribution is the same, but the main contribution rate is 8.2 per cent, not 10 per cent. Members of personal pension schemes run by private insurance companies pay contributions at the contracted-in rate for SERPS, but the state pays the private scheme a sum equal to the difference between the contracted-in and the contracted-out contribution. Self-employed earners pay at a lower rate on the assumption they are responsible for their own pensions.

Employer's contributions

The employer also has to pay a contribution for each of his or her employees and the amount depends on the wages or salaries of the worker. For an employer in 1995/6 whose employees were in SERPS the rates were:

Weekly earnings (£s per week)	Rate of contribution (%)
58–104.99	3.0
105–149.99	5.0
150–204.99	7.0
205 and above	10.2

If the worker was contracted out of SERPS the employer paid 3 per cent less.

The United Kingdom raises less in the form of a separate social security tax than most European countries. In particular, it levies less on employers. Economists doubt the validity of these distinctions. They argue that if the market sets the labour cost per employee, the combined employee and employer social security tax merely forms part of the labour cost faced by the employer. Thus the higher it is set, the smaller the market wage actually paid to the employee. The extent to which the tax is passed on in lower wages, rather than absorbed in lower profit levels or passed on in higher prices, will reflect the price elasticities and market power of employers and workers. International comparisons do suggest that social security contributions are levied at the expense of lower wages – they are shifted on to wage earners (Brittain, 1972). In that sense all contributions are paid by employees.

Funding

As we saw above, the National Insurance Fund does not carry a huge surplus invested in government securities or company shares. Private schemes run a balance sufficient to pay out the promised pension or benefit even if no more income came in tomorrow. These schemes are fully 'funded' – or are supposed to be! The pension is secured by the investments – the security and value of which vary with economic fortune. With National Insurance, if the government decides to cut the income to the fund and thus cut the benefits, or simply to wipe out a benefit, it can do so. The Conservative government did indeed do just that in 1982 when the earnings-related sickness and unemployment benefits were abolished. Why is the state scheme not funded in the same way? The reasons are partly political and partly economic, as follows:

1. If a large surplus accumulates, political pressure mounts to use the surplus to increase benefits to current pensions.
2. Conservatives in general and City institutions in particular fear the huge sums that government would be able to build up and the power this would give it in the market. For the opposite reasons, socialists have argued for at least the partial funding of a National Superannuation Scheme (Labour Party, 1958).

3. 'Pay-as-you-go' schemes enable governments to pay out pensions now. A full-funded scheme would mean either waiting many years for the fund to build up or imposing very high contributions to build up a surplus quickly, or a bit of both.
4. The major economic problem has been that inflation has so rapidly eroded the value of pension funds whether public or private. With pay-as-you-go schemes, both benefits and contributions can rise in line with inflation each year.
5. Since the state can enforce sufficient contributions to ensure payment of benefits it does not need a large investment fund to guarantee its income.

Pay-as-you-go schemes were particularly attractive when real incomes were rising. The cost of a given pension seemed less if it was to be paid in the future by a richer population. As real income growth has slowed, past promises are going to be expensive to honour. This had led some to argue that fiscal responsibility demands that governments adopt a funding policy or require membership of private schemes that do so (Johnson and Falkingham, 1994; World Bank, 1994; Bosworth, 1996).

Tax expenditures

Subsidies to individual taxpayers who invest in their own retirement constitute a major cost to the Exchequer. Just how large a cost is a technical argument that rests essentially on one's view as to what form of tax ought to be levied (Board of Inland Revenue, 1983).

There is some disagreement about whether pensions should be treated as deferred pay and not taxed twice and, if so, whether original income should be fully taxed and pensions not at all, or vice versa. Tax relief is thus a way of avoiding double taxation and not a subsidy at all. Another view says that pensions are not deferred pay but an investment. If I choose to invest in shares or capital, I get no relief. I pay tax on my original income and on the interest my savings earn. To be consistent, the same should happen if I invest in a pension scheme. If we want to encourage any form of savings, for example, through an expenditure tax or relief on income from savings of all kinds, as in the 1995 Budget, that is another matter (see Chapter 7).

Occupational pension schemes

Running alongside, but regulated by government, are the occupational pension schemes. An employee must be a member of the state scheme or an employers' occupational scheme, or, under the 1986 Social Security Act, a personal private pension scheme with a private insurance company. Moreover, the minimum level of contribution an employee must pay is also set by the state. It does not want to permit *employees* to free-ride and make no provision for their old age. Thus, in the United Kingdom an employed person can effectively choose only whether to be taxed directly by the state or indirectly by his or her employer, or alternatively to pay into his or her own pension scheme up to a given sum set by government.

Most private schemes used to have no inflation proofing at all and others have only partial proofing. After twenty years of inflation even an apparently generous private pension will be tiny in real terms. To try to rectify this weakness the Conservative government in 1986 required new pensions schemes in the private sector to guarantee the *minimum* pension level required in the legislation against inflation up to 5 per cent per annum. This inflation proofing comes in two stages. First, schemes must arrange for the value of contributions that finance the minimum pension to rise by the rate of inflation or 5 per cent, whichever is less. Similarly, after retirement the minimum pension must be raised with inflation up to 5 per cent but no more. This is only meagre protection, however, especially if you change job. Pension contributions are not raised in line with earnings and preserved pension rights from a succession of jobs will look very low in relation to earnings in thirty or twenty years' time. Secondly, there is no inflation proofing above 5 per cent and inflation has often reached those levels. Individuals may get less generous pensions than they are expecting from a lifetime of work. The third worry is that pension schemes run by employers are at risk of being syphoned off to help out a company in difficulty. British law has been particularly lax in this respect. The Maxwell case prompted the Conservative government to see whether the law could be tightened and the Goode Committee (1994) proposed a range of reforms, including the appointment of a Pensions Regulator, the enforcement of minimum solvency requirements, and restrictions on withdrawals. The government did not fully implement the report and even the report itself did not go as far as many felt necessary. There is no recompense if an employer goes bankrupt, increasingly common, and early leavers' rights are not properly secured. (For a brief but good discussion of these points see the Social Justice Commission, 1994: 281–3).

Personal pensions

These were greatly stimulated after 1988 with significant tax advantages and heavy selling by pension companies. They do enable individuals to move jobs or have their own pension scheme as self-employed persons. But for many who were persuaded to move from SERPS or occupational schemes they were a bad buy, and many of the companies concerned now face legal action from the would-be pensioners who were poorly advised. Despite their problems, such schemes, if properly regulated, do secure pension rights against assets that are invested and to which individuals can lay some claim, which is more than can be said of government benefits.

Towards 2000

It is difficult to discuss alternative ways of financing social security without discussing major changes to the whole system of social benefits. To do this in detail is beyond the scope of this chapter, but it is possible to sketch the broad outlines of very different financing strategies that have been under discussion and will form the basis of a new system of social security in the next century.

The compulsory private model

The Conservative government's 1986 reforms began to move in this direction. The state gradually phases out the basic pension. By the year 2000 this will be well on its way to being complete. The basic pension will be worth little more than 10 per cent of average earnings and may be dispensed with little fuss. Income support remains for existing pensioners, but in order to ensure that people do not simply rely on it, membership of an occupational pension scheme or personal private pension scheme has become compulsory.

The logic of these trends will lead eventually to the following system. The state sets minimum levels of pensions and sickness benefits which employers must provide. These are fixed at, or above, the level of income support. The pensions are financed by contributions paid by the employee and the employer aided by government tax reliefs. Pension rights would be transferable. The only state benefits would be income support or a negative income tax payment financed out of general taxation.

The *advantages* claimed for such schemes are as follows:

1. Their low cost in terms of direct public spending and taxation.
2. The choice that workers would be able to exercise in negotiating more or less generous or flexible pension arrangements.
3. The creation of large pension funds that would finance economic growth.

The main *disadvantages* of such schemes in the past – failure to inflation-proof or transfer pension rights – can be overcome, it is claimed, though the government did not feel able to insist on full inflation proofing in 1986. Other *disadvantages* or objections levelled at such proposals are as follows:

1. The lower tax burden argument is spurious. Enforced membership of a pension scheme and a compulsory contribution up to a given level are merely systems of taxation under another name.
2. In practice, workers' representatives have little or no choice in the form of their pension scheme.

A unified funded pension scheme

Many in the population, especially women but increasingly all sections of the population, are outside employment and have little financial capacity to buy into personal pension schemes.

This has led to a compromise proposal: compulsory membership of personal pension schemes, with the state meeting the contributions of those not in the labour force (Falkingham and Johnson, 1995). Every individual would build up a personal retirement fund which would be used to buy a pension annuity. These would have to offer a minimum pension. A set percentage of earnings would have to be put in to such a fund. For those falling below a threshold, or with no employment or income, the state would contribute a capital sum each year to the personal fund. These would be run by private competing companies.

There are many problems with this idea. It is not clear what percentage of earnings would be required to generate a minimum pension linked to future average earnings. There is a wide range of uncertainties – for example changing asset values – where risks would be difficult to spread. Then there would be incentives for individuals to defraud the system, organizing their incomes into phases that made them poor some years in order to qualify for a capital grant.

At the same time, it would generate large savings, vesting pensions in assets that belonged to individuals not governments or husbands. However, it would also raise in a more acute form the issue posed by Richard Titmuss (1976) many years ago: that of large sums levied compulsorily by private pension schemes being invested with major economic and distributive effects by socially 'irresponsible' or unaccountable insurance firms.

The libertarian residual model

Those who see the state's compulsion as pernicious, whether operated through employers or its own agencies, prefer a more libertarian approach. They would encourage individuals to make their own pension arrangements, for example with private companies. The state would confine its activity to emergency last-resort help for those not able to make such provision. The *advantages* are seen to be those of the previous model, but without the element of compulsion embodied in it. The *disadvantages* are as follows:

1. If the state supplementary pension or benefit scheme is relatively generous or humane, this constitutes, for most people, a strong disincentive to taking out a private pension. People obtain little benefit from private pensions that merely reduce

entitlement to their state means-tested pension. If the basic pension scheme is very inadequate, then encouragement of private provision will lead to suffering on the part of those who have to rely on the state.

2. Private pension funds could borrow inflation-proofed bonds from government, enabling them to inflation-proof pensions to some extent, but that is in effect to give private pension schemes a large open-ended grant from the Exchequer. They already receive major tax reliefs. These are effectively paid for by all the population, but disproportionately benefit the better-off who gain the highest pensions.

Back to Beveridge

Some writers simply advocate that the principle of the Beveridge Report should be implemented, something that was never fully done because benefits were never generous enough to live on. Contributors should receive an *adequate* benefit or pension so that they do not need supplementary benefit. The basic principle would be as follows:

1. Payment of flat-rate social security benefits to all those not in work at a level set at the minimum needs of a single person or married couple, as appropriate. These needs could be set relative to average earnings. Benefits would be taxed.
2. Unconditional child benefit set at a level sufficient to meet the minimum needs of children of different ages.
3. Means-tested benefits only as a last resort; thus the benefit levels would be set sufficiently generously to eliminate most means-tested extras.
4. A tax structure that began to tax above these minimum levels.

The *advantages* of the system would be as follows:

1. It removes the disincentives of the poverty trap, and the indignities and low take-up that result from means-testing.
2. It is simple to understand and administer.
3. It leaves individuals free to add their own private arrangements on top of the basic provision, and gives them an incentive to do

so because they know the income they gain from a private scheme cannot reduce the value of their state pension of benefit.

The *disadvantages* would be as follows:

1. The Beveridge contribution principle gives rights to benefit to those who have the most fortunate employment histories, and discriminates against the disabled, the marginal worker and women, especially divorced and separated women. This can be overcome only by an extensive and generous system of crediting such groups with 'contributions' paid by the Exchequer. The more this is done the more notional becomes the contribution principle.
2. Employers' contributions are passed on in reduced wages or higher prices or result in reduced employment. It would be much more democratic to make the costs clear to those who are paying. National Insurance contributions are taxes. We may as well be honest about them.

One alternative is to continue to give contingent-based benefits – for old age, sickness, and so on – but to finance the benefits out of general taxation or a social security tax that carries no link with benefits and is proportional to income. The 'back to Beveridge' strategy was best discussed in the Meade Report (Meade, 1978).

A two-tier national social security scheme

This model largely accepts the objections to both the occupational benefit and 'back to Beveridge' schemes, but does not wish to break with the contribution principle entirely. It argues for both an adequate means-tested bottom benefit for all categories of need, regardless of whether contributions have ever been paid, and on top of that a second-tier pension. This could be an improved SERPS scheme or funded personal pensions of the kind discussed above, an earnings-related state benefit corresponding to previous earnings and hence previous contributions. The first part would be financed from taxation, the second by earnings-related employee and employer contributions.

The *advantages* claimed for such a scheme are as follows:

1. It provides adequate benefits for the disabled, late entrants to the labour market, those who have spent most of their lives bringing up children or looking after dependants without recourse to means-testing, and at the same level as the flat-rate benefit received by those who have not been in work.
2. The second level provides benefits for all categories of worker, not merely those whose employers can afford an occupational scheme, and also has the advantages advanced above.

A social dividend scheme or a citizen's income

Such a scheme (Pigou, 1920; Rhys Williams, 1943; Jordan, 1987; Parker, 1989; Atkinson, 1995) would give each man, woman and child a sum sufficient for him or her to live on by itself by virtue of their citizenship rather than past contributions, or their capacity to work. It should be paid out of general taxation. Those who worked would pay the taxes to finance the scheme. All other cash benefits and tax reliefs would be abolished. The scheme has a beautiful simplicity which has attracted many. Only a birth certificate would be sufficient to claim benefit.

However, it suffers from major disadvantages which have led many initially attracted to be wary of it, as follows:

1. The guarantee of a living income regardless of work or education could lead to withdrawal from both for the less motivated. Such a scheme for young people in Belgium does seem to have produced these results. The same might be true of married women.
2. It does also mean very high tax rates. A citizen's income of only £40 a week would require a basic tax rate of 38 per cent and higher rates above that.
3. Many of those who would gain would be families with high earnings where the wife did not work.

These difficulties have led Professor Atkinson (1994) to suggest a 'participation income' only available to those who participate in the workforce or undertake functions such as caring. A modified version of such a scheme was put forward for discussion by the Social Justice Commission (1994).

Stakeholder's welfare

Frank Field (1995) advanced a set of proposals that drew on some of these ideas but had a different emphasis. He pointed to the pernicious effects of overlapping and extended means-testing and benefits that derived from no contributory work record. This, he argued, led to a scrounging society. Instead, a stakeholding society would reward those with a contributory work record. A new insurance agency should be created, separated from government, collecting contributions from employers, employees and government. They would each appoint members to a governing board. The government would pay the contributions for the lowest paid, but the board would set the contribution rates and benefits, which would be high enough to take people off means-tested benefits. The government would merely have a veto power.

The difficulties are illustrated by the problems the French have had with a system very like this. It leaves the government in a weak position, having to pick up the costs of benefits non-elected representatives vote for with tax implications they do not have to defend to the electorate. That was precisely why the French government were in the end prepared to battle the issue out on the streets.

Further reading

Do read the Beveridge Report (Cmd 6404 (1942), Social Insurance and Allied Services, London: HMSO), the first part of which is still the most lucid exposition of his case. For a discussion of the ways in which the old Beveridge model no longer meets modern social conditions see S. Baldwin and J. Falkingham (1994), *Social Security and Social Change*, Hemel Hempstead: Harvester. For a full-blooded attack on the Beveridge principle see A. W. Dilnot, J. A. Kay and C. N. Morris (1984), *The Reform of Social Security*, Oxford: Oxford University Press. A good discussion of many of the various alternative models summarized at the end of this chapter is to be found in: Social Justice Commission (1994), *Social Justice: Strategies for national renewal*, London: Vintage, chapter 6.

The economics of social security are best found in N. A. Barr (1993), *The Economics of the Welfare State*, 2nd edn, London: Weidenfeld; A. Dilnot and I. Walker (1989), *The Economics of Social Security*, Oxford: Clarendon Press; and A. B. Atkinson (1989), *Poverty and Social Security*, Hemel Hempstead: Harvester Wheatsheaf.

A useful review of pensions policy options is to be found in A. W. Dilnot, R. Disney, P. Johnson and E. Whitehouse (1994), *Pensions Policy in the UK*, London: Institute of Fiscal Studies.

PART V

The future: towards 2000

CHAPTER 15

CAN WE AFFORD THE WELFARE STATE?

In the first chapter of this book I began by emphasizing that welfare, as I defined it, could be financed and provided in a variety of ways. In the chapters that followed I showed that the ways in which Britons pay for their welfare state have changed significantly in the past decade. Direct income taxation on the highest-income groups has been reduced, but other forms of taxation have risen. The average earner and the poorer households have had to bear a larger part of the burden. Central government determination of both taxes and spending has increased at the expense of local determination. Social spending stabilized as a share of the economic activity in the United Kingdom and other countries in the aftermath of the crises of the mid-1970s. The scale of welfare spending by governments in the largest OECD nations reached a plateau after the rapid increases of the 1960s and early 1970s. The slower growth, or actual decline, in national incomes in the 1970s, and the growing burden of financing unemployment, shook the complacent view that such growth in publicly financed services was inevitable or even desirable. Some writers swung to the opposite extreme, claiming that welfare states were in crisis and that major changes in their finance were necessary and unavoidable (Gough, 1979; OECD, 1981; Mishra, 1983; Offe, 1984). This crisis view was shared by those with very different political values – free-market Conservatives and Marxists. Both believed that a mixed economy with a largely publicly provided element was inherently incompatible with a capitalist economic structure. The radical right argued that the balance must shift decisively towards individual purchases in a private market and that voters would support such a move. Marxists argued that either a *financial* crisis would result from trying to pay for the welfare sector out of taxation, or a *legitimacy* crisis would result from trying to dismantle it.

Neither of these predictions have been borne out by the experience of the 1980s and 1990s. The 1980s were a decade in which radical right ideas were influential with Conservative governments, and others in such diverse countries as Chile and Israel (Glennerster and Midgley, 1991). Yet, overall, as we have seen earlier, there has been neither a collapse of welfare spending with a major move to the market nor a revolutionary crisis as a result of restraining growth in social spending. Instead, there has been an adjustment to the slower growth of the western economies and a stabilization of state spending. The United Kingdom has, however, gone further than most other economies in shifting responsibility for future *pensions* from the taxpayer to the individual. The erosion of the real value of the state pension in relation to average earnings and the scaling down of the benefits derived from SERPS mean that the United Kingdom will enter the next century with lower commitments to its elderly than any other advanced country. A study by OECD in 1995 showed that by the year 2025, or soon after, Japan, France, Germany and Italy will be spending 15 per cent of the national incomes on social security pensions. Even Canada and the United States will be spending 8 per cent or more. The United Kingdom will only be spending 6 per cent (OECD, 1995). The bulk of the burden of supporting ourselves in old age will fall on families direct.

The forms of provision in the United Kingdom have changed too. There has been more emphasis on mixed forms of provision and on market-type forms of organization within the state sector (Glennerster and Le Grand, 1995). There has been an attempt to increase the efficiency of the social welfare systems and to get more value for taxpayers' money. The political system in the United Kingdom has responded incrementally to the severe economic pressures since 1976 (Glennerster, 1995b) and is likely to continue to do so.

The market for welfare

It is possible to think of the political market for welfare services as an extension of the traditional market for other goods and services

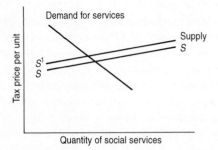

Figure 15.1 The political market for social services

(see Figure 15.1). On the horizontal axis in the figure we measure the quantity of service provided; on the vertical axis we measure the price the public has to pay for the services it receives – the tax price or the level of taxation that has to be set in order to pay for a given level of service or a given policy. This might be the expansion of higher education or a higher level of old age pension.

The supply

It will be clear that the more units of tax-based social services are provided, the higher the total cost. It is also probable that unit costs tend to rise the larger the sector grows. The most expensive resource is the staff employed, and the more highly qualified the staff, the more difficult it is to recruit them. The more physics teachers you need, the more you are likely to have to pay to employ the same quality of staff. The supply curve therefore *slopes* upwards to the right. The cost per unit of service provided rises the more you seek to provide.

The price of a service like education or health is also likely to rise as wages in the rest of the economy rise. It is a very labour-intensive activity. As the workers in the Ford Motor car plants raise their productivity and earn more, so it becomes necessary to pay public sector workers more to retain the services of staff who are as well qualified. This has the effect of *shifting* the supply curve upwards, from S to S^1. It increases the price of supplying a given policy: setting a maximum class size of twenty-five for all secondary science pupils, for example. The price of medical treatments and procedures tends to rise faster than general costs in the economy too. These costs are pulled up by advances in medical science in other countries where prices and wages are higher. Other factors can have the same price effect. A change in the population structure is a case in point. The policy of giving an adequate pension to all over 65 becomes more expensive if the number of over-65s increases.

The cost of producing social services has risen for all these reasons and has an inherent tendency to do so. In short, S^1 has kept shifting upwards. The tax price people must pay to buy the same quantity of care or service has risen. In a traditional supply and demand model we would expect the demand to fall off. The quantity of services supplied through the political marketplace will tend to fall as voter resistance to tax increases builds up. At the same time, however, demand may increase.

The demand

Pressure groups representing service users, their carers, or those who work in the services will articulate demands on the political system. They will press for higher standards in education, better old age pensions or shorter waiting times for hospital. Politicians will have to respond if they want votes, but they will also know that many voters want lower taxes, or at least taxes not to be increased. Hence the downward sloping demand curve. The demand falls more as the price of responding to these demands for better services increases. Different parties compete by offering different mixes of high benefits and high taxes and low benefits and low taxes. It may not be that clear in their manifestos, but the public are pretty quick to see what the issues are. The debate may not simply centre on the tax price of an improved service but on other supposed effects. It may be possible to persuade the electorate that an increase in social welfare spending is bad for the economy because it takes people away from really 'productive work'. Others may try to persuade the voters that more education is necessary for the health of the economy. There are also other extraneous things in the electoral basket, like feelings towards the Falklands war, or Europe, that cloud the clear choice on that one issue. But in a competitive electoral situation parties will make adjustments to the contents of their baskets to appeal more closely to the revealed preferences of the electorate.

Over time, those preferences may change too, shifting between tax cuts with low benefits to higher taxes with higher benefits. There is evidence that major shifts have occurred in such attitudes during the past twenty years in the United Kingdom. Thus the balance between supply and demand factors will vary through time with no predictable resting place.

Supply-side factors into the next century

Population changes

It is in the early and late years of life that we are heavy users of the social services. The costs of schooling and further and higher education are also heavily age based. Even if the size of a population remains constant, the fact that it has a higher number of elderly in it will affect the costs of providing the same level of services. Over the last half century this has been one of the most important

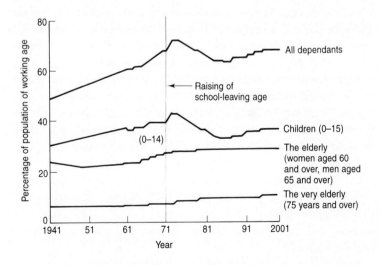

Figure 15.2 The dependent age population of the United Kingdom, 1941–2001 (Source: Central Statistical Office, *Social Trends*, various editions)

factors increasing the cost of social policy. It is not just that more has to be paid out in terms of pensions or care but that the size of the working population relative to the 'economically inactive' one has declined. This means that the tax cost per worker is higher because the number of workers paying taxes is relatively low. The traditional way to think about this problem is in terms of a dependency ratio – the number of people in the age groups that do not work, expressed as a percentage of those that do. This is done in Figure 15.2.

It can be seen from Figure 15.2 that the United Kingdom went through its major adjustment to a more age-dependent population in the period between 1941 and 1971. Since then it has benefited from a demographic bonus followed by a period of relative stability. Much of that bonus has been dissipated, of course, by the reduction in the numbers of working age who were actually working. This illustrates the weakness of the dependency ratio as a policy tool. It ignores critical features of the labour market, above all the percentage of women who are working and the unemployed. The period of apparently rising dependency from 1941 to 1971 was relieved by the rapid rise in the number of women who entered the labour market. In the late 1980s and the 1990s the total size of the dependent age groups has begun to rise again but nothing like as fast. By the year 2030 the United Kingdom will have a higher ratio of workers to retired people than other major economies (see Figure 15.3). Moreover, recent policy changes – notably, the falling level of state pensions relative to earnings and raising the pension age for women to 65 – are going to reduce the level of social security contributions that will be necessary to finance pensions in the next century. The government actuary, who has the task of forecasting the state of the National Insurance Fund which we discussed in the last chapter, has calculated that the combined employer/employee contribution should be able to fall from the 18.5 per cent in 1994/5 to 15.8 per cent or 15.9 per cent by the year 2040/1. No one should take the precise figure seriously, but the *downward* trend should correct the alarmist talk of demographic time bombs. For more discussion of this see Hills (1993, 1995b).

Pensions are not the only additional demands that an older population will put on the welfare system. We have seen that health spending and personal social services spending are both

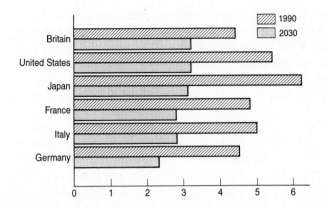

Figure 15.3 Ratio of people of working age to retired people in different countries, 1990–2030 (Source: *The Economist*, 27 January 1996; World Bank; ILO)

heavy spenders at the older age ranges. Hills (1993) reviewed all these demands and modelled what would happen if a future government were to *stop* reducing the real pension in relation to earnings and were to retain the standards of health and education spending as they were in 1993. This was an attempt to see what it would cost to retain the welfare state in its traditional form, taking account of the more elderly population. He showed that the impact of population change made some difference but not an unsustainable one. Over the next half century, up to 2040, the share of the GDP that would have to be devoted to the services we have discussed in this book would need to rise by 0.5 per cent every decade until that date – from about 25 per cent to about 30 per cent, in short. That would bring the United Kingdom up to the level currently spent in the rest of Europe, which is not inconceivable in political or economic terms. It is difficult to square, though, with a commitment to a 20 per cent rate of income tax. The choice at this point becomes political, not economic.

The economy

The ultimate supply-side factor is the health of the economy. The faster the economy grows, the more revenue the government can raise, while still keeping the tax *rates* the same. If we buy more goods with our higher incomes, VAT receipts rise automatically. No Chancellor has to come to the dispatch box in the House of Commons and announce a tax increase to pay for better schools.

In the decades immediately after the Second World War the UK growth rate was, on average, half that of its major industrial rivals in Europe. That meant that politicians had a smaller growth dividend to allocate in those years for service improvements than their continental counterparts. In the 1980s – indeed, since the United Kingdom became an oil state – its rate of growth recovered to its long-run average since the war of over 2 per cent per annum. Countries in Europe have fallen nearer to the same kind of rate of growth. Productivity gains are more difficult to make in already advanced service societies. The poor growth of the US economy in the past two decades is a warning. Modest long-term growth seems the best prospect we can look forward to in the next century. It means a modest growth in individual and family income and in the absolute levels of personal prosperity. That is likely to constrain politicians' capacity to raise taxes and increase the standard of social services merely by spending a lot more.

However, growth brings costs as well as benefits. The main costs may be environmental, and to counter environmental damage is going to be both expensive and higher on the political agenda.

Welfare spending: burden or boost?

In the 1970s social welfare spending was widely blamed for the economic crisis of the time. Bacon and Eltis (1976) were two of the most influential critics, but similar critiques appeared in other countries. Social services took resources that could be better used to build up the productive growth-related sectors of the economy. They crowded out capital expenditure by laying first claim on the savings of the population, thus denying them to industry. They took labour from the rest of the economy, thus increasing the shortages faced by industry and forcing up wages. These arguments convinced many people in all political parties.

In fact, the massive reduction in public sector investment in the late 1970s and 1980s has not produced an equivalently massive increase in manufacturing investment. The notion that there is an overall shortage of labour, when unemployment levels are so much higher than in the decades after the war, is implausible. There are shortages of skilled people and it has begun to dawn, even on politicians, that maybe this is the consequence of too little, rather than too much, spending on education and training. Professor Moser's (1990) address to the British Association on the subject making this point drew a quite unprecedentedly favourable response, and was followed by the report of the National Commission for Education (1993) which he inspired. The view that economic prosperity depends on the quality of human capital and the lifetime education of the population has become an orthodoxy of all political parties. Titmuss's (1968) 'welfare as a burden' model could be waning again in the light of the experience of the 1980s and 1990s.

In Chapter 2 we saw that modern economics has developed an increasing understanding of why some forms of social provision may be more efficient than the private market. Not to allocate resources publicly in those circumstances reduces the efficiency of the economy and wastes resources that could be available elsewhere. If the UK National Health Service can deliver the same or similar standard of health with 7 per cent of the total national income as a country like the United States can with 15 per cent, that means that UK citizens have 8 per cent more income to spend on other things.

The health example also illustrates another point that is often lost in political argument. The fact that tax-funded services are reduced does not leave the individual with a lot more money to spend on summer vacations and posh restaurants. He or she needs to look carefully at the cost of taking out private health insurance and school fees. There *is* no free lunch or health care either. Faced with that possibility, the family may find itself in for a rude shock. The average American family will have to pay at least $5,000 a year for a health scheme with reasonable cover and even that will not cover the range of risks that the NHS does. Moreover, tax bills to pay for the very elderly and mentally ill and disabled will still be there unless we let them die on the streets.

The argument comes down to which form of funding you believe is most efficient and equitable. For those who, like Professor Snower (1993), believe that the efficiency effects of paying for a large welfare sector through taxation are too high a price to pay, then the case for reducing that share stands, whatever the politics. For those who think the efficient and equitable balance lies with the present kind of system, the politics of raising the money matters.

The demand side

How much are people prepared to support political parties that raise taxes *and* service standards? Again the story of the last part of the 1990s may be different from the 1980s. Public opinion polls in the period between 1960 and the mid-1970s suggested that support for social spending was steadily declining. By 1974 (Whitely, 1981), support for *increasing* taxes and service levels had disappeared. Most people favoured the existing levels of spending and taxation to support social services, but about 30 per cent thought service spending and social benefits were too generous. By the 1979 General Election this view had gained more support. Mrs Thatcher therefore had identified a real underlying shift in public priorities. The economic crisis of the mid-1970s had reduced the growth in incomes. The higher levels of taxation had reduced the real levels of take-home pay for the average family. Their private standard of living had fallen. It was not surprising that so many welcomed the chance to keep more of their pay and enjoy a reduction in taxation, especially if they were told that this could all be done by cutting out inefficiency and waste and not by reducing service standards.

It soon became evident, however, that things were not that simple. Very soon some reductions in service levels became apparent. Even where they did not, and services grew in scale, so did the demands upon them. The level of service per person at risk sometimes fell. This more complex story is set out in some detail in Hills (1990).

Thus the government were right to claim that more money was being devoted to social policy, but social needs and expectations were outpacing it. Evidence for this last point is of two kinds. The first kind of evidence is that private spending on services like education went on rising at the same rate as, or rather faster than, incomes (see Chapter 12 and Glennerster and Low, 1990). In short, people were prepared to spend more on education out of their own pockets as their incomes rose, but the state was not. In local authority areas that had cut education spending most in the 1980s, the rise in private school spending was greatest, standardizing for relevant factors. The rising expectations of families for their children's education were not being matched by the state and people voted with their feet, or their children's feet. The same kind of story was found in health (Besley *et al.*, 1996).

The second kind of evidence is to be found in surveys of social attitudes. Over the 1980s the British Social Attitudes Survey

(Jowell *et al.*, 1983–95) has put the same set of questions to a national sample of the British population on these issues. They have also asked the same questions of people in other countries (Jowell *et al.*, 1989). The results are striking.

British attitudes to spending and taxing

Despite the Thatcher years, the British population's support for the view that the government has prime responsibility for certain aspects of social life remains strong and stronger than in many other countries. Nearly the whole sample respond by saying that

Table 15.1 Attitudes to the state in different countries, 1988

Question	Percentage of respondents replying positively				
	Britain	United States	Australia	West Germany	Italy
Is it definitely the government's responsibility to:					
Provide health care for the sick?	86	36	60	54	87
Provide a decent standard of living for elderly people?	79	43	62	56	82
Provide a decent standard of living for unemployed people?	45	16	15	24	40
Reduce income differences between rich and poor people?	48	17	24	28	48

Source: Jowell *et al.* (1989).

they feel it is the government's responsibility to provide health care for the sick, and the percentage saying so had not changed since 1985. The same was true of its obligation to provide a decent standard of living for the elderly. Thus the view that government should, or perhaps could, provide an economic climate in which everyone had a job has declined. However, the idea that society has a collective responsibility for health, education, support for the elderly and income support and redistribution more generally has not, and remains very strong in the United Kingdom. Just how strong can be seen by comparing the responses to the same set of questions addressed to people in other countries (see Table 15.1).

In Britain in 1988, 86 per cent of people believed it was *definitely* the state's job to provide health care, but only 36 per cent of those in the United States thought that. Only Italians felt as strongly about this as the British. In every society, providing a decent standard of living for the unemployed is given a much lower priority. Even so, 45 per cent of British respondents felt this was definitely the government's job, compared with only 16 per cent of those in the United States and only 24 per cent in West Germany. When it comes to wanting to see more spent on these services by the state, again the British are way ahead (see Table 15.2). Even before the easing of east–west relations and the end of the Berlin wall, defence expenditure came low on most people's priorities; only

Table 15.2 Those wanting more state spending on various services in different countries, 1988

Service	Percentage wanting more/much more state spending				
	Britain	United States	Australia	West Germany	Italy
Health	88	60	62	52	81
Old age pensions	75	44	55	46	76
Education	75	66	64	40	63
Unemployment benefit	41	25	13	35	57
Police and law enforcement	40	51	67	30	48
The environment	37	43	32	83	61
Military and defence	17	20	46	6	12
Culture and the arts	10	16	10	14	33

Source: Jowell *et al.* (1989).

17 per cent of Britons and 6 per cent of West Germans put it on their shopping list. Culture and the arts came even lower, it is fair to say, in all countries except Germany and Italy!

How did these preferences stand up to the tougher question, 'Would you be prepared to pay higher taxes to get these better services?', and how did the Thatcher years change things? The number of British people saying that they wanted government to reduce taxes and spend less was never great – 9 per cent in 1983, but it had fallen to only 3 per cent in 1990 and risen only slightly to 4 per cent in 1994 (see Table 15.3). By contrast the number who said they wanted to increase taxes and spend more rose in the same period from 32 per cent to 58 per cent.

Health was the top priority, but with more people wanting to spend more on pensions and education as the decade passed. A class analysis of these results is interesting. The desire to *reduce* taxes and service levels is greatest amongst the working class and least amongst the 'salaried'. Support for high-quality services like health and education is strong amongst the new middle class, and they are the fastest-growing part of the population.

Levels of dissatisfaction with state social services rose in the 1980s, but this led not to more support for privatization, but to a view that more resources and more taxes were necessary to improve them (Taylor-Gooby, 1991). The shift in attitudes, at least as expressed in these surveys, does seem to be more favourable to paying for welfare than it was in the late 1970s.

Table 15.3 Attitudes in Britain to raising taxes, 1983–94

Question	Percentage of respondents replying positively			
	1983	1986	1990	1994
If the government had to choose, it should:				
Reduce taxes and spend less on health, education and social benefits?	9	5	3	4
Keep the taxes and spending at the same level as now?	54	44	37	33
Increase taxes and spend more?	32	46	54	58

Source: Taylor-Gooby (1995).

At the same time, if public services do not keep pace with the rising standards and expectations that families have for their children or their own health, they will hesitate much less than their parents did before they have recourse to the private market. And more families will have the money to do so. The shadow of the war and collective feelings of communality have long since waned. Frustrated by state schools or the local hospital, people will do what they can afford to obtain the services they want.

Forty-five years ago, in a ravaged economy, when real incomes were less than half what they are today, people voted for what came to be called the welfare state, and paid the price, and voted to continue affording it. Will their grandchildren do the same in the next century?

Further reading

Perhaps the most lucid discussion of the issues discussed in this chapter is to be found in J. Hills (1993) *The Future of Welfare*, York: Joseph Rowntree Foundation. See also his more recent discussion in J. Hills (1995b), 'Funding the welfare state', *Oxford Review of Economic Policy*, **11**, no. 3, pp. 27–43. The whole issue is devoted to the 'Future of the Welfare State'. For a very different view, see D. Snower (1993), 'The future of the welfare state', *Economic Journal*, **103**, pp. 700–17.

The *British Social Attitudes Survey*, published annually, reports regular surveys of British public opinion including its views about social service spending and taxation (see R. Jowell *et al.* (1983–95), *British Social Attitudes*, Aldershot: Gower and Dartmouth Press).

BIBLIOGRAPHY

Aaron, H. J. (1982), *The Economic Effects of Social Security*, Washington, DC: Brookings Institution.

Aaron, H. J. and Swartz, B. (1984), *The Painful Prescription*, Washington, DC: Brookings Institution.

Abel-Smith, B. (1958), 'Whose welfare state?', in N. MacKenzie (ed.), *Conviction*, London: McGibbon & Kee.

Abel-Smith, B. (1964), *The Hospitals 1800–1948*, London: Heinemann.

Abel-Smith, B. (1976), *Value for Money in Health Services*, London: Heinemann.

Abel-Smith, B. (1984), *Cost Containment in Health Care*, Occasional Papers on Social Administration no. 73, London: Bedford Square Press.

Abel-Smith, B. and Townsend, P. (1984), *Social Security: The real agenda*, London: Fabian Society.

Advisory Council for Adult and Continuing Education (1982), *Continuing Education: From policies to practice*, London: ACACE.

Alt, J. E. (1971), 'Some social and political correlates of county borough expenditures', *British Journal of Political Science*, **1**, pt 1, pp. 49–62.

Armstrong Committee (1980), *Budgetary Reform in the United Kingdom*, Oxford: Oxford University Press.

Arrow, K. (1963), 'The welfare economics of medical care', *American Economic Review*, **53**, pp. 941–73.

Ashford, A. E., Berne, R. and Schramm, R. (1976), 'The expenditure-financing decision in British local government', *Policy and Politics*, **5**, no. 1, pp. 5–24.

Atkinson, A. B. (1969), *Poverty in Britain and the Reform of Social Security*, Cambridge: Cambridge University Press.

Atkinson, A. B. (1975), 'Income distribution and social change revisited', *Journal of Social Policy*, **4**, pt 1, pp. 57–68.

Atkinson, A. B. (1981), *On the Switch to Indirect Taxation*, Taxation and Incentives Research Project Paper no. 24, London: LSE.

Atkinson, A. B. (1989), *Poverty and Social Security*, Hemel Hempstead, Harvester Wheatsheaf.

Atkinson, A. B. (1994), *Pensions for Today and Tomorrow*, London: Institute for Gerontology.

Atkinson, A. B. (1995), *Public Economics in Action: In the basic income/ flat tax proposal*, Oxford: Oxford University Press.

Atkinson, A. B. and King, M. A. (1982), 'Housing policy taxation and reform', *Midland Bank Review*, Spring, pp. 7–15.

Atkinson, A. B. and Stiglitz, J. E. (1980), *Lectures in Public Economics*, London and New York: McGraw-Hill.

Audit Commission (1984), *The Impact on Local Authorities' Economy, Efficiency and Effectiveness of the Block Grant System*, London: HMSO.

Audit Commission (1986a), *Managing the Crisis in Council Housing*, London: HMSO.

Audit Commission (1986b), *Making a Reality of Community Care*, London: HMSO.

Audit Commission (1989), *Better Financial Management*, Management Paper no. 3, London: HMSO.

Audit Commission (1991), *Two B's or Not?: Schools' and colleges' 'A' level performance*, London: HMSO.

Audit Commission (1996), *What the Doctor Ordered: A study of GP fundholders in England and Wales*, London: HMSO.

Bacon, R. and Eltis, W. (1976), *Britain's Economic Problem: Too few producers*, London: Macmillan.

Bailey, S. J. (1995), *Public Sector Economics*, London: Macmillan.

Bailey, S. J. and Bruce, A. (1994), 'Funding the NHS: the continuing search for alternatives', *Journal of Social Policy*, **23**, pt 4, pp. 489–516.

Bains Committee (1972), *The New Local Authorities: Management and structure*, London: HMSO.

Baldwin, P. (1990), *The Politics of Social Solidarity*, Cambridge: Cambridge University Press.

Baldwin, S. and Falkingham, J. (1994), *Social Security and Social Change*, Hemel Hempstead: Harvester.

Banks, T. (1979), 'DHSS programme budgeting', in T. Booth (ed.), *Planning for Welfare*, London: Martin Robertson and Basil Blackwell.

Barclay Committee (1982), *Social Workers: Their roles and tasks*, London: Bedford Square Press.

Barnes, J. and Barr, N. (1988), *Strategies for Higher Education: The alternative White Paper*, David Hume Paper no. 10, Aberdeen: Aberdeen University.

Barr, N. A. (1981), 'Empirical definitions of the poverty line', *Policy and Politics*, **9**, no. 1, January, pp. 1–21.

Barr, N. A. (1989), *Student Loans: The next steps*, David Hume Paper no. 15, Aberdeen: Aberdeen University.

Barr, N. A. (1992), 'Economic theory and the welfare state: a survey and interpretation', *Journal of Economic Literature*, **30**, June, pp. 741–803.

Barr, N. A. (1993), *The Economics of the Welfare State*, 2nd edn, London: Weidenfeld.

Barr, N. A. (1994), *Labour Markets and Social Policy in Central and Eastern Europe: Transition and beyond*, Oxford: World Bank and Oxford University Press.

Barr, N. A. and Carrier, J. (1977), 'Women's aid groups: the economic case for state assistance to battered wives', *Policy and Politics*, **6**, no. 3, pp. 333–50.

Barr, N. A. and Coulter, F. (1990), 'Social security: solution or problem?', in J. Hills (ed.), *The State of Welfare*, Oxford: Oxford University Press.

Barr, N. A., Falkingham, J. and Glennerster, H. (1994), *Funding Higher Education*, Poole: BP Educational.

Barr, N. A., Glennerster, H. and Le Grand, J. (1988), *Reform and the National Health Service*, Welfare State Discussion Paper no. 32, Suntory and Toyota International Centres for Economics and Related Disciplines, London: LSE.

Barr, N. A., Glennerster, H. and Le Grand, J. (1989), 'Working for patients: the right approach?', *Social Policy and Administration*, **23**, no. 2, pp. 117–27.

Bartlett, W. (1991), 'Quasi markets and contracts: a markets and hierarchies perspective on NHS reform', *Public Money*, **11**, no. 3, pp. 53–61.

Baumol, W. (1967), 'Macroeconomics of unbalanced growth: anatomy of urban crisis', *American Economic Review*, **57**, no. 3, pp. 415–26.

Bebbington, A. and Davies, B. (1993), 'Effective targeting of community care: the case of the home help service', *Journal of Social Policy*, **22**, pt 3, pp. 373–91.

Bebbington, A. and Kelly, A. (1995), 'Expenditure planning in the personal social services: unit costs in the 1980s', *Journal of Social Policy*, **24**, pt 3, pp. 385–411.

Becker, G. S. (1976), *The Economic Approach to Human Behavior*, Chicago: University of Chicago Press.

Bennett, R. (ed.) (1990), *Decentralisation, Local Governments and Markets: Towards a post welfare agenda*, Oxford: Oxford University Press.

Besley, T., Hall, J. and Preston, I. (1996), *Private Health Insurance and the State of the NHS*, London: Institute for Fiscal Studies.

Beveridge, W. (1948), *Voluntary Action*, London: Allen & Unwin.

Beveridge Report (1942), *Social Insurance and Allied Services*, Cmd 6404, London: HMSO.

Billis, D. (1989), *A Story of the Voluntary Sector: Implications of policy and practice*, Centre for Voluntary Organisation, London: LSE.

Billis, D. (1993), *Organising Public and Voluntary Agencies*, London: Routledge.

Billis, D. and Glennerster, H. (1995), 'Human service non profits: towards a theory of comparative advantage', paper given to the Social Policy Association Annual Conference Sheffield, London: LSE.

Blackstone, T. (1971), *A Fair Start*, London: Allen Lane.

Blackstone, T. and Plowden, W. (1988), *Inside the Think Tank: Advising the Cabinet 1971–1983*, London: Heinemann.

Blair, P. (1991), 'Fees and charges: an underdeveloped local authority resource', *Local Government Studies*, **17**, no. 2.

Blake, D. and Ormerod, P. (1980), *The Economics of Prosperity*, London: Grant McIntyre.

Blau, P. (1964), *Power and Exchange in Social Life*, New York: Wiley.

Boaden, N. (1971), *Urban Policy Making*, Cambridge: Cambridge University Press.

Board of Inland Revenue (1983), *Cost of Tax Reliefs for Pension Schemes: Appropriate statistical approaches*, London: Inland Revenue.

Booth, T. (1979), *Planning for Welfare*, Oxford: Martin Robertson and Basil Blackwell.

Borcherding, T. E. (1977), *Budgets and Bureaucrats: The sources of government growth*, Durham, NC: Duke University Press.

Bosanquet, N. (1984), *Extending Choice for Mentally Handicapped People: The case for service credits*, London: MIND.

Bosworth, B. (1996), 'Fund accumulation: How much, how managed?', in Diamond, P. A., Lindeman, D. C. and Young, H. (eds), *Social Security: What role for the future?*, Washington, DC: Brookings Institution and National Academy of Social Insurance.

Bowley, M. (1945), *Housing and the State 1919–44*, London: Allen & Unwin.

Bradford, D. F., Malt, R. A. and Oates, W. E. (1969), 'The rising cost of local public services: some evidence and reflections', *National Tax Journal*, June.

Bradshaw, J. (1991), 'Social security expenditure in the 1990s', *Public Money and Management*, **11**, no. 4, pp. 25–9.

Bradshaw, J. and Piachaud, D. (1980), *Child Support in the European Community*, Occasional Paper on Social Administration, London: Bedford Square Press.

Bramley, G., Evans, A., Leather, P. and Lambert, C. (1983), *Grant Related Expenditure: A review of the system*, Working Paper no. 29, Bristol: School of Advanced Urban Studies.

Brannan, J. and Wilson, G. (eds) (1987), *Give and Take in Families*, London: Allen & Unwin.

Brennan, G. and Buchanan, J. M. (1980), *The Power to Tax: Analytical foundations of a fiscal constitution*, Cambridge: Cambridge University Press.

Breton, A. (1974), *The Economic Theory of Representative Government*, London: Macmillan.

British Medical Association (1970), *Health Service Financing*, London: BMA.

Brittain, J. A. (1972), *The Pay Roll for Social Security*, Washington, DC: Brookings Institution.

Brown, C. V. (1983), *Taxation and the Incentive to Work*, Oxford: Oxford University Press.

Brown, C. V. and Levin, E. (1974), 'The effects of income tax on overtime: the results of a national survey', *Economic Journal*, **84**, no. 336, pp. 833–48.

Bull, D. (1980), *What Price 'Free' Education?*, Poverty Pamphlet no. 48, London: Child Poverty Action Group.

Burtless, G. and Housman, R. (1978), 'The effect of taxation on labour supply: evaluating the Gary negative income tax experiment', *Journal of Political Economy*, pp. 1103–30.

Butler, D., Adonis, A. and Travers, T. (1994), *Failure in British Government: The politics of the poll tax*, Oxford: Oxford University Press.

Buxton, M. J. and Klein, R. (1975), 'Distribution of hospital provision: policy themes', *British Medical Journal*, **8**, February.

Buxton, M. J. and Klein, R. (1978), *Allocating Health Services: A commentary on the report of the Resource Allocation Working Party*, Royal Commission on the National Health Service, Research Paper no. 3, London: HMSO.

Byrne, T. (1995), *Local Government in Britain: Everyone's guide to how it all works*, Harmondsworth: Penguin.

Carr-Hill, R. (1990), 'RAWP is dead: long live RAWP', in A. J. Culyer, A. K. Maynard and S. W. Posnett (eds), *Competition in Healthcare: Reforming the NHS*, London: Macmillan.

Carr-Hill, R., Hardman, G., Martin, S., Peacock, S., Sheldon, T. A. and Smith, P. (1994), *Formula for Distributing NHS Revenues Based on Small Area Use of Hospital Beds*, Centre for Health Economics, York: University of York.

Central Statistical Office (1995a), *Social Trends 1995*, London: HMSO.

Central Statistical Office (1995b), *United Kingdom National Accounts*, London: HMSO.

Central Statistical Office (1995c), *Economic Trends*, November, London: HMSO.

Central Statistical Office (1995d), *Economic Trends*, December, London: HMSO.

Centre for Policy Studies (1983), *Personal and Portable Pensions – For All*, London: CPS.

Charities Aid Foundation (1990), *Charity Trends 1990*, Tonbridge: Charities Aid Foundation.

Charities Aid Foundation (1995), *Dimensions of the Voluntary Sector*, Tonbridge: Charities Aid Foundation.

Chartered Institute of Public Finance and Accountancy (CIPFA) (1984), *Health Care UK 1984*, London: CIPFA.

Child Poverty Action Group (1995a), *Rights Guide to Non-Means Tested Benefits*, London: CPAG.

Child Poverty Action Group (1995b), *National Welfare Benefits Handbook*, London: CPAG.

Chubb, J. E. and Moe, T. E. (1990), *Politics, Markets and America's Schools*, Washington, DC: Brookings Institution.

Clotfelter, C. (1985), *Tax Incentives and Charitable Giving*, Chicago: University of Chicago Press.

Cmd 1581 (1922), *Report of the Committee on National Expenditure*, London: HMSO.

Cmd 6404 (1942), *Social Insurance and Allied Services*, London: HMSO.

Cmd 6730 (1946), *Report by the Government Actuary on the Financial Provisions of the National Insurance Bill*, London: HMSO.

Cmnd 1432 (1961), *Control of Public Expenditure*, Plowden Report, London: HMSO.

Cmnd 4755 (1971), *Strategy for Pensions*, London: HMSO.

Cmnd 7615 (1979), *Royal Commission on the National Health Service, Report*, London: HMSO.

Cmnd 7746 (1979), *The Government's Expenditure Plans 1980/81*, London: HMSO.

Cmnd 7866 (1980), *The Government's Public Expenditure Plans 1980/81 to 1983/84*, London: HMSO.

Cmnd 8449 (1981), *Alternatives to Domestic Rates*, London: HMSO.

Cmnd 8789 (1983), *The Government's Public Expenditure Plans 1983/4 to 1985/6*, London: HMSO.

Cmnd 9008 (1983), *Rates*, London: HMSO.

Cmnd 9058 (1983), *Financial Management in Government Departments*, London: HMSO.

Cmnd 9135 (1984), *Training for Jobs*, London: HMSO.

Cmnd 9143 (1984), *The Government's Expenditure Plans 1984/5 to 1986/7*, London: HMSO.

Cmnd 9189 (1984), *The Next Ten Years: Public expenditure and taxation into the 1990s*, London: HMSO.

Cmnd 9428 (1985), *The Government's Expenditure Plans 1985/86 to 1987/88*, London: HMSO.

Cmnd 9714 (1986), *Paying for Local Government*, London: HMSO.

Cm 555 (1989), *Working for Patients*, London: HMSO.

Cm 849 (1989), *Caring for People*, London: HMSO.

Cm 1021 (1990), *The Government's Expenditure Plans 1990/91 to 1992/93*, London: HMSO.

Cm 1513 (1991), *The Government's Expenditure Plans 1991/92 to 1993/94*, Department of Health and Office of Population Censuses and Surveys, Departmental Report, London: HMSO.

Cm 1514 (1991), *The Government's Expenditure Plans 1991/92 to 1993/94: Social security*, London: HMSO.

Cm 1541 (1991), *Higher Education: A new framework*, London: HMSO.

Cm 1867 (1992), *Budgetary Reform*, London: HMSO.

Cm 2812 (1995), *The Government's Expenditure Plans: Department of Health 1995/6 to 1997/8*, London: HMSO.

Cm 2813 (1995), *The Government's Expenditure Plans: Social security 1995/6 to 1997/8*, London: HMSO.

Cockburn, C. (1977), *The Local State*, London: Pluto Press.

Collard, D. (1978), *Altruism and Economy: A study in non-selfish economics*, Oxford: Martin Robertson.

Coons, J. and Sugarman, S. (1978), *Education by Choice: The case for family control*, Berkeley: University of California Press.

Coughlin, R. M. (1980), *Ideology, Public Opinion and Welfare Policy*, Institute of International Studies, Berkeley: University of California.

CPRS (1975), *A Joint Framework for Social Policy*, London: HMSO.

CPRS (1980), *Education, Training and Industrial Performance*, London: HMSO.

Crew, M. and Young, A. (1977), *Vouchers for Students*, London: Institute of Economic Affairs.

Crosland, C. A. R. (1956), *The Future of Socialism*, London: Jonathan Cape.

Crosland, C. A. R. (1962), *The Conservative Enemy*, London: Jonathan Cape.

Culyer, A. J. (1976), *Need and the National Health Service*, London: Martin Robertson.

Culyer, A. J. (1980), *The Political Economy of Social Policy*, Oxford: Martin Robertson.

Culyer, A. J. (1990), *The Internal Market: An acceptable means to a desirable end*, Discussion Paper no. 67, Centre for Health Economics, York: University of York.

Danziger, J. N. (1978), *Making Budgets: Public resource allocation*, London: Sage.

Davies, B. P. (1968), *Social Needs and Resources in Local Services*, London: Michael Joseph.

Davies, B. P. (1978), *Universality, Selectivity and Effectiveness in Social Policy*, London: Heinemann.

Davies, B. P. and Bebbington, A. C. (1980), 'Territorial need indicators: a new approach. Parts I and II', *Journal of Social Policy*, **9**, pts 2 and 4, pp. 145–68 and 433–62.

Davies, B. P. and Challis, D. (1986), *Matching Resources to Needs in Community Care*, Aldershot: Gower.

Davies, G. and Piachaud, D. (1983), 'Social policy and the economy', in H. Glennerster, *The Future of the Welfare State*, London: Heinemann.

Davies, H. and Joshi, H. (1994), 'Sex sharing and the distribution of income', *Journal of Social Policy*, **23**, pt 3, pp. 301–40.

Day, P. and Klein, R. (1990), *Inspecting the Inspectorates*, Centre for the Analysis of Social Policy, Bath: Bath University.

Deakin, N. (1983), *The Voluntary Sector and the Future of London Government*, London: London Voluntary Services Council.

Demone, H. W. and Gibelman, M. (eds) (1989), *Services for Sale: Purchasing health and human services*, New Brunswick, NJ and London: Rutgers University Press.

DES (1967), *Children and their Primary Schools*, The Plowden Report, London: HMSO.

DES (1968), *Public Schools Commission: First report*, London: HMSO.

DES (1970), *Public Schools Commission: Second report*, London: HMSO.

DES (1983), *Statistics of Finance and Awards 1981–2*, London: HMSO.

DES (1988), *Top Up Loans for Students*, Cm 520, London: HMSO.

DES (1991), *Higher Education: A new framework*, Cm 1541, London: HMSO.

DFE (1995), *Government Expenditure Plans 1995/6–1997/8, Department for Education*, London: HMSO.

DHSS (1976a), *Priorities for Health and Personal Services in England*, London: HMSO.

DHSS (1976b), *Sharing Resources for Health in England*, London: HMSO.

DHSS (1976c), *The National Health Service Planning System*, London: HMSO.

DHSS (1976d), *Sharing Resources for Health in England*, Report of the Resource Allocation Working Party, London: HMSO.

DHSS (1977), *The Way Forward*, London: HMSO.

DHSS (1980), *Inequalities in Health: Report of a research working group*, The Black Report, London: HMSO.

DHSS (1981), *Care in Action*, London: HMSO.

DHSS (1983), *Health Care and its Costs*, London: HMSO.

DHSS (1984), *Population, Pension Costs and Pensioners' Incomes*, London: HMSO.

DHSS and the Thames Region (1979), *Assessing Target Allocations within the Thames Region*, London: HMSO.

DHSS (1989), *Review of the RAWP Formula*, London: HMSO.

Dilnot, A. and Walker, I. (1989), *The Economics of Social Security*, Oxford: Clarendon Press.

Dilnot, A. W., Disney, R., Johnson, P. and Whitehouse, E. (1994), *Pensions Policy in the UK*, London: Institute of Fiscal Studies.

Dilnot, A. W., Kay, J. A. and Morris, C. N. (1984), *The Reform of Social Security*, Oxford: Oxford University Press.

Disney, P. (1990), *Proceedings on Medium Term Prospects for Public Expenditure*, London: Public Finance Foundation.

Dixon, J. and Glennerster, H. (1995), 'What do we know about fundholding in general practice?', *British Medical Journal*, **311**, pp. 727–30.

DoE (1977), *Housing Policy: A consultative document*, Cmnd 6851, London: HMSO.

DoE (1981), *Alternatives to Domestic Rates*, Cmnd 8449, London: HMSO.

DoE (1982a), *Housing Subsidies and Accounting Manual*, London: HMSO.

DoE (1982b), *Housing Statistics*, London: HMSO.

DoE (1986), *Paying for Local Government*, London: HMSO.

DoE (1991), *A New Tax for Local Government*, Scottish and Welsh Offices, London: HMSO.

DoH (1988a), *Community Care: Agenda for action*, London: HMSO.

DoH (1988b), *Inspection of Cleveland Social Services Department's Arrangements for Handling Child Sexual Abuse*, London: HMSO.

DoH (1988c), *Inspection of Child Protection Services, London Borough of Southwark*, London: HMSO.

DoH (1989), *Caring for People: Community care in the next decade and beyond*, Cm 844, London: HMSO.

DoH (1991), *Purchase of Service*, Social Services Inspectorate, London: HMSO.

DoH (1995) *The Government's Expenditure Plans 1995/6 to 1997/8: Department of Health*, Cm 2812, London: HMSO.

DoH (1996) *A New Partnership for Care in Old Age*, London: HMSO.

Donnison, D. V. and Ungerson, C. (1982), *Housing Policy*, Harmondsworth: Penguin.

Douglas, J. (1983), *Why Charity? The case for a third sector*, London: Sage.

Downs, A. (1957), *An Economic Theory of Democracy*, New York: Harper & Row.

Downs, A. (1967), *Inside Bureaucracy*, Boston: Little, Brown.

Dunleavy, P. (1983), *The Politics of Mass Housing in Britain 1945–75*, Oxford: Clarendon Press.

Dunleavy, P. (1991), *Democracy, Bureaucracy and Public Choice*, Hemel Hempstead: Harvester Wheatsheaf.

Dunleavy, P. and O'Leary, B. (1987), *Theories of the State*, London: Macmillan.

Easam, P. and Oppenheim, C. (1989), *A Charge on the Community*, London: Child Poverty Action Group.

Eckstein, H. (1964), *The English Health Service*, Cambridge, Mass.: Harvard University Press.

Else, P. K. and Marshall, G. P. (1981), 'The unplanning of public expenditure', *Public Administration*, **59**, Autumn, pp. 253–78.

Enthoven, A. C. (1985), *Reflections on the Management of the National Health Service*, London: Nuffield Provincial Hospitals Trust.

Enthoven, A. C. (1991), 'NHS market reform', *Health Affairs*, **10**, no. 3, pp. 60–70.

Equal Opportunities Commission (1980), *The Experience of Caring for Elderly and Handicapped Dependants*, Manchester: EOC.

Ermisch, J. (1983), *The Political Economy of Demographic Change*, London: Heinemann.

Esping-Anderson, G. (1990), *The Three Worlds of Welfare Capitalism*, Oxford: Polity Press and Blackwell.

Etzioni, A. (1976), 'What to do about the nursing homes', *Juris Doctor*, **6**.

Eurostat (1994), *Basic Statistics of the Community*, Luxembourg: Eurostat.

Evandrou, M. (1990), *Challenging the Invisibility of Carers: Mapping informal care nationally*, Welfare State Programme Discussion Paper no. 49, London: LSE; repr. in C. Victor and F. Lasko (eds) (1992), *Social Policy and Older People*, Aldershot: Gower.

Evandrou, M. and Falkingham, J. (1995), 'Gender, lone parenthood and lifetime incomes', in J. Falkingham and J. Hills (eds), *The Dynamics of Welfare: The welfare state and the life cycle*, Hemel Hempstead: Harvester.

Evandrou, M., Falkingham, J. and Glennerster, H. (1990), 'The personal social services: everyone's poor relation but nobody's baby', in J. Hills (ed.), *The State of Welfare*, Oxford: Oxford University Press.

Evandrou, M., Falkingham, J., Hills, J. and Le Grand, J. (1991), *The Distribution of Welfare Benefits in Kind*, Welfare State Discussion Paper no. 68, London: LSE.

Falkingham, J. and Hills, J. (eds) (1995), *The Dynamics of Welfare: The welfare state and the life cycle*, Hemel Hempstead: Harvester.

Falkingham, J. and Johnson, P. (1995), 'Funding pensions over the life cycle', in J. Falkingham and J. Hills (eds), *The Dynamics of Welfare: The welfare state and the life cycle*, Hemel Hempstead: Harvester.

Farmer, N. and Barrell, R. (1982), 'Why student loans are fairer than grants', *Public Money*, **2**, no. 1, pp. 19–24.

Feldstein, M. (1974), 'Social security, induced retirement and aggregate capital accumulation', *Journal of Political Economy*, **82**, no. 5, pp. 905–26.

Feldstein, M. (1975), 'The income tax and charitable contributions', *National Tax Journal*, **28**, pp. 209–26.

Feldstein, M. (1980), 'International differences in social security spending', *Journal of Public Economics*, **14**, pp. 225–44.

Feldstein, M. (1995), 'The effect of marginal tax rates on taxable income: a panel study of the 1986 Tax Reform Act', *Journal of Political Economy*, **103**, no. 3, pp. 551–72.

Feldstein, M. and Boskin, S. (1975), *Effects of charitable deductions on contributions by low and middle income households*, Discussion Paper no. 427, Cambridge, Mass.: Harvard Institute of Economic Research.

Feldstein, M. and Clotfelter, C. (1974), *Tax incentives and charitable contributions in the US*, Discussion Paper no. 381, Cambridge, Mass.: Harvard Institute of Economic Research.

Ferlie, E. and Judge, K. (1981), 'Retrenchment and rationality in the personal social services', *Policy and Politics*, **9**, no. 3, pp. 333–50.

Field, F. (1995) *Making Welfare Work*, London: Institute of Community Studies.

Finch, J. (1987), 'Family obligations and the life course', in B. Bryman, B. Blytheway, P. Alliat and T. Keil (eds), *Rethinking the Life Cycle*, London: Macmillan.

Finer Committee (1974), *Report of the Committee on One-Parent Families*, Cmnd 5629, London: HMSO.

Flora, P. and Heidenheimer, A. (eds) (1981), *The Development of Welfare States in Europe and America*, London: Transaction Books.

Flynn, R. (1988), 'Political acquiescence, privatisation and residualisation in British housing policy', *Journal of Social Policy*, **17**, pt 3, pp. 289–312.

Fogarty, M. (1982), *Retirement Policy: The next fifty years*, London: Heinemann.

Foot, M. (1973), *Aneurin Bevan*, vol. ii, London: Davis Pointer.

Foster, C. D., Jackman, R. and Perlman, M. (1980), *Local Government Finance in a Unitary State*, London: Allen & Unwin.

Friedman, M. (1962), *Capitalism and Freedom*, Chicago: Chicago Press.

Friedman, M. and Friedman, R. (1979), *Free to Choose*, Harmondsworth: Penguin Books.

Garnham, A. and Knights, E. (1994), *Putting the Treasury First: The truth about child support*, London: Child Poverty Action Group.

Gauldie, E. (1974), *Cruel Habitations: A history of working-class housing 1780–1918*, London: Allen & Unwin.

Geddes Committee (1922), *Reports of the Committee on National Expenditure*, Cmd 1581, London: HMSO.

Gerard, D. (1983), *Charities in Britain: Conservatism or change*, London: Bedford Square Press.

Gibson, J. (1990), *The Politics and Economics of the Poll Tax: Mrs Thatcher's downfall*, Worley: EMAS.

Gilbert, B. B. (1966), *The Evolution of National Insurance in Great Britain*, London: Michael Joseph.

Gilbert, N. (1983), *Capitalism and the Welfare State*, New Haven and London: Yale University Press.

Glazer, N. (1988), *The Limits of Social Policy*, Cambridge, Mass.: Harvard University Press.

Glendenning, C. (1983), *The Costs of Unshared Care*, London: Routledge.

Glendenning, C. (1992), *The Costs of Informal Care: Looking inside the household*, London: HMSO.

Glennerster, H. (1971), *The Finance of Education*, Milton Keynes: Open University Press.

Glennerster, H. (1975), *Social Service Budgets and Social Policy*, London: Allen & Unwin.

Glennerster, H. (1979), 'The determinants of public expenditure', in T. Booth (ed.), *Planning for Welfare*, Oxford: Martin Robertson.

Glennerster, H. (1980), 'Prime cuts: public expenditure and social service planning in an hostile environment', *Policy and Politics*, **8**, no. 4, pp. 367–82.

Glennerster, H. (1981a), 'The role of the state in financing recurrent education', *Public Choice*, **36**, 3, pp. 551–71.

Glennerster, H. (1981b), 'From containment to conflict? Social planning in the seventies', *Journal of Social Policy*, **10**, pt 1, pp. 31–51.

Glennerster, H. (ed.) (1983), *The Future of the Welfare State*, London: Heinemann.

Glennerster, H. (1991), 'Quasi markets and education', *Economic Journal*, **101**, no. 408, pp. 1256–67.

Glennerster, H. (1994), *Implementing GP Fundholding*, Milton Keynes: Open University Press.

Glennerster, H. (1995a), 'Opportunity costs', *New Economy*, May, pp. 110–14.

Glennerster, H. (1995b), *British Social Policy Since 1945*, Oxford: Blackwell.

Glennerster, H. and Billis, D. (1995), 'Human service non profits: towards a theory of comparative advantage', paper given at the Social Policy Association Annual Conference 1995, London: LSE.

Glennerster, H. and Le Grand, J. (1995), 'The development of quasi markets in welfare provision in the UK', *International Journal of Health Services*, **25**, no. 2, pp. 203–18.

Glennerster, H. and Low, W. (1990), 'Education and the welfare state: does it add up?', in J. Hills (ed.), *The State of Welfare*, Oxford: Oxford University Press.

Glennerster, H. and Midgley, J. (1991), *The Radical Right and the Welfare State: An international assessment*, Hemel Hempstead: Harvester.

Glennerster, H. and Turner, T. (1993), *Estate Based Housing Management: An evaluation*, London: HMSO.

Glennerster, H. and Wilson, G. (1970), *Paying for Private Schools*, London: Allen & Unwin.

Glennerster, H., Falkingham, J. and Barr, N. (1995), 'Education funding, equity and the life cycle', in J. Falkingham and J. Hills (eds), *The Dynamics of Welfare: The welfare state and the life cycle*, Hemel Hempstead: Harvester.

Glennerster, H., Korman, N. and Marslen-Wilson, F. (1982), *Social Planning: A local study*, Department of Social Science and Administration, London: LSE.

Glennerster, H., Korman, N. and Marslen-Wilson, F. (1983), *Planning for Priority Groups*, Oxford: Martin Robertson.

Glennerster, H., Matsaganis, M. and Owens, P. (1992), *A Foothold for Fundholding*, London: Kings Fund.

Glennerster, H., Power, A. and Travers, T. (1991), 'A new era for social policy: a new enlightenment or a new leviathan?', *Journal of Social Policy*, **20**, no. 3, pp. 389–414.

Glennerster, H., Wilson, G. and Merrett, S. (1968), 'A graduate tax', *Higher Education*, **1**, no. 1, pp. 26–38.

Goldberg, E. M. and Hatch, S. (1981), *A New Look at the Personal Social Services*, Research Paper no. 4, London: Policy Studies Institute.

Goldberg, E. M. and Warburton, R. W. (1979), *Ends and Means in Social Work*, London: Allen & Unwin.

Goldberg, E. M., Warburton, R. W., McGuinness, B. and Rowlands, S. H. (1977), 'Towards accountability in social work: one year's intake into an area office', *British Journal of Social Work*, **7**, Autumn.

Goode Committee (1993), *Pensions Law Reform*, Cm 2342, London: HMSO.

Goodin, R. and Le Grand, J. (1987), *Not Only the Poor: The middle classes and the welfare state*, London: Allen & Unwin.

Golding, P. and Middleton, S. (1982), *Images of Welfare: Press and public attitudes to poverty*, Oxford: Martin Robertson.

Goldman, S. (1973), *The Developing System of Public Expenditure Management and Control*, Civil Service College Studies no. 2, London: HMSO.

Gordon, A. (1982), *Economics and Social Policy*, Oxford: Martin Robertson.

Gough, I. (1979), *The Political Economy of the Welfare State*, London: Macmillan.

Gould, F. (1983), 'The development of public expenditures in Western industrialised countries', *Public Finance*, **38**, no. 1, pp. 38–69.

Goss, S. and Lansley, S. (1982), *What Price Housing?*, London: SHAC, London Housing Centre.

Gray, H. (1968), *The Cost of Council Housing*, London: Institute of Economic Affairs.

Green, C. (1967), *Negative Income Taxes and the Poverty Problem*, Washington, DC: Brookings Institution.

Green, D. (1990), *The NHS Reforms: Whatever happened to consumer choice?*, London: Institute of Economic Affairs.

Green, H. (1988), *General Household Survey 1985: Informal carers*, London: HMSO.

Greenwood, R. (1979), 'Local authority budgetary process', in T. Booth (ed.), *Planning for Welfare*, Oxford: Martin Robertson.

Greenwood, R., Hinings, C. R., Ranson, S. and Walsh, K. (1980a), 'Incremental budgets and the assumption of growth', in M. Wright (ed.), *Public Spending Decisions, Growth and Restraints in the 1970s*, London: Allen & Unwin.

Greenwood, R., Hinings, C. R., Ranson, S. and Walsh, K. (1980b), *Patterns of Management in Local Government*, Oxford: Martin Robertson.

Gretton, J. and Posnett, J. (1983), 'Academic salaries: how to distinguish payment for teaching and research in universities', *Public Money*, **2**, no. 4, pp. 29–34.

Grey, A., Hepworth, N. and Olding-Smee, J. (1981), *Housing Rents Costs and Subsidies: A discussion document*, London: CIPFA.

Griffith, J. A. G. (1965), *Central Departments and Local Authorities*, London: Allen & Unwin.

Gupta, S. P. (1968), 'Public expenditure and economic development: a cross section analysis', *Finanzarchiv*, October.

Hadley, R. (1981), 'Social service departments and the community', in E. M. Goldberg and S. Hatch (eds), *A New Look at the Personal Social Services*, London: Policy Studies Institute.

Hakim, C. (1982), 'The social consequences of high unemployment', *Journal of Social Policy*, **11**, pt 4, pp. 433–67.

Halfpenny, P. (1990), 'Volunteering in Britain', in *Charity Trends*, 13th edn, Tonbridge: Charities Aid Foundation.

Halfpenny, P. and Lowe, D. (1994), *Individual Giving and Volunteering in Britain in 1993*, Tonbridge: Charities Aid Foundation.

Hall, A. (1974), *The Point of Entry*, London: Allen & Unwin.

Hall, P., Land, H., Parker, R. and Webb, A. (1975), *Change, Choice and Conflict in Social Policy*, London: Heinemann.

Hall, R. E. (1973), 'Wages income and hours of work in the US labour force', in G. Cain and H. Watts (eds), *Income Maintenance and Labour Supply Econometric Studies*, Chicago: Markham.

Ham, C., Hunter, D. and Robinson, R. (1995), 'Evidence based policy making: research must inform policy making as well as medical care', *British Medical Journal*, **301**, pp. 71–2.

Hambleton, R. (1978), *Policy Planning and Local Government*, London: Hutchinson.

Hansman, H. (1980), 'The role of non profit enterprise', *Yale Law Journal*, **89**, pp. 835–901.

Hansman, H. (1987), 'Economic theories of non profit organisation', in W. Powell (ed.), *The Non Profit Sector: A research handbook*, Yale: Yale University Press.

Hanuschek, E. A. (1986), 'The economics of schooling', *Journal of Economic Literature*, **23**, no. 3, pp. 1141–77.

Harrison, A. S. (1989), *The Control of Public Expenditure 1979–89*, New Brunswick, NJ and Oxford: Transaction Books.

Harwin, J. (1990), 'Parental responsibilities in the Children Act 1990', in *Social Policy Review 1989–90*, London: Longman.

Hatch, S. (1980), *Outside the State*, London: Croom Helm.

Hatch, S. and Mocroft, I. (1979), 'The relative costs of services provided by voluntary and statutory organisations', *Public Administration*, Winter.

Hatch, S. and Mocroft, I. (1983), *Components of Welfare*, London: Bedford Square Press.

Heald, D. (1983), *Public Expenditure*, Oxford: Martin Robertson.

Heald, D. (1995), 'Steering public expenditure with defective maps', *Public Administration*, **73**, no. 2, pp. 213–40.

Heclo, H. and Wildavsky, A. (1981), *The Private Government of Public Money*, 2nd edn, London: Macmillan.

Heigham, D. (1982), 'Grant related expenditures: an invisible push towards efficiency in local government', *Public Money*, June, pp. 39–42.

Hemming, R. and Kay, J. (1982), 'The future of occupational pension provision in Britain', in M. Fogarty (ed.), *Retirement Policy in the Next Fifty Years*, London: Heinemann.

Hewitt, P. (1989), 'A way to cope with the world as it is', *Samizdat*, **6**, pp. 3–4.

Hill, M. (1990), *Social Security Policy in Britain*, Aldershot: Edward Elgar.

Hills, J. (1988), *Changing Tax: How the tax system works and how to change it*, London: Child Poverty Action Group.

Hills, J. (ed.) (1990), *The State of Welfare: The welfare state in Britain since 1974*, Oxford: Oxford University Press.

Hills, J. (1991a), *Unravelling Housing Finance: Subsidies, benefit and taxation*, Oxford: Oxford University Press.

Hills, J. (1991b), *Thirty Nine Steps to Housing Finance Reform*, York: Rowntree Trust.

Hills, J. (1993), *The Future of Welfare*, York: Joseph Rowntree Foundation.

Hills, J. (1995a), *Inquiry into Income and Wealth*, vol. ii, *A Summary of the Evidence*, York: Joseph Rowntree Foundation.

Hills, J. (1995b), 'Funding the Welfare State', *Oxford Review of Economic Policy*, **11**, no. 3, pp. 27–43.

Hills, J. and Sutherland, H. (1991), *Banding, Tilting, Gearing, Gaining and Losing: An anatomy of the proposed council tax*, Welfare State Discussion Paper no. 63, London: LSE.

Hills, J., Ditch, J. and Glennerster, H. (1994), *Beveridge and Social Security: An international retrospective*, Oxford: Oxford University Press.

Hirsch, F. (1977), *Social Limits to Growth*, London: Routledge.

Hirschman, A. O. (1970), *Exit, Voice and Loyalty: Responses to decline in firms, organisations and states*, Cambridge, Mass.: Harvard University Press.

Hirst, M. (1984), *Moving On: Transfer from child to adult services for young people with disabilities*, Social Policy Research Unit, York: University of York.

HM Treasury (1981), *Economic Progress Report*, London: HMSO.

HM Treasury (1984), *The Next Ten Years: Public expenditure and taxation into the 1990s*, Cmnd 9189, London: HMSO.

HM Treasury (1993), *Autumn Statement 1993*, London: HMSO.

Hochman, H. M. and Rodgers, J. D. (1969), 'Pareto optimal redistribution', *American Economic Review*, **59**, pp. 542–7.

Hogwood, B. W. (1989), 'The hidden face of public expenditure: trends in tax expenditures in Britain', *Policy and Politics*, **17**, no. 2.

Holmans, A. E. (1987), *Housing Policy in Great Britain*, London: Croom Helm.

Honnigsbaum, F. (1979), *The Division of British Medicine*, London: Kogan Page.

Hood, C. and Wright, M. (1981), *Big Government in Hard Times*, Oxford: Martin Robertson.

Houseman, J. A. (1981), 'Labour supply' in H. Aaron and J. A. Pechman (eds), *How Taxes Affect Economic Behavior*, Washington, DC: Brookings Institution.

House of Commons (1980), *The Funding and Organisation of Courses in Higher Education*, Fifth Report from the Science and Arts Committee, HC 787 1979/80, London: HMSO.

House of Commons (1995), *National Insurance Fund Account 1993/4*, HC 404 1994/5, London: HMSO.

House of Commons General Sub-Committee of the Expenditure Committee (1976), *Report*, HC 718 1975–76, London: HMSO.

House of Commons Select Committee on Estimates (1958), *Treasury Control*, House of Commons Paper no. 294, London: HMSO.

House of Commons Social Services Committee (1990), *Third Report: Community care funding for local authorities*, HC 277, 1989/90, London: HMSO.

House of Commons Treasury and Civil Service Sub-Committee (1983), *The Structure of Personal Income Taxation and Income Support*, HC 386, Session 1982/3, The Meacher Report, London: HMSO.

Housing Corporation (1989), *Rent Policy and Principles*, Circular HC/89, London: Housing Corporation.

Howson, J. (1982), 'Variations in local authority provision of education', *Oxford Review of Education*, **8**, no. 2.

Hulme, G. (1991), 'Expenditure on Personal Social Services in the 1980s and 1990s', *Public Money and Management*, **11**, no. 4, pp. 31–4.

Hunter, D. J. and Judge, K. (1988), *Griffiths and Community Care: Meeting the challenge*, London: Kings Fund Institute.

Independent Schools Information Service (ISIS) (1984), *How Grandparents can help with School Fees*, London: ISIS.

Independent (1991), *Schools Charter*, London: Independent Newspaper.

International Labour Office (1984), *Into the Twenty-First Century: The development of social security*, Geneva: International Labour Office.

Irving, D. (1983), 'Territorial need indicators: a comment', *Journal of Social Policy*, **12**, pt 2, pp. 241–5.

Isaacs, B. and Neville, I. (1972), *The Measurement of Need in Old People*, Scottish Health Services Studies, Edinburgh: Scottish Home and Health Department.

Jackman, R. (1982), 'Does central government need to control the total of local government spending?', *Local Government Studies*, **8**, no. 3, pp. 75–90.

Jacob, J. (1991), 'Lawyers go to hospital', *Public Law*, Summer, pp. 255–81.

James, C. (1984), *Occupational Pensions: The failure of private welfare*, London: Fabian Society.

Jencks, C. (1971), 'Evidence to the US Senate Select Committee on Equal Opportunity', quoted in J. A. Mecklenberger and R. A. Hostrop (eds), *Education Vouchers from Theory to Allum Rock*, Harewood, Ill.: ETC Publications.

Jenkin, P. (1980), 'Evidence to the House of Commons Social Services Committee', HC 702, pp. 99–100.

Jerome-Forget, M., White, J. and Wiener, J. M. (1995), *Health Care Reform Through Internal Markets: Experience and proposals*, Washington, DC: Brookings Institution and IRPP.

Johnson, N. (1981), *Voluntary Social Services*, Oxford: Martin Robertson and Basil Blackwell.

Johnson, P. and Falkingham, J. (1994), 'Is there a future for the Beveridge pension scheme?', in S. Baldwin and J. Falkingham (eds), *Social Security and Social Change*, Hemel Hempstead: Harvester.

Jones, A. and Posnett, S. (1990), 'Giving by covenant in the UK', in *Charity Trends*, 13th edn, Tonbridge: Charities Aid Foundation.

Jones, D. R. and Masterman, S. (1976), 'NHS resources: scales of variation', *British Journal of Preventive and Social Medicine*, **30**.

Jones, G. and Stewart, J. (1983), *The Case for Local Government*, London: Allen & Unwin.

Jones, P. R. (1983), 'Aid to charities', *International Journal of Social Economics*, **10**, no. 2, pp. 3–11.

Jordan, B. (1987), *Rethinking Welfare*, Oxford: Blackwell.

Joshi, H. and Davies, H. (1994), 'Sex, sharing and the distribution of income', *Journal of Social Policy*, **23**, no. 3, pp. 301–40.

Jowell, R., Witherspoon, S. and Brook, L. (1989), *British Social Attitudes: Special international report*, Aldershot: Gower.

Jowell, R. *et al.* (eds) (1983–1995), *British Social Attitudes*, annual reports, Aldershot: Gower and Dartmouth Press.

Judge, K. (1978), *Rationing Social Services*, London: Heinemann.

Judge, K. (ed.) (1980), *Pricing the Social Services*, London: Macmillan.

Judge, K. (1981), 'State pensions and the growth of social welfare expenditure', *Journal of Social Policy*, **10**, pt 4, pp. 503–30.

Judge, K. (1982a), 'The public purchase of social care: British confirmation of American experience', *Policy and Politics*, **10**, no. 4, pp. 397–416.

Judge, K. (1982b), 'The growth and decline of social expenditure', in A. Walker (ed.), *Public Expenditure and Social Policy*, London: Heinemann.

Judge, K. and Hampson, R. H. (1980), 'Political advertising and the Growth of social welfare expenditure', *International Journal of Social Economics*, **2**, no. 2, pp. 61–92.

Judge, K. and Matthews, J. (1980), *Charging for Social Care*, London: Allen & Unwin.

Kaldor, N. (1955), *An Expenditure Tax*, London: Allen & Unwin.

Kamerman, S. B. and Kahn, A. J. (1983), *Income Transfers for Families with Children*, Philadelphia: Temple University Press.

Kanter, R. M. (1984), *The Changemasters: Corporate entrepreneurs at work*, London: Allen & Unwin.

Kay, J. (1984), '*Financial Times* Conference on: "Pensions – time for a change"', *Financial Times*, 14 March 1984.

Kay, J. and King, M. (1996), *The British Tax System*, Oxford: Oxford University Press.

Kelly, A. (1989), 'An end to incrementalism: the impact of expenditure restraint on social services budgets, 1979–1986', *Journal of Social Policy*, **18**, no. 2, pp. 187–210.

Kendall, J. and Knapp, M. (1995a), *Shifting Frontiers: The UK voluntary sector*, Manchester: Manchester University Press.

Kendall, J. and Knapp, M. (1995b), 'The Kent Hopkins mapping: summary of the UK statistical mapping', in S. Saxon-Harrold and J. Kendall (eds), *Dimensions of the Voluntary Sector*, Taunton: Charities Aid Foundation.

Ketner, P. and Martin, G. (1987), *Purchase of Service Contracting*, New York: Sage.

Kilroy, B. (1978), *Housing Finance: Organic reform?*, London: Labour Economic Finance and Taxation Association.

Kilroy, B. (1982), 'Public expenditure on housing', in A. Walker (ed.), *Public Expenditure and Social Policy*, London: Heinemann.

King, D. (1990), 'Accountability and equity in British local finance: the poll tax', in R. Bennett (ed.), *Decentralisation, Local Governments and Markets*, Oxford: Oxford University Press.

Kings Fund Institute (1988), *Health Finance: Assessing the options*, London: Kings Fund Institute.

Klein, R. (1980), 'The welfare state: a self inflicted crisis', *Political Quarterly*, Jan.–March.

Klein, R. (1984), 'Privatisation and the welfare state', *Lloyds Bank Review*, January, pp. 12–29.

Klein, R. (1988), *Joint Approaches to Social Policy: Rationality and Practice*, Cambridge: Cambridge University Press.

Klein, R. (1995), *The Politics of the National Health Service*, London: Longman.

Klein, R. and Hall, P. (1974), *Caring for Quality in Caring Services*, London: Centre for Studies In Social Policy.

Kogan, M. and Kogan, D. (1983), *The Attack on Higher Education*, London: Kogan Page.

Kramer, R. (1981), *Voluntary Agencies in the Welfare State*, Berkeley: University of California Press.

Kramer, R. (eds), *Privatisation in 4 European Countries*, New York: Sharpe Amonk.

Kramer, R. and Grossman, B. (1987), 'Contracting for social services: process management and resource dependencies', *Social Service Review*, March, pp. 32–55.

Labour Party (1958), *National Superannuation*, London: Labour Party.

Laffont, J-J. (1989), *The Economics of Uncertainty and Information*, London and Cambridge, Mass.: MIT Press.

Laing, W. (1982), 'Contracting out in the NHS', *Public Money*, Dec.

Laing, W. (1993), *Financing Long Term Care: The crucial debate*, London: Age Concern.

Laing, W. (1994), *Laing's Review of Private Health Care*, London: Laing and Buisson Publications.

Land, H. (1975), 'Family allowances', in P. Hall *et al.*, *Change, Choice and Conflict in Social Policy*, London: Heinemann.

Land, H. (1978), 'Who cares for the family', *Journal of Social Policy*, **7**, pt 3, pp. 257–84.

Lansley, S. (1979), *Housing and Public Policy*, London: Croom Helm.

Lansley, S. (1982), *Housing Finance: New Policies for Labour*, London: Labour Housing Group.

Lawson, N. (1993), *The View from No 11*, London: Corgi Books.

Layfield Committee (1976), *Local Government Finance*, Cmnd 6453, London: HMSO.

Leather, P. (1983), 'Housing (dis?)investment programmes', *Policy and Politics*, **11**, no. 2, pp. 215–39.

Lee, P. and Raban, C. (1988), *Welfare Theory and Social Policy: Reform or Revolution?*, London: Sage.

Lee, T. (1990), *Carving Out the Cash for Schools LMS and the New ERA for Schools*, Bath Social Policy Paper no. 17, Bath: Bath University.

Lee, T. (1992a), *Local Management of Schools*, Milton Keynes: Open University Press.

Lee, T. (1992b), 'Local management of schools and special education', in T. Booth, W. Swann, M. Masterdon and P. Potts (eds), *Policies for Diversity in Education*, London: Routledge.

Lee, T. (1995), 'The search for equity', PhD thesis, Bath University.

Lees, D. S. (1966), *Economic Consequences of the Professions*, London: Institute of Economic Affairs.

Le Grand, J. (1982), *The Strategy of Equality*, London: Allen & Unwin.

Le Grand, J. (1983), 'Making redistribution work: the social services', in H. Glennerster (ed.), *The Future of the Welfare State*, London: Heinemann.

Le Grand, J. (1989a), 'Markets, welfare and equality', in J. Le Grand and S. Estrin (eds), *Market Socialism*, Oxford: Oxford University Press.

Le Grand, J. (1989b), 'An International Comparison of Health Inequalities', in J. Fox (ed.), *Health Inequalities in European Countries*, London: Gower.

Le Grand, J. (1991), 'The theory of government failure', *British Journal of Political Science*, **21**, pp. 423–42.

Le Grand, J. (1995), '"Knights" and "knaves": strategies in social policy', Inaugural Lecture, London: LSE.

Le Grand, J. and Bartlett, W. (1993), *Quasi-Markets and Social Policy*, London: Macmillan.

Le Grand, J. and Robinson, R. (1984a), *The Economics of Social Problems*, 2nd edn, London: Macmillan.

Le Grand, J. and Robinson, R. (eds) (1984b), *Privatisation and the Welfare State*, London: Allen & Unwin.

Le Grand, J. and Winter, D. (1987), 'The middle classes and the welfare state under Conservative and Labour Governments', *Journal of Social Policy*, **6**, pp. 399–430.

Le Grand, J., Glennerster, H. and Maynard, A. (1991), 'Quasi markets and social policy', *Economic Journal*, **101**, no. 408, 1256–67.

Leibenstein, H. (1966), 'Allocative efficiency versus X efficiency', *American Economic Review*, **56**, pp. 392–415.

Letwyn, D. and Redwood, J. (1988), *Britain's Biggest Enterprise*, London: Centre for Policy Studies.

Lewis, J. (1983), *Women's Welfare, Women's Rights*, London: Croom Helm.

Lewis, J. (1993) (ed.), *Women and Social Policies in Europe: Work, family and the state*, Aldershot: Edward Elgar.

Lewis, J. (1995), *The Problem of Lone Mothers in Twentieth Century Britain*, Welfare State Discussion Paper no. 114, London: LSE STICERD.

Lewis, J. and Glennerster, H. (1996), *Implementing Community Care*, Milton Keynes: Open University Press.

Lewis, J. and Meredith, B. (1988), *Daughters Who Care: Daughters caring for mothers at home*, London: Routledge.

Likierman, A. (1988), *Public Expenditure: Who really controls it and how*, Harmondsworth: Penguin.

Lord, R. (1983), 'Value for money in the education service', *Public Money*, **3**, no. 2, pp. 15–22.

Lowe, R. (1989), 'Resignation at the Treasury: The social services committee and the failure to reform the welfare state 1955–7', *Journal of Social Policy*, **18**, pt 4, pp. 505–26.

McLachlan, G. and Maynard, A. (eds) (1982), *The Public/Private Mix for Health*, London: Nuffield Private Hospitals Trust.

Macnicol, J. (1980), *The Movement for Family Allowances 1918–45*, London: Heinemann.

Malpass, P. (1990), *Reshaping Housing Policy: Subsidies, rents and residualisation*, London: Routledge.

Martin, J. (1995), 'Individual giving and volunteering in Britain 1993', in S. Saxon-Harrold and J. Kendall (eds), *Dimensions of the Voluntary Sector*, Tonbridge: Charities Aid Foundation.

Martin, J. and White, A. (1988), *The Financial Circumstances of Disabled Adults Living in Private Households*, London: HMSO.

Matsaganis, M. and Glennerster, H. (1994), 'The threat of cream skimming in the post reform NHS', *Journal of Health Economics*, **13**, pp. 31–60.

Maynard, A. (1975), *Experiment with Choice in Education*, London: Institute of Economic Affairs.

Maynard, A. (1978), 'The medical profession and the efficiency and equity of health services', *Social and Economic Administration*, **12**, no. 1, pp. 3–19.

Maynard, A. (1979), 'Pricing insurance and the National Health Service', *Journal of Social Policy*, **8**, pt 2, pp. 157–76.

Maynard, A. (1982), 'Private health care sector in Britain', in G. McLachlan and A. Maynard, *The Public/Private Mix for Health*, London: Nuffield Provincial Hospitals Trust.

Maynard, A. (1986), 'Performance Incentives in General Practice in G. Teeling Smith (ed.), *Health Education and General Practice*, London: Office of Health Economics.

Maynard, A. (1991), 'Developing the health care market', *Economic Journal*, **101**, pp. 1277–86.

Mays, N. and Bevan, G. (1987), *Resource Allocation in the National Health Service*, Occasional Paper in Social Administration, London: Bedford Square Press.

Mayston, D. (1990), 'NHS resourcing: a financial and economic analysis', in A. J. Culyer, A. Maynard and S. W. Posnett (eds), *Competition in Health Care; Reforming the NHS*, London: Macmillan.

Meacher Report (1983), *The Structure of Personal Income Taxation and Income Support*, House of Commons Treasury and Civil Service Committee, 1982–83, HC 386, London: HMSO.

Meade, J. F. (1978), *The Structure and Reform of Direct Taxation*, London: Allen & Unwin.

Merrett, S. (1979), *State Housing in Britain*, London: Routledge.

Minford, P., Peel, M. and Ashton, P. (1987), *The Housing Morass*, London: Institute of Economic Affairs.

Mishra, R. (1983), *The Welfare State in Crisis*, Brighton: Harvester Press.

Morris, L. (1989), *The Workings of the Household: A US/UK comparison*, Oxford: Polity Press.

Mortimore, P., Sammons, P., Stall, L., Leiris, D. and Ecob, R. (1988), *The Junior School Project: Understanding school effectiveness*, Research and Statistics Branch, London: ILEA.

Moser, Sir Claus (1990), *Presidential Address to the British Association*, London: British Association.

Mueller, D. C. (1979), *Public Choice*, Cambridge: Cambridge University Press.

Mueller, D. C. (1989), *Public Choice II*, Cambridge: Cambridge University Press.

Murray, G. J. (1969), *Voluntary Organisations and Social Welfare*, Edinburgh: Oliver & Boyd.

Musgrave, R. A. (1959), *The Theory of Public Finance*, London and Tokyo: McGraw-Hill.

Musgrave, R. A. (1969), *Fiscal Systems*, New Haven: Yale University Press.

Musgrave, R. A. and Musgrave, P. B. (1980), *Public Finance in Theory and Practice*, London and Tokyo: McGraw-Hill.

National Commission on Education (1993), *Learning to Succeed*, London: Heinemann.

National Federation of Housing Associations (1991), *Inquiry into British Housing* Second Report, London: NFHA.

National Institute for Social Work (1982), *Social Workers, Their Role and Tasks*, Barclay Report, London: NISW.

Nevitt, A. A. (1966), *Housing, Taxation and Subsidies*, London: Nelson.

Newton, K. (1976), *Second City Politics*, London: Clarendon Press.

Newton, K. (1981), *Urban Political Economy*, London: Frances Pinter.

Newton, K. and Sharpe, L. J. (1977), 'Local outputs research', *Policy and Politics*, **5**, no. 3, 61–82.

Niskanen, W. (1971), *Bureaucracy and Representative Government*, Chicago: Aldine Atherton.

Nissel, M. and Bonnerjea, L. (1982), *Family Care of Handicapped Elderly: Who pays?*, London: Policy Studies Institute.

Novick, D. (ed.) (1965), *Program Budgeting*, Cambridge, Mass.: Harvard University Press.

O'Connor, J. (1973), *The Fiscal Crisis of the State*, New York: St Martins Press.

Occupational Pensions Board (1981), *Improved Protection for the Occupational Rights and Expectations of Early Leavers*, Cmnd 8721, London: HMSO.

OECD (1976a), *Public Expenditure on Income Maintenance Programmes*, Paris: OECD.

OECD (1976b), *Public Expenditure on Education*, Paris: OECD.

OECD (1977), *Public Expenditure on Health*, Paris: OECD.

OECD (1978), *Public Expenditure Trends*, Paris: OECD.

OECD (1981), *The Welfare State in Crisis*, ed. A. H. Halsey, Paris: OECD.

OECD (1984), 'Social expenditure: erosion or evolution', *OECD Observer*, January.

OECD (1987), *The Control and Management of Government Expenditures*, Paris: OECD.

OECD (1988), *Ageing Population: Social policy implications*, Paris: OECD.

OECD (1992), *The Reform of Health Care Systems: A comparative analysis of seven OECD countries*, Paris: OECD.

OECD (1994), *The Reform of Health Care Systems: A review of seventeen countries*, Health Policy Studies no. 5, Paris: OECD.

OECD (1995), 'Pension liabilities in seven major economies', *Economic Outlook*, June, Paris: OECD.

Offe, C. (1984), *Contradictions of the Welfare State*, London: Hutchinson.

O'Higgins, M. (1980), 'The distributive effects of public expenditure and taxation: an agnostic view of the CSO analysis', in C. Sandford, C. Pond and R. Walker (eds), *Taxation and Social Policy*, London: Heinemann.

O'Higgins, M. (1983), 'Rolling back the welfare state: rhetoric and reality', in C. Jones and J. Stevenson (eds), *The Yearbook of Social Policy 1982*, London: Routledge.

Osbourne, D. and Gaebler, T. (1992), *Reinventing Government: How the entrepreneurial spirit is transforming the public sector from the school house, city hall to the Pentagon*, Reading, Mass.: Addison-Wesley.

Owens, P. and Glennerster, H. (1990), *Nursing in Conflict*, London: Macmillan.

Pahl, J. (1980), 'Patterns of money management within marriage', *Journal of Social Policy*, **9**, pt 3, pp. 313–45.

Pahl, J. (1989), *Money and Marriage*, Basingstoke: Macmillan.

Paine, T. (1969), *Rights of Man*, London: Penguin.

Painter, J. (1991), 'Compulsory competitive tendering in local government: the first round', *Public Administration*, **69**, pp. 191–210.

Papadakis, E. and Taylor-Gooby, P. (1987), *The Private Provision of Public Welfare: State, market and community*, Hemel Hempstead: Wheatsheaf.

Parker, G. (1990), *With Due Care and Attention*, 2nd edn, London: Family Policy Studies Centre.

Parker, G. (1992), 'Counting care, numbers and types of informal carers', in *Carers Research and Practice*, London: HMSO.

Parker, G. (1993), *With this Body*, Milton Keynes: Open University Press.

Parker, H. (1989), *Instead of the Dole*, London: Routledge.

Parker, H. (1995), *Taxes Benefits and Family Life: The seven deadly traps*, London: Institute of Economic Affairs.

Parker, R. (1967), *The Rents of Council Houses*, Occasional Paper in Social Administration no. 22, London: Bell.

Parker, R. (1976), 'Charging for the social services', *Journal of Social Policy*, **5**, pt 4, pp. 359–73.

Passey, A. (1995), 'Corporate support for the voluntary sector 1993/4', in S. Saxon-Harrold and J. Kendall (eds), *Dimensions of the Voluntary Sector*, Tonbridge: Charities Aid Foundation.

Pateman, C. (1973), *Participation and Democratic Theory*, Cambridge: Cambridge University Press.

Pauly, M. (1974), 'Over insurance and public provision of insurance: the roles of moral hazard and adverse selection', *Quarterly Journal of Economics*, **88**, pp. 44–62.

Peacock, A. J. and Wiseman, J. (1967), *The Growth of Public Expenditure in the United Kingdom*, London: Allen & Unwin.

Peacock, A. T., Glennerster, H. and Lavers, R. (1968), *Educational Finance: Its sources and uses in the UK*, London and Edinburgh: Oliver & Boyd.

Peacock, S. and Smith, P. (1994), *Resource Allocation Consequences of the New NHS Needs Formula*, Discussion Paper no. 103, Centre for Health Economics, York: University of York.

Pechman, J. (ed.) (1980), *What Should Be taxed: Income or expenditure?*, Washington, DC: Brookings Institution.

Pechman, J. (1985), *Who Paid the Taxes 1966–85*, Washington, DC: Brookings Institution.

Pechman, J. and Okner, B. (1974), *Who Bears the Tax Burden?* Washington, DC: Brookings Institution.

Pechman, J. and Timpane, T. M. (1975), *Work Incentives and Income Guarantees*, Washington, DC: Brookings Institution.

Pendlebury, M. W. (1994), 'Management accounting in local government', *Financial Accountability and Management*, **10**, no. 2, pp. 117–29.

Piachaud, D. (1982), 'Patterns of income and expenditure within families', *Journal of Social Policy*, **11**, pt 4, pp. 464–82.

Pigou, A. C. (1920), *The Economics of Welfare*, London: Macmillan.

Pinker, R. (1971), *Social Theory and Social Policy*, London: Heinemann.

Pirie, M. and Butler, E. (1988), *The Health of Nations*, London: Adam Smith Institute.

Plowden Report (1961), *Control of Public Expenditure*, Cmnd 1432, London: HMSO.

Plowden, W. J. L. (1977), 'Developing a joint approach to social policy', in K. Jones (ed.), *Yearbook of Social Policy 1976*, London: Routledge.

Posnett, J. and Chase, J. (1985), *Independent Schools in England and Wales Charitable Status in Charity Statistics*, Tonbridge: Charities Aid Foundation.

Power, A. (1984), *Local Housing Management: Priority estates project report*, London: Department of the Environment.

Power, A. (1987a), *Property Before People*, London: Allen & Unwin.

Power, A. (1987b), *The PEP Guide to Local Housing Management*, London: HMSO.

Power, A. (1991), *Running to Stand Still: Progress in local management on twenty unpopular housing estates*, London: HMSO.

Power, A. (1992), *Hovels to High Rise*, London: Allen & Unwin.

Pratt, J., Travers, T. and Burgess, T. (1978), *Costs and Control in Further Education*, Windsor: National Foundation for Education Research.

Prest, A (1966), *Financing University Education*, London: Institute of Economic Affairs.

Prest, A. R. and Barr, N. (1985), *Public Finance in Theory and Practice*, 6th edn, London: Weidenfeld & Nicholson.

Price, R. W. R. (1979), 'Public expenditure, policy and control', *National Institute Economic Review*, November, pp. 68–75.

Propper, C. and Maynard, A. (1990), 'Whither the private health care sector', in A. J. Culyer, A. K. Maynard and J. W. Posnett (eds), *Competition in Health Care: Reforming the NHS*, London: Macmillan.

Pruger, K. (1973), 'Social policy: unilateral transfer or reciprocal exchange', *Journal of Social Policy*, **2**, pt 4, pp. 289–302.

Rainwater, L., Rein, M. and Schwartz, J. E. (1986), *Income Packaging in the Welfare State*, Oxford: Oxford University Press.

Rathbone, E. (1924), *The Disinherited Family*, London: Allen & Unwin.

Rathbone, E. (1940), *The Case for Family Allowances*, Harmondsworth: Penguin.

Reddin, M. (1980), 'Taxation and Pensions' in C. Sandford, C. Pond and R. Walker (eds), *Taxation and Social Policy*, London: Heinemann.

Rees, P. M. and Thompson, F. P. (1972), 'The relative price effect in public expenditure: its nature and method of calculation', *Statistical News*, **18**, August.

Rhodes, R. A. W. (1979), 'Research into central–local relations: a framework for analysis', *Central–Local Government Relationships*, London: Social Science Research Council, app. 1, pp. 1–45.

Rhodes, R. A. W. (1986), '"Corporate bias" in central—local relations: a case study of the consultative council on local government finance', *Policy and Politics*, **14**, no. 2, pp. 221–45.

Rhys-Williams, Lady (1943), *Something to Look Forward To*, London: MacDonald.

Richards, E. (1996), *Estimating the Costs of Long Term Care*, London: Institute of Public Policy Research.

Rimlinger, G. (1971), *Welfare Policy and Industrialisation in Europe, America and Russia*, New York: Wiley.

Rimmer, L. (1982), *The Intra-Family Distribution of Income*, London: Study Commission in the Family.

Rivlin, A. and Wiener, J. M. (1988), *Caring for the Disabled Elderly: Who will pay?*, Washington, DC: Brookings Institution.

Robbins Committee (1963), *Higher Education*, Cmnd 2154, London: HMSO.

Robbins, P. K. (ed.) (1982), *A Guarenteed Annual Income: Evidence from a local experiment*, New York: Academic Press.

Robinson, R. (1988), *Efficiency and the NHS: A case for an Internal Market*, London: Institute of Economic Affairs.

Robinson, R. (1991), 'Health Expenditure: Recent trends and prospects for the 1990s', *Public Money and Management*, **11**, no. 4, pp. 19–24.

Robinson, R. and Le Grand, J. (1994), *Evaluationg the NHS Reforms* London: Kings Fund.

Robson, M. H. and Walford, G. (1989), 'Independent schools and tax policy under Mrs Thatcher', *Journal of Education Policy*, **4**, no. 2, pp. 149–62.

Robson, W. A. (1954), *Development of Local Government*, London: Allen & Unwin.

Rose, R. and Davies, P. L. (1994), *Inheritance and Public Policy: Change without choice in Britain*, New Haven: Yale University Press.

Rose-Ackerman, S. L. (ed.) (1986), *The Economics of Non Profit Institutions*, Oxford: Oxford University Press.

Rothschild, M. and Stiglitz, J. (1976), 'Equilibrium and competitive insurance markets: an essay on the economics of imperfect information', *Quarterly Journal of Economics*, **9**, pp. 629–49.

Royal Commission on the Distribution of Income and Wealth (1979), *The Distribution of Wealth in Ten Countries*, Background Paper no. 7, London: HMSO.

Royal Commission on the National Health Service (1979), *Report*, Cmnd 7615, London: HMSO.

Rubenstein, P., Munday, R. E. and Rubenstein, M. L. (1979), 'Proprietary social services', in *Social Welfare Forum 1978*, New York: Columbia University Press.

Rutter, M., Maughan, B., Mortimore, P. and Ouston, S. (1979), *15,000 Hours: Secondary schools and their effects on children*, London: Open Books.

Salamon, L. M. (1992), 'Social Services', in C. Clotfelter (ed.), *Who Benefits from the Non Profit Sector?*, Chicago: University of Chicago Press.

Salamon, L. M. and Anheier, H. K. (1995), 'The emerging sector: the non profit sector in comparative perspective – an overview', in S. Saxon-Harrold and J. Kendall (eds), *Dimensions of the Voluntary Sector*, Tonbridge: Charities Aid Foundation.

Saltman, R. and von Otter, C. (1992), *Planned Markets and Public Competition: Strategic reform in northern European health systems*, Milton Keynes: Open University Press.

Saltman, R. and von Otter, C. (eds) (1995), *Implementing Planned Markets in Health Care*, Milton Keynes: Open University Press.

Sammons, P. (1991), *The Impact of LMS and Formula Funding on Resource Allocation to Inner London Schools*, Centre for Educational Research, London: LSE.

Savas, E. S. (1977), 'Policy analysis for local government: public v private refuse collection', *Policy Analysis*, **3**, pp. 44–74.

Savas, E. S. (1982), *Privatising the Public Sector: How to shrink government*, Chatham, NJ: Chatham House.

Schick, A. (1966), 'The road to PPB: the stages of budget reform', *Public Administration Review*, **26**, no. 4, pp. 243–58.

Schieber, G. S., Poullier, J-P. and Greenwald, M. (1991), 'Health care systems in twenty four countries', *Health Affairs*, **10**, no. 3, pp. 22–38.

Schlesinger, M., Dwort, R. A. and Pulice, R. T. (1986), 'Competitive bidding and states' purchase of services', *Journal of Policy Analysis and Management*, **5**, no. 2, pp. 245–63.

Schuller, T. (1983), 'Plums, paper bags and pensions', *New Society*, 18 August.

Schuller, T. and Walker, A. (1990), *The Time of Our Life: Education, employment and retirement in the third age*, London: Institute for Public Policy Research.

Scott, D. and Wilding, P. (1984), *Beyond Welfare Pluralism*, Manchester: Manchester Council for Voluntary Service and Manchester Social Administration Department.

Scousen, C. R. (1990), 'Budgeting practices in local government', *Financial Accountability and Management*, **6**, no. 3, pp. 191–202.

Seebohm Committee (1968), *Report of the Committee on Local Authority and Allied Personal Social Services*, Cmnd 3703, London: HMSO.

Seldon, A. (1957), *Pensions in a Free Society*, London: Institute of Economic Affairs.

Seldon, A. (1960), *Pensions for Prosperity*, London: Institute for Economic Affairs.

Seldon, A. (1977), *Charge*, London: Temple Smith.

Self, P. (1993), *Government by the Market: The politics of public choice*, London: Macmillan.

Showler, B. (1982), 'Public expenditure on employment', in A. Walker (ed.), *Public Expenditure and Social Policy*, London: Heinemann.

Sinfield, A. (1983), 'The necessity for full employment', in H. Glennerster (ed.), *The Future of the Welfare State*, London: Heinemann.

Slack, K. (1960), *Councils, Committees and Concern for the Old*, Occasional Papers on Social Administration, London: Bell.

Smith, A. (1974), *The Wealth of Nations*, Harmondsworth: Penguin.

Smith, G. (1980), *Social Need*, London: Routledge.

Smith, S. (1988), 'Should UK local government be financed by a poll tax?', *Fiscal Studies*, **9**, no. 1, pp. 18–28.

Smith, T. and Noble, M. (1995), *Education Divides*, London: Child Poverty Action Group.

Smyth, M. and Robins, N. (1989), *The Financial Circumstances of Families with Disabled Children Living in Private Households*, London: HMSO.

Snower, D. (1993), 'The future of the welfare state', *Economic Journal*, **103**, pp. 700–17.

Social Justice Commission (1994), *Social Justice: Strategies for national renewal*, London: Vintage.

Steadman-Jones, G. (1971), *Outcast London*, Oxford: Clarendon Press.

Stevens, R. (1956), *Medical Practice in Modern England*, London: Yale University Press.

Stewart, J. D. (1974), *The Responsive Local Authority*, London: Charles Knight.

Stubblebine, W. (1965), 'Institutional elements in the financing of education', *Southern Economic Journal*, July, pp. 15–34.

Sugarman, S. D. (1980), 'Family choice in education', *Oxford Review of Education*, **6**, no. 1, pp. 31–40.

Sutherland, G. (1973), *Policy-Making in Elementary Education 1870–1895*, Oxford: Oxford University Press.

Taylor-Gooby, P. (1991), 'Attachment to the welfare state', in R. Jowell *et al.* (eds), *British Social Attitudes: 8th Report*, Aldershot: Dartmouth.

Taylor-Gooby, P. (1995), 'Comfortable, marginal and excluded' in *British Social Attitudes: 12th Report*, R. Jowell *et al.* (eds), Aldershot: Dartmouth.

Thain, C. and Wright, M. (1990), 'Coping with difficulty: the Treasury and public expenditure 1976–89', *Policy and Politics*, **18**, no. 1, pp. 1–15.

Thain, C. and Wright, M. (1992a), 'Planning and controlling public expenditure in the UK – Part I: the Treasury's public expenditure survey', *Public Administration*, **70**, no. 1, pp. 3–24.

Thain, C. and Wright, M. (1992b), 'Planning and controling public expenditure in the UK – Part II: the effects and effectiveness of the survey', *Public Administration*, **70**, no. 2, pp. 193–224.

Thain, C. and Wright, M. (1995), *The Treasury and Whitehall: The planning and control of public expenditure, 1976–93*, Oxford: Oxford University Press.

Thane, P. (1982), *The Foundations of the Welfare State*, London: Longman.

Thomas, S., Pan, H., Goldstein, H. and Metropolitan, A. (1994), *Report on the Analysis of the 1992 Examination Results*, London: London University Institute of Education.

Thompson, E. P. (1980), *The Making of the English Working Class*, Harmondsworth: Penguin.

Tiebout, C. (1956), 'A pure theory of local expenditure', *Journal of Political Economy*, **64**, no. 5, pp. 416–24.

Titmuss, R. M. (1950), *Problems of Social Policy*, London: HMSO.

Titmuss, R. M. (1958, 1976), *Essays on the Welfare State*, London: Allen & Unwin.

Titmuss, R. M. (1962), *Income Distribution and Social Change*, London: Allen & Unwin.

Titmuss, R. M. (1968), *Commitment to Welfare*, London: Allen & Unwin.

Titmuss, R. M. (1970), *The Gift Relationship*, London: Allen & Unwin.

Townsend, P. (1962), *The Last Refuge*, London: Routledge.

Townsend, P. (1971), *The Fifth Social Service*, London: Fabian Society.

Townsend, P. and Bosanquet, N. (1972), *Labour and Inequality*, London: Fabian Society.

Travers, T. (1986), *The Politics of Local Government Finance*, London: Allen & Unwin.

Trinder, C. (1990), *Proceedings on Medium Term Prospects for Public Expenditure*, London: Public Finance Foundation.

Tullock, G. (1965), *The Politics of Bureaucracy*, Washington, DC: Public Affairs Press.

Tunley, P., Travers, T. and Pratt, J. (1979), *Depriving the Deprived*, London: Kogan Page.

Twigg, J. (1994), *Carers Perceived: Policy and practice in informal care*, Milton Keynes: Open University Press.

UK Efficiency Unit (1988), *Improving Management in Government: the next steps – a report to the Prime Minister*, London: HMSO.

UK Efficiency Unit (1991), *Making the Most of Next Steps: The management of ministers' departments and their executive agencies*, London: HMSO.

United States Congressional Budget Office (1983), *Tax Expenditures: Current issues and five year budget projections, fiscal years 1984–88*, Washington, DC: CBO.

Uttley, S (1980), 'Welfare exchange reconsidered', *Journal of Social Policy*, **9**, pt 2, pp. 187–205.

Van de Ven, W. P. M. M. and van de Vleit, R. C. S. A. (1990), 'How can we prevent cream skimming in a competitive health insurance market?', *Second World Congress on Health Economics*, Rotterdam: Erasmus University.

Vandenburge, V. (1995), *Education in Quasi-Markets: The Belgian experience*, SAUS/LSE Seminar on quasi-markets, Bristol: School of Advanced Urban Studies.

Waldfogel, J. (1993), *Women Working for Less*, Welfare State Discussion Paper no. 93, London: LSE.

Walker, A. (ed.) (1982a), *Community Care*, Oxford: Martin Robertson and Basil Blackwell.

Walker, A. (ed.) (1982b), *Public Expenditure and Social Policy*, London: Heinemann.

Walker, A. (1983), 'A caring community', in H. Glennerster (ed.), *The Future of the Welfare State*, London: Heinemann.

Walker, A. (1984), *Social Planning: A strategy for socialist planning*, Oxford: Blackwell.

Walker, R., Lawson, R. and Townsend, P. (1984), *Responses to Poverty: Lessons from Europe*, London: Heinemann.

Warburton, M. (1983), *Housing Finance: The case for reform*, London: Catholic Housing Aid Society.

Washington State Department of Health and Human Services (1979), *Report of Proceedings of a Conference on the Denver and Seattle Income Guarantee Experiment*, Washington State: Olympia.

Webster, C. (1981), 'A social market answer on housing', *New Society*, 12 November.

Webster, C. (1988), *The Health Services Since the War*, vol. 1, London: HMSO.

Weisbrod, B. (1986), 'Towards a theory of the voluntary non profit sector in a three sector economy', in S. Rose-Ackerman (ed.), *The Economics of Non Profit Institutions*, Oxford: Oxford University Press.

West, E. G. (1965), *Education and the State*, London: Institute of Economic Affairs.

West, E. G. (1975), *Education and the Industrial Revolution*, London: Batsford.

Whitehead, C. (1984), 'Privatisation and housing', in J. Le Grand and R. Robinson (eds), *Privatisation and the Welfare State*, London: Allen & Unwin.

Whiteley, P. (1981), 'Public opinion and the demand for social welfare in Britain', *Journal of Social Policy*, **10**, pt 4, pp. 453–75.

Whiteside, N. (1983), 'Private agencies for public purposes', *Journal of Social Policy*, **12**, pt 2, 165–93.

Whiteside, N. and Krafchik, L. (1983), 'Interwar health insurance revisited', *Journal of Social Policy*, **12**, pt 4, pp. 525–9.

Whittaker, J. K. and Gabarino, J. (1983), *Social Support Networks: Informal helping in the human services*, New York: Aldine.

Wiener, J. M., Illston, L. H. and Hanley, R. J. (1994), *Sharing the Burden*, Washington, DC: Brookings Institution.

Wildavsky, A. (1975), *Budgeting: A comparative theory of budgetary processes*, Boston: Little, Brown.

Wildavsky, A. (1979), *The Politics of the Budgetary Process*, 3rd edn, Boston: Little, Brown.

Wilding, P. (1972), 'Towards exchequer subsidies for housing 1906–14', *Social and Economic Administration*, **6**, no. 1.

Wilding, P. (1982), *Professional Power and Social Welfare*, London: Routledge.

Wilensky, H. L. (1981), 'Leftism, Catholicism and democratic corporatism: the role of political parties in recent welfare state development', in P. Flora and A. J. Heidenheimer (eds), *The Development of Welfare States in Europe and America*, London: Transaction Books.

Wilkinson, M. and Wilkinson, R. (1982), 'The withdrawal of mortgage tax relief: a survey and evaluation of the debate, *Policy and Politics*, **10**, no. 1, pp. 43–63.

Willetts, D. and Goldsmith, M. (1988), *Managed Healthcare: A new system for a better NHS*, London: Centre for Policy Studies.

Williamson, O. E. (1975), *Markets and Hierarchies: Analysis and anti-trust implications*, New York: Free Press.

Willis, J. R. M. and Hardwick, P. J. W. (1978), *Tax Expenditures in the United Kingdom*, London: Institute of Fiscal Studies and Heinemann.

Wistow, G. (1983), 'Joint finance and community care', *Public Money*, **3**, no. 2, pp. 33–7.

Wistow, G., Knapp, M., Hardy, B. and Allen, C. (1994), *Social Care in a Mixed Economy*, Milton Keynes: Open University Press.

Wistow, G. and Webb, A. (1982), 'The personal social services', in A. Walker (ed.), *Public Expenditure and Social Policy*, London: Heinemann.

Wolf, C. (1979), 'A Theory of Non Market Failure', *Journal of Law and Economics*, **22**, pp. 107–39.

Wolfenden Committee (1978), *The Future of Voluntary Organisations*, London: Croom Helm.

Wolpert J. (1990), 'Generosity and civic commitment: the local public and voluntary sector', in R. Bennett (ed.), *Decentralisation, Local Governments and Markets*, Oxford: Oxford University Press.

Woodhall, M. (1982), *Student Loans: Lessons from recent international experience*, London: Policy Studies Institute.

Woodhall, M. (1989), *Financial Support for Students: Grants, loans or a graduate tax?*, London: Kogan Page.

World Bank (1994) *Averting the Old Age Crisis*, Washington DC: World Bank.

Wright, A., Stewart, S. and Deakin, N. (1984), *Socialism and Decentralisation*, London: Fabian Society.

Wright, M. (ed.) (1980), *Public Spending Decisions: Growth and Restraint in the 1970s*, London: Allen & Unwin.

INDEX

Abel-Smith, Brian, 167
adverse selection, 21–3
AIDS specific grant, 20
Arrow, Kenneth, 16
assigned revenue, 211
Attlee, Clement, 140
Audit Commission, 52, 84–5, 193,
   228
Autumn Statement, 70

Bevan, Aneurin, 136, 140, 176, 179,
   195
Beveridge, William, 159, 175, 264,
   270
   Report, 259, 261–2, 264, 278–9
Budget
   Unified, 69–70
   Report, 67
   Schools, 217–19
budgeting
   cuts, 103–7
   incrementalism, 103–4
   local, 107–9
   theories, 49–51
bureaucracy, 33–5

Cabinet, 52–4, 64–7
   EDX Committee, 63–4, 70
capital
   Annual Capital Guidelines, 87–8
   controls, 86–8

Credit Approvals, 87
   receipts, 86–8
capping, 91–2, 114
care
   child, 193–4
   day, 137–8
   informal, 6, 149–51
   management, 202–3
   residential, 192–3
   unpaid, 149–51
cash
   limits, 58, 62, 73, 81
   planning, 59–62, 70–1
Central Policy Review Staff
   (CPRS), 57, 73
Chancellor of the Exchequer,
   52–3, 69–71, 102, 292
charges, 135–47
   case against, 144–7
   case for, 141–4
   children's services, 193–4
   day care, 137–8
   health service, 140–1
   home helps, 194–5
   meals on wheels, 194
   nursery, 137–8
   overseas visitors, 177
   personal social service, 191
   pre school, 138–9
   prescription, 175–6
   residential care, 191–2

charges (*continued*)
  school meals, 141
charity, 4, 18, 148–63
  tax relief, 153–6
Child Support Agency, 10, 23
citizens' income, 280–1
Clarke, Kenneth, 67
Commission for Local Authority
    Accounts, 52
community care, 199–204
  Kent experiment, 202–3
competition
  between schools, 227–9
  imperfect, 18
compulsory competitive tendering,
    101
Contingency Reserve, 71
contract compliance, 45
contract culture, 203–4
contracting, 33–4
  NHS, 186–7
  personal social services, 202–4
control
  capital, 86–8
  central, 77–9
  total, 63–4, 66–7
cream skimming, 22–3, 45–6

Davies, Bleddyn, 141
district health authorities, 41–3,
    172, 177, 179–81, 186–90

education finance, 208–35
efficiency, 35–8, 50–1, 120–2
Enthoven, Alan, 42
entitlement to higher education,
    234
equity, 32, 38–9, 218, 234, 241
European Social Chapter, 260
exit, 29, 36, 42, 141–2, 248
expenditure
  Autumn Statement on, 70
  education, 212–14
  general government, 67–9
  House of Commons Committee,
    58
  housing, 243–4
  local authority, 71–110, 244–8

NHS, 72–5
  personal social services, 196–8
  real terms, 61–2
  social security, 266–9
  volume terms, 58, 61–2, 72
externalities, 17–18

family allowances, 263–4
family income supplement, 264–5
fees, 135–47
Finer Committee, 10
flow of funds, 8–13
full employment, 4
fundholding general practitioners,
    181–2, 187–90
Further Education Funding
    Council, 221

Geddes Committee, 211–12
general practice, 170–2, 181–3
Gift Aid, 153–4
giving, 148–63
  corporate, 155
  limits to, 156–9
Goode Committee, 274
grants
  education, 208–12, 215, 226–7
  housing association, 249
  improvement, 251
  matching, 80
  mental illness, 200–1
  percentage, 80, 211–12, 215
  personal social services, 200–2
  revenue support, 89–90
  special transitional, 201–2
  unit, 80
  voluntary organizations, 204–5
grant maintained schools, 216–17

Hatch, Stephen, 204
Higher Education Funding
    Councils, 221–2
Hills, John, 13, 257, 290
home helps, 194–5
homelessness, 252
hospitals
  amenity beds, 176
  funding, 167–9, 178–81

hospitals (*continued*)
Poor Law, 169
private pay beds, 176
Trusts, 6, 180–1
voluntary, 167–9
House of Commons, 53, 58, 292
housing
associations, 31, 248–51
benefit, 251–2, 254–5
Corporation, 249–50
finance, 236–57
improvement grants, 251
mortgage tax relief, 240–2, 255
owner-occupiers, 240–4, 255–6
private landlord, 239–40, 251
Rent Acts, 239–40
rent guideline, 246–7
rent support, 242–3
revenue accounts, 244–8
sale of council houses, 247–8
subsidies, 238–9, 252–4

Inner London Education
Authority (ILEA), 215, 228
information failure, 20–4
inspectorates, 31, 85–6, 198–9, 200,
209, 227, 231
internal markets, 30–46, 180–90,
202–4, 228
international comparisons
attitudes to taxation, 295–7
education, 213–14
elderly population, 291
health spending, 172–4, 293–6
markets, 25–8
personal social services, 206–7
social security, 267–8, 295
taxes, 125–8, 131–2, 296

job seekers allowance, 262–3

labour markets, 44–5
Lawson, Nigel, 185
Layfield Committee, 78, 80, 94–5,
97–9
local authorities
budgets, 100–10
spending control, 71–2, 77–110

long-term care, 192–3, 206–7
loyalty, 36

Manpower Services Commission,
161
market failure, 15–24
markets
internal, 30–46, 180–90, 202–4,
228
labour, 44–5
quasi, 30–46, 180–90, 202–4, 228
meals on wheels, 194
mental illness specific grant, 200–1
minimum standards, 31
mixed economy of welfare, 8
monopoly, 18, 35–6
moral hazard, 23–4
Moser, Claus, 293

National Audit Office, 52
National Commission for
Education, 293
National Health Service, 32
contracts, 186–7
expenditure, 172–5
finance, 175–85
national insurance, 113–14, 120,
129–30, 133, 269–73
National Insurance Fund, 269–73,
290
Newcastle Commission, 208–9
Next Steps Agencies, 51
non-domestic rates, 89–90
not-for-profit organizations, 7–9,
204–5

occupational welfare, 4, 13, 265–6,
274–5
OFSTED (Office for Standards in
Education), 86, 231
owner-occupier tax relief, 240–2

PAR (programme analysis and
review), 57, 69
parental contributions, 219
pensions
funded, 272
occupational, 265–6, 274–5

pensions (*continued*)
  pay as you go, 272–3
  personal, 275
  population impact on, 290–1
  private, 275–8
  Regulator, 274–5
  residual, 277–8
  SERPS, 271–2, 275, 279, 286
personal social services,
    191–207
PES (Public Expenditure Survey),
    57, 59, 66, 71, 74–5, 226
Plowden Committee, 54–8, 63–4
political economy theories,
    24–7
Polytechnic and Colleges Funding
    Council, 221
population, impact on spending,
    289–91
private
  education, 7, 220–1, 232–3
  health care, 183–5
  housing, 239–44, 255–6
  pensions, 265
  personal social services, 205
  residential care, 191–3, 196–9,
    206
privatization, 5–8, 102
PSBR (Public Sector Borrowing
    Requirement), 62
Public Accounts Committee, 51–2
public assistance, 259–60
public choice theories, 27–9
public goods, 16–17, 19
Public Schools Commission, 141–2,
    233
purchaser–provider split, 180–2,
    187, 202

quasi markets, 30–46, 180–90,
    202–4, 228

rate capping, 91–2, 114
rates, 82, 88–9, 91–2, 114
RAWP (Resource Allocation
    Working Party), 179
road traffic contribution, 176
Robbins Committee, 234

schools
  competition, 229
  denominational, 209–10
  Funding Agency, 216
  grant maintained, 216–17
  inspectors, 31, 85–6, 209, 227,
    231
  local management, 217–19
  meals, 141
  opted out, 216–17
  poor law, 210
  private, 7, 220–1, 232–3
SCRAW (Scottish Health Service
    resource allocation
    formula), 179
Seebohm Committee, 196
Snower, Dennis, 293
social capital, 25
social dividend scheme, 280–1
social goods, 16–17
social insurance, 260–3
Social Justice Commission, 234,
    281
social security finance, 258–82
  expenditure, 266–9
Social Services Inspectorate, 198–9
Social Work Advisory Service, 198
stakeholder welfare, 281
standard spending assessments,
    100–1, 201–2
Star Chamber, 64
statutory employer benefits, 265–6
stigma, 136, 147, 157, 259, 262
students, 224–5
  loans, 225, 233–4
Supplementary Benefits
    Commission, 242

tax, 113–34
  attitudes to, 295–8
  capital, 116–17
  capital gains, 116–17
  community charge, 82, 89, 91–4,
    114–15, 123
  corporation, 116
  council, 92–4, 131
  direct, 115–18, 121–3
  earmarked, 114

tax (*continued*)
    expenditure, 10, 41, 118
    graduate, 234
    incentives and, 123–7
    incidence, 127–31
    income, 115–16
    indirect, 118–19, 121–3
    international comparisons, 131–2
    local income, 94–5
    mortgage relief, 240–2
    poll, 82, 89, 91–4, 114–15, 123
    property, 94, 117–18
    relief for charities, 153–6
    VAT (Value Added Tax), 119,
        122, 130, 133, 153, 292
    vehicles, 118
technical education, 211
Thatcher, Margaret, 28, 50, 56, 62,
    82, 93, 139, 184, 199, 262,
    269, 294
Titmuss, Richard, 13, 75, 277, 293
Townsend, Peter, 196
training, 225–6
Treasury, Her Majesty's
    Chief Secretary, 52, 64–5
    control of spending, 43–4, 49–76
    education and, 211–12
    local authorities and, 71–2

reorganization, 66

ultra vires, 83–4
unitary government, 32
universality, 32
university grants committee,
    222

voice, 36
voluntary organizations, 159–63,
    191, 196
voluntary sector, 204–5
volunteers, 161
vouchers, 9, 40–1, 226, 229–32

welfare
    courts, 10–12
    defined, 3–4, 195
    future of, 285–98
    market for, 286–9
    mixed economy, 7
    occupational, 4, 13
    private, 7–9
    state, 3
Wilson, Harold, 140
Wolfenden Committee, 160–3

X-inefficiency, 37–8